Katherine Govier won the Toronto Book Award for her most recent novel, *Hearts of Flame*, in 1992. Her other short stories and novels, including *Between Men*, *Fables of Brunswick Avenue*, *Going Through the Motions* and *Random Descent* have been critically acclaimed and published internationally. Born in Alberta, Govier has lived in the United States and England, and currently resides in Toronto.

Without a Guide

Without a Guide

CONTEMPORARY WOMEN'S TRAVEL
ADVENTURES

EDITED BY

Katherine Govier

An Imprint of HarperCollins*Publishers*

Pandora
An Imprint of HarperCollins*Publishers*
77–85 Fulham Palace Road,
Hammersmith, London W6 8JB

First published in Canada by
Macfarlane Walter & Ross, Toronto 1994
Published by Pandora 1996
1 3 5 7 9 10 8 6 4 2

Selection and introduction © 1994 by Katherine Govier
See Sources for copyright information on individual stories

Katherine Govier asserts the moral right to
be identified as the author of this work

A catalogue record for this book
is available from the British Library

ISBN 0 04 440961 3

Printed in Great Britain by
HarperCollinsManufacturing Glasgow

Acknowledgements

I would like to acknowledge, gratefully, the following people who assisted in preparing this book. Phyllis ("Pat") Grosskurth encouraged me to put together an anthology of women writing about travel. Lisa Canton's administrative assistance allowed me to communicate with dozens of writers from Lahore to Helsinki. Greg Gatenby at the Harbourfront Reading Series shared a few of his precious addresses. Sara Borins did great detective work in the Metro Toronto Reference Library, and also handled a confusing number of drafts of seventeen different articles. Finally, without Jan Walter's immediate enthusiastic response to the idea, this book would not exist.

Contents

Introduction

I LOVE TO TRAVEL. ONE OF MY EARLY GRIEFS WAS that I did not grow up in the kind of family where the Grand Tour of Europe was an automatic graduation gift. Full of self-pity, I saw my roommate off for a year in a Parisian walk-up. She ended up living in a cave with Greek shepherds, only to be dragged home and forced into a mauve dress to be my bridesmaid. I had dedicated myself instead to an early marriage, a more affordable voyage of discovery. After that came my first epic journey: moving my household goods in a Ford Econoline van from Alberta to Toronto, taking the route North of Lake Superior through Wawa, Ontario, home of the giant Canada goose and famed nemesis of hitchhikers. Culture shock while adapting to Eastern Canadian mores absorbed the next five years. All in all I was twenty-eight before I stepped foot off North America. I've been trying to make up for lost years as a tourist ever since.

Travel is what people did when they had private incomes; today we practise tourism, the middle-class alternative. But who claims to be a "tourism writer"? No one. We travel, we want to write about it, we become "travel writers." Travel writing may be, as Jan Morris says in her introduction to Mary Lee Settle's *Turkish Reflections: A Biography of a Place*, "demeaned" by its own name.

"Ms Settle could experience such insights anywhere, encounter such characters in her own imagination," writes Morris. Says who? Not Ms Settle, I warrant. Writers travel precisely to collect insights and characters they can't find at home. A footloose wordsmith promises a double treat: a person of imagination and insight, pitched into a foreign environment fraught with danger, mystery, unforeseen delights.

And if that writer on the road is a woman? Even more exciting, because less frequently encountered.

Travel writing is writing about *place*, a subject which, more and more, begins to seem the subject most worth pursuing. But it is writing about place by a visitor, by someone with peeled eyes and a stranger's point of view; that is how it gains its authority. Authority is all, in travel writing. And historically, travel writing was predominantly male. This is hardly mysterious. Men had money; a man could leave his home, his children, his responsibilities in the hands of another — usually a wife — and set off in search of botanical specimens or insights into primitive ritual. On arrival at his destination, the male traveller is draped in even greater privilege: he has his membership in the touring culture (as opposed to the toured), his comparative wealth (no small issue), and his expert status, encouraging him to pronounce opinions on what he sees so that others may learn.

But how did he become an expert, we might ask, that we can believe what he says? Why, by leaving home. This is the opposite of "Don't leave home without it." The travel writer must leave home to get it. He gains credibility by being one of *us* in a nation of *them*.

"It's a man's world," my mother used to say. By this token women are lifelong travellers. Our expertise, our authority, arises from being women, *other*, from the eye we have developed for delineating the practices of the culture under scrutiny. Women have not easily won that authority, but they have certainly begun to travel. There are today, as there were not even ten or twenty years ago, many ordinary women of ordinary means moving around the globe freely, determinedly, independently, though not always easily.

Why then are we not able to read more travel writing by women, I wondered. The travel literature shelves of most bookstores carry nearly nine books by men to every one by a woman. In 1991 the literary magazine *Granta* published a "Best of Granta Travel" issue. Two pieces out of twenty-one were by women. Is travel writing the last bastion of macho journalists? Is it because of this question of authority? There can be no excuse on those grounds, considering today how large are the numbers of women war correspondents writing and travelling in the most dangerous parts of the world, sending back dispatches.

Travel is a release into the unknown. Writing about it, and finding an audience for that work, is a different sort of journey. Few of the stories here have been published before. Most were written for this anthology. Clearly there must be more where they came from.

Despite its maleness, there was always a corner, a cul-de-sac, of the travel writing genre reserved for women. Here we find what I call the Doughty Dowager Diarist, in her heavy skirts, who set out to go where no white female had ever dared tread, notebook in hand. She and her spiritual descendants gave us our first women's-eye view of places on earth as remote to the nineteenth-century layman as the Hawaiian Islands, Labrador, and Kenya, perhaps no longer in grand style of Karen Blixen: "Once I had a farm in Africa, at the foot of the Ngong Hills."

Areas of the globe which had fallen to empires were the stomping grounds of these early women travellers, and the former colony of Canada, my home, saw its share. Now, like Australians, we retaliate and cover a lot of territory.

Round about the time Queen Victoria was ascending the throne, Anna Brownell Jameson (*Winter Studies and Summer Rambles in Canada*) nipped across the top of Manitoulin Island in a canoe paddled by native Indians. She had arrived in Toronto in 1836 to lend respectability to her estranged husband, who was to be installed as Vice-Chancellor of Upper Canada. Before giving up on him and departing for home, she took a sleigh ride from Toronto to Niagara Falls, falling out when it overturned in the snow. Similarly, sisters Susanna Moodie and Catharine Parr Traill, though resident in Canada, were hobbled travellers, making their new land a home.

There are others: Isabella Bird went to the Rocky Mountains, Anna

Leonowens to Siam. Always, they defied convention, though some-times in the most upright way. Isabelle Eberhardt, whose life, with other women's, is chronicled in Lesley Blanche's *Wilder Shores of Love*, found scandal, romance, and finally death in the Arab world. In the last fifty years we've seen the heirs of the Dowagers visit still further colonized areas of the globe. Margaret Laurence went to Somalia and wrote *The Prophet's Camel Bell*. She set off, she begins, "prepared for anything, prepared for nothing, burdened with baggage, most of it useless, unburdened by knowledge, assuming all will go well because it is you and not someone else going to the far place."

Still, authority seemed to be elusive. Many of these later women travel writers went to some lengths to carve out their territory. Eccen-tricity became the rule: they undertook trips no ordinary mortal should have considered, like riding a bicycle from Ireland to India, clip-clopping to Ethiopia with a mule. The Dowagers are not included here, wonderful as they are, nor are their descendants, the Eccentrics. Their work has been amply collected, their lives noted in such works as Lesley Blanche's. Besides, there are so many fascinating contemporary women who travel and write.

Today's women writers travel as a matter of course. They travel light-heartedly or because their life depends on it; they go more often to see what is there than to prove a point. While there is nothing cow-ardly about their travel, they take no more than their share of risks and are not particularly eccentric. To be free of domesticity, to be anony-mous in a hotel room, to discover how other people live, to explore the world with the senses, perhaps even on expenses! What could be finer? Okay, it isn't travel but tourism, and it is often three weeks in-stead of three years, and none of these women could say, "Once I had a farm in Africa. . . ."

The contributors to this anthology are primarily novelists and poets, not professional travel writers. Nonetheless, their travel is not mere sightseeing. It is escape — from domesticity, from enclosure, from small talk and small children, from a man or from an outgrown life, by way of a man or with no thought of a man — and it is escapade. Can I generalize about what is in this collection? Only to say that the stories are not exactly what I expected when I asked for "travel adventures."

The ghastly train ride E. Annie Proulx writes about was a routine working trip until the train "lost its slot in the great flow of rail traffic" and became a mythical beast bolting through the sagging, sickening outskirts of industrial northern North American cities. Ann Beattie watches other people travel, hooking up with a photographer to capture the ironies of a busload of Japanese tourists being hustled through Southern California.

These stories can simply be read for the pleasure of the writers' powers of observation. Bapsi Sidhwa describes the awe-inspiring gorge of the Indus River in Pakistan's Unadministered Territories. Kirsti Simonsuuri takes us into the experience of day-long, utter darkness in the winter of northern Finland.

Travel is sometimes a quest, as it was for Irene Guilford in "The Cold Sea"; she seeks the displaced persons camp where her mother spent the last year of the war. Hanan al-Shaykh scours the collapsing stone jungle of Cairo for a figure from Arab folklore and fiction: the dominant, man-defying, hookah-smoking woman impresario, the *miallima*

Here's a delightful surprise: women travellers dare to have mothers, in defiance of literary conventions that most frequently render female parents silent and invisible. The Irish writer Clare Boylan recalls a trip not long, but long *awaited*, one of those wished-for journeys of youth taken too late. Her mother once longed to travel the earth, but her years were consumed by children's and husband's demands. She responds with a kind of dismay to her daughter's insistent, "We could go anywhere now."

We are slightly puritanical about travel: to have a Task is helpful. Braveries are small but the capacity to be altered by what is there is large. I imagined daring adventures; I got them, but as often I discovered that a trip was significant to a writer mainly because of her travelling companion. There is this business of travelling *with*, rather than *where*. I know, I know: this is a cliché. I didn't particularly want to discover that the company they kept on the journey *was* the journey. But frequently I did.

Not that there was a shortage of danger. Ysenda Maxtone Graham sings hymns to overcome her fear; it's that or die of thirst in Arizona. Wendy Law-Yone's urge to travel lands her in prison in Burma. Speaking of daring, I have included Robyn Davidson's account of her trek across Australia from Alice Springs to the ocean, on camelback. Originally published in *National Geographic* in 1978, "Alone Across the Outback" has become a classic, the seed for her book *Tracks,* and now a CD-ROM, *From Alice to Ocean.* Davidson contradicts any notions that women travellers by definition move more easily through alien territory, that they blend in, empathizing all the way. She engaged in combat with almost everyone she met; full of rage, and on a desperate mission, she learned to castrate a tame bull camel and shoot a wild one, and how to outsmart the various human shysters she encountered.

But death-defiance is the exception rather than the rule. Here are also some light-hearted adventures, stories of the serendipity of travel, the ghastliness, the mundane tribulations, the fears and, especially, the moments of insight, whether experienced in a blinding flash or the slow dawning light, which we see on the road.

There is a dark side to all of this exploration. Travel being as easy as it has become, and commerce as irresistible, today any hot country lined with beaches is targeted to become a tart for Western dollars, its citizens to decline to waiters, peddlars of souvenirs, and prostitutes. Tourism has been called the great evil of the twentieth century. But Margaret Atwood cites another possibility in her piece about the Galápagos Islands: because the tourists who visit them want to see the rich and abundant flora and fauna, they must be preserved intact.

The French still come to see Chateaubriand's Niagara Falls, and go away disappointed. The reason is that Chateaubriand's Niagara Falls were thoroughly his own, aggrandized — as if they needed it! — and romanticized, and yet still a backdrop, a mirror to reflect his own grandeur. If there is a kind of travel writing I don't like it is that.

The women who have travelled and written for this anthology go inquisitively, acceptingly, wishing to feel what is there and to partake of it rather than to call it into being with the power of their important naming.

These women have made inroads on our earth. Words are more violent than we think. The gentle "inroads" in fact means, according to the *Oxford English Dictionary*, "a hostile incursion into a country; a raid or foray; an opening or passage in." In all senses the word is fitting. Travel writing by women is an invasion of territory, as well as a road which leads, though outward, finally, to a richer self.

I am a member of the generation for which the most frequently quoted lines of poetry were T.S. Eliot's: The end of all our exploring will be to arrive where we started and to know the place for the first time. What a depressing thought, and how like a man to say it.

I believe in destinations. Now that we're travelling, what are our preferred routes, where shall we go? What is out there? What *is* out there, beyond our gender, beyond our means, beyond our privilege, beyond what protects us and encloses us?

Katherine Govier

Cairo Is a Grey Jungle

I was always tempted to write about my travels, but I never did, apart from seven articles on my visit to North Yemen in 1982, until I was asked to contribute to this anthology. Cairo still attracts me more than any other place. It is the first Arab city that can carry the title "Mother of the World." I lived in Cairo for four years beginning in 1963; ever since, it has remained alive in my mind, urging me to visit it.

"IT'S A GREY JUNGLE," SAID MY FRIEND.
"I want to fly around with a sprinkler in my hand," I said, "spray the trees and houses, the roads, hose down the children to get rid of the flies and dust and dirt that changes the colour of their skin. Or maybe get a vacuum cleaner and suck up the dust to make sure it doesn't escape, and be drawn up by the winds and delivered to the clouds, which will send it down again as dirty rain. Now it's settling in my mouth, my nostrils, and in the veins of the branches, the cracks in the concrete, the curves of balconies, so that it's like a new form of life, coexisting alongside people and animals and plants."

We're talking about Cairo while the Nile flows past, grass and little fish choked by its polluted waters floating on its surface. A child reaches out from a felucca; he and other members of his family are harvesting nature's excretions, handed out freely. We watch as he carefully picks his treasure from the water as if he has found diamonds, and shake our heads pityingly. This confirms the painful impact of our first few hours wandering around; we have been dulled until now by our absorption in the planning of our program, which we have come to Cairo specifically to carry out. What had assaulted our eyes at the start was the general corrosion: we saw a city suffering from leprosy. Wear and decay had ravaged its buildings, streets, pavements, and above all its ancient heritage. We couldn't acclimatize to this general sense of degeneration which, as we gradually registered it, left us with an accumulation of surprise, regret, pain, and amusement.

We would escape somewhere peaceful, which meant somewhere not eroded by decay where our eyes could rest from the chaos and remember that beauty and harmony still existed. We sought refuge on the banks of the Nile or in our hotel, which had been built in the nineteenth century to receive the Empress Eugenie and other foreign princesses who took part in the celebrations for the inauguration of the Suez Canal. The coloured engravings on the woodwork, the mashrabiyas, high ceilings, and marble pillars had all been made so that their hearts would lift when they encountered them and their dreams would be happy, whether they were asleep or awake. Everywhere, on balconies and in the garden, birds competed with one another to express their joy at finding themselves in this pleasant spot, although the birds in the run-down areas of town also sang loudly, to my surprise, in spite of the dust adorning their heads and clogging their throats.

I had come to Cairo, with a friend who made documentaries, in an attempt to give physical substance to the snapshot of a "miallima" which flashed through my mind every time I was asked for the truth about the Arab woman and the repression she suffered. About the walls surrounding her on all sides. About the sword poised permanently over her neck. As if millions of Arab women were frozen into a single figure with no past or future and all Arab countries had the same customs and were narrow-minded or open in equal measure. I

couldn't blame these people asking the questions, with their precon-
ceived ideas about Arab women, because my novels and the novels of
other Arab writers which have been translated portray the reality of
this repression, this submission.

The miallima: a female boss, Egyptian, a woman with a penetrating
gaze exuding severity and also desire, plump under the gallabiya
which is designed to hide her curves but in fact accentuates them, her
sleeves rolled up to the elbow like a man's, suggesting she's serious
about her work (running a small business or a café, owning property). I
see her bringing the hookah up to her mouth and taking a long drag.
The water gurgles like a mineral spring exploding underground. Then
she blows the smoke out hard as if transmitting her aura of power
combined with allure to the men around her, and incidentally demon-
strating her material well-being with the gold bangles which jingle
each time she moves her arm. She causes an earthquake whenever she
explodes into laughter, debates with a man, rages and shouts at him,
criticizes him and calls him names, seduces and ensnares him, tires of
him, drives him away, exploits him. Her grip on him is as determined
as her grip on the water-pipe.

Having shaken off the awe which invariably descended on me
when I saw such a character in a film, it was as if I wanted to discover
for myself what factors combined to create her in real life. Was it he-
redity, material circumstances, or a feeling of liberation and control
which was generated in her instinctively?

We had relied on a close friend of a friend of mine to produce a key
from his shirt or trouser pocket to unlock Cairo for us (in my friend's
words), for the city wraps itself round with hundreds of arms from
which thousands of fingers reach out to take the winding alleys and
basement rooms in their claw-like grasp. But he wasn't waiting for us
on our arrival as promised, nor did he contact us the following day. We
had no way of contacting him, so we walked to the Nile Casino, passing by beautiful crumbling buildings and men sitting in total lethargy
as if the world had stopped. From the Nile Casino, Cairo appeared
spread out around us, well within reach, not needing a key. Perhaps it

3

was the still waters of the Nile, on whose surface a person could have happily slept, that gave us the confidence and resolve to begin our search for the miallima, even if she turned out to be just an old woman remembering. But when we stopped a taxi we felt as if we were points on a compass needing to define our direction. Falteringly I said to the taxi driver, "Al-Hussein."

The taxi weaves in and out of the crowds, over bridges, through tunnels, then over the Azhar bridge, which towers above the neighbouring streets. We see buildings from all sides, instead of just from the front, and it's as if they've been scratched and mauled and not yet had their wounds bound. We have a good view of their upper stories, the individual features of different apartments, the furniture and other junk on their balconies abandoned and lifeless, as if poised in a vacuum. Only the signs hanging on the balconies or in the windows indicating the existence of a consultant surgeon, an engineer, a lawyer, refocus the gaze on the present, the age of medical technology, of operations on foetuses in the womb. Then when we are confronted on either side of the street by buildings with archways, and land which seems to be abandoned, judging from the state of the stony, churned-up ground and the animals straying there, and realize the buildings are inhabited, we again have to remind ourselves what age we are living in.

For me the quarter of Al-Hussein is the heart of Cairo, the shrine to be visited. In it are the Azhar, Khan al-Khalili, the Moski, the Ghoury Palace and bazaar, the Muayyid Mosque built in Mameluke times, Anderson's house, the Sahimi Palace where cats sleep in the garden, the ceiling of the public baths with its glass windows like a lotus with different-coloured petals. From the mashrabiyas and windows we look down on the noisy streets. I rush to the roofless lavatory in the Barquq Mosque, after asking permission from Sheikh Hanafi, the blind Quran reciter, who says to me, "We see with our minds, and our hearts are only for loving."

We'd caught sight of him enjoying a stroll around the mosque thinking of Paradise, where he knows his sight will be restored.

We come to the Fishawi Café, where the mirrors on the walls

drowse, reluctant to reflect people's faces. The café walls distance us from the noise of Khan al-Khalili and all we hear is the waiter's call: "One mint tea, one coffee without sugar, one water-pipe with spiced tobacco."

We walk in the Ghoury bazaar, in the tent-maker's market, past the Fatimid engravings in the plaster walls. Against these ancient walls beggars squat and traders prop their barrows laden with ducks and chickens, spices, earthenware containers, baked potatoes. I suddenly remember Nagi Turguman, the guide who showed me round this bazaar some years before, refused to take anything for his troubles and even invited me to eat in a restaurant, which he conjured up from a place resembling the inside of a walnut. He selected the cut of meat off the lamb before it was killed and prepared for roasting and then asked if I minded him giving it a bunch of clover. "Eat, my dear, eat," he murmured gently to it as he fed it.

I inquire about Nagi, and some indicate with a backward flick of their heads where I might find him, while others insist that he's left the area and gone to Sinai. Then I notice a young woman with her head covered and an armful of textbooks who arouses my curiosity. Except for her and all the plastic goods for sale, which are so incongruous that you look twice at them, this place is still buried in Mameluke times. I ask her if she's from around here and if she knows Nagi. She answers my questions simply, without surprise or curiosity, as if she's known me for a thousand years: my friend and I normally expect to attract attention when we walk around areas like these, as we are neither foreign tourists nor the normal sort of Arab visitor, who probably wouldn't come here. The girl lives in a house in one of the nearby alleys and is a university student, so when we ask her about the miallima figure, she smiles and proceeds to dissect the character for us in a precise and reasoned manner. We reach a steep flight of steps, where she waves to a sign proclaiming SAID TURGUMAN, then says goodbye, adding, "Go to the abattoir. You might find a miallima there."

Said Turguman is not Nagi Turguman. Said is a squat figure, sitting behind a large desk surrounded by hundreds of papyrus paintings which hang on the walls of his extensive warehouse: Nefertiti,

Tutankhamen, Ramses, and so on, all in vivid colours. Two sales-women are almost reeling with the kind of fatigue engendered by boredom rather than unremitting hard work. This is confirmed by Said, who talks non-stop, switching rapidly between topics: his import-ance as king of a papyrus empire, which he illustrates by showing us tourist brochures where his name figures prominently, the collapse of the tourist trade, and the story of Nagi Turguman, who has moved to Suez and who was, according to him, a friend and a brother. They were like twins, deliberately copying each other's clothes and fash-ions: if Nagi wore a jacket with leather trimmings, Said would adopt this innovation, and if Said had an unusual haircut, then Nagi would rush to the barber's asking for the same, until they became like "two bums in one pair of pants." He also informs me in passing that Nagi has talked a lot about me. I think that perhaps I should buy a painting from him, because he starts hinting at the slump in business again, casting angry looks at the salesgirls as if they are responsible for this disaster, but I don't like any of them. They look to me like the two girls, who yawn at the staleness of their own thoughts and passions and only show signs of life when we don't finish our glasses of Seven-Up and they insist this is a bad omen and means they'll never marry, and implore us to drink up. They are eighteen at the most.

We go down the steps with Said Turguman. I can't imagine any jacket big enough to fit his waist and hips, still less see him with leather trimmings and an original hairstyle. But this time I take in what I only vaguely noticed before I went into the building with my hopes pinned on finding Nagi there: goat droppings on the uneven, swampy ground, the din from the surrounding offices, and a white goat roaming freely. Said walks along the street with us and points out a shop selling Ramadan lanterns whose owner is a miallima and an-other, similar shop nearby. Then, urging us to visit him again, he van-ishes before his eyes can fill with tears at the thought of parting from us. My friend and I release all the laughter we've been holding in while he was speaking, and she begins to laugh again when I tell her how thin Nagi was, how his hair was light-coloured and straight.

We make for the first miallima and find a dignified woman sitting among Ramadan lanterns of various shapes and sizes, as silent and still as if she is one herself. Then we transfer our attention to the second miallima a few feet away, who stands unabashedly devouring a sandwich, her long earrings trembling and gold tooth glinting. When I ask if the shop belongs to her, she answers with much laughter and gesticulating, "Of course. Otherwise I wouldn't be standing here eating like this. I'd have sneaked off into a corner where no one could see me."

She is wearing a black jersey and long skirt, plastic earrings and modern-type makeup, as if she's determined to keep up with the fashions. Everything about her proclaims her desire to be up to date, even the Ramadan lanterns, which are in the shape of Mickey Mouse, instead of the traditional ones in red, green, blue, and orange which proliferate in the weeks before Ramadan in preparation for the festive month when the children run up and down with them singing:

Open up for Ramadan
Open your purses and give us your coins
Then we'll go and leave you alone
Open up for Ramadan

We both try to construct shots of this miallima, devise scenes, imagine her responses, and delve into her life, entranced by her mannerisms and gestures, convincing ourselves that we have found what we are looking for. But as soon as our taxi carries us away over the bridge leaving this complicated world behind, and the lights of the huge hotels and the apartments overlooking the Nile come into view, we begin searching for an objective angle on the subject of the "miallima of the lanterns" and come to the conclusion that she doesn't conform to the image we've drawn previously of a miallima's character. She gave orders to her assistant, but they were perfectly normal requests to do with the running of the business and he had talked to her on an equal footing, quite at ease. At the same time she seemed in awe of her husband, who came and went in the shop more freely than her. It was as if he had assigned the work in the shop to her so that he could get on with more demanding activities such as amusing himself with the lads in the market. A few more moments and we're in another world which envelops us as we brush the dust off our hair and shoes, distancing us from what we've seen, leaving only faint echoes of the words of Said Turguman, his two assistants, and the modern miallima to drift back to us from time to time.

There's a cross section of people in the hotel foyer: the veiled woman, the glamorous girl looking as if she's about to be part of a film shot, businessmen, young male tourists from the Gulf with the latest clothes, hairstyles, spectacles, portable telephones, and cologne. Observing this mix, and especially the female part of it, prompts us to resume our search for a miallima, encouraged by the fact that my friend's friend has put in an appearance at last. However, I hadn't pictured he would be so young, handsome, elegant, intense, and serious as he tries to warn us against the error of looking at Cairo through orientalists' eyes.

His meticulous cross-questioning convinces us that he really does have the key to Cairo, and we're so positive and confident that we feel we're floating on air. The business of finding a miallima moves particularly fast: he frowns and says seriously, "I'll take you to the cycle woman, and the café woman and her daughters. We must be there when they start work."

So the following morning we leave our oasis with him, full of energy and enthusiasm even though he's late, and hail a taxi. Before we set off he informs the driver that he's dealing with a native of Gamaliyya (part of the quarter of Al-Hussein). This pronouncement makes us determined to hold on to our key to Cairo. I picture him taking me up and down alleys, into basement rooms, up staircases, onto rooftops, into hidden cafés, and I see the miallima — a different miallima.

We walk along beside him, surrounded by domes and minarets. He takes us into mosques, up onto their roofs, down the alleys which give their names to Naguib Mahfouz's trilogy: Qasr al-Shawq (*Palace of Desire*), Bayn al-Qasrayn (*Palace Walk*), Al-Sukariyya (*Sugar Street*). He

8

points up at a window in one of the ancient buildings and says, "That's my home."

We gasp in surprise: it's hard to imagine somebody with his personality and wearing a shirt and glasses like his living in one of these buildings, which seem to belong to another age. However, we are impatient to meet the miallima. He takes us down some narrow, dusty streets and finally comes to a halt by an open-fronted shop where a woman is sitting on the ground. At first I think she's crippled because of the pain written on her face. On either side of her bicycles hang, and her round face, encircled by its black headcover merges with their black wheels. She looks at us coldly and the bearer of Cairo's key begins to address her: "I'm from around here. You must know such-and-such alley. Mr. So-and-So? That's where I'm from."

"Glad to see you," she answers politely.

He tells her that we want to talk to her.

Some youths have gathered at the shop entrance and one of them calls, "Are you another lot from the TV? They filmed her already hiring out bikes and blowing up tires."

I'm disappointed and annoyed by the answer she gives when I ask her how she comes to be doing this strange work, but the goodness in her face and her air of desperation make me warm to her in spite of myself. "It's my husband. He said you've got to help me. The thing is he's got a government job. It's not well paid. He said you've got to help me because of the kids and all the expenses. He's got a job, so he and I take it in turns to work here."

Does she encounter any difficulties working in a man's world? Looking at the ground, she answers, "Never. I've never put anything on my lips. I only wear black and I only talk to children. I just sit here as if I'm on guard and wait for my husband. Thanks be to God."

Does she sometimes wish she could stay at home? Does she ever miss chatting with the neighbours? She answers mechanically, like a robot, "How could I? The work nearly kills me. It's backbreaking. I don't have any friends. After I've finished here I go home and cook, wash the clothes, clean."

9

You mean you're not financially independent? "If I want to stay out longer I ask my husband's permission and he always says no."

So you're not free to do what you want? Working doesn't make you free? Again she doesn't understand what I mean. She pulls at the black dress which envelops her completely and turns her face to mine; it is sad, suffering, silent, immobile, patiently enduring. The bicycles, hanging motionless, seem to reflect her expression as if they too have abandoned themselves to waiting for the riders who rarely come. If times are hard, as you say, do you hire bikes to girls and young women? "That would be awful! A girl on a bike isn't right."

As we leave, I try to put her out of my mind: her submissiveness, the glimpse of life she gets courtesy of her husband. But then I think maybe she's not so badly off: she gets away from the housework for a while, escapes from the prison of the four walls into the real world. The gloom of the shop's interior comes back to me, the bicycles suspended overhead, the woman crouching there hour after hour, only ever looking at the ground or the bicycles because it's up to her to protect her reputation and that of her family. I change my mind again and wish for her the gloom of her home and familiar things around her reminding her of life, like the roar of the gas stove, the pots and pans, the chair, the neighbours' racket.

The man with the keys to Cairo doesn't notice our disappointment until we explain again to him what we mean by a miallima. A liberated woman in a position to tell other people what to do. A woman who's chosen the hard way. Autocratic, seductive, unjust. She counts her money, makes plans. He nods his head, guides us along. Is he taking us to the café owner and her daughters? But he wants us to go somewhere to eat and rest. What about the woman who runs a café? He seems uninterested in the subject and we are left sunk deep in a mood of frustration.

But the life around us soon removes our frustration, which was changing our eyes into lenses and our ears into oversensitive receiving equipment. My friend realizes that the soft whistling, the refrain "hss hss wss," isn't someone pestering her but a warning sign used by those

on bicycles, pushing laden carts, or carrying huge loads, while I remember the elevator in the Hussein Hotel which used not to work unless one of the passengers kept his hand on a certain spot the whole
time. We make for this hotel and I'm praying that it's still like it was
the last time I visited it some years back. My foreboding seems justi-
fied when I see the clean floors and the almost sparkling elevator, but
I ask eagerly if it still needs someone to help it go up, and am told,
"Yes, Amm Girgy will go up with you as soon as he comes."

A tall old man appears shortly like a genie from a bottle wearing the
hotel uniform. I shake him by the hand and greet him warmly. I seem
to feel a need to show him how close I feel to Cairo, how keen to express my affection for its people. Instead of responding as I anticipate,
he shouts, "Girgy? Who's Girgy?"

Stunned by his anger, I reply, "They told me you were Amm
Girgy."

His face burns darkly as if I've set it alight and he shouts again,
"I'm Girgy? I'm Muhammad Tawfiq. Girgy! Who told you that?"

I realize that the group of men at the desk wanted to annoy him.
He is a suitable candidate, reacting in a comic and dramatic way when
provoked, his anger spreading to encompass an ever-increasing area
like ink on blotting paper. He begins threatening his tormenters,
swearing he's Muhammad Tawfiq, calling out that he's decided to
give all this up, his hand never leaving the side of the elevator so that
we keep rising. But then at a particular floor he stops, leans out of the
door and shouts, "They told her my name was Girgy. I swear by the
Prophet I'll take these lousy things off (pulling at his uniform as if he's
about to tear it off) and leave you all in the shit."

Then he brings his head back in and leans his hand on the side of
the elevator and clamps his jaws shut, trying to control himself in case
he opens his mouth and consumes us and the elevator and the laughter
welling up in our throats and in danger of exploding. Girgy/Muhammad
Tawfiq leaves us on the roof terrace; and our minds are preoccupied by
a different kind of sensation as we look out over Al-Hussein Square and
see the Azhar with crowds of pedestrians round it, Khan al-Khalili, the

domes and minarets of dozens of mosques, the walls and one of the seven gates of the old city of Cairo, the stones which in days gone by were hoisted up on men's shoulders to construct these buildings that are still standing today, indifferent to the vagaries of a hotel elevator and to Muhammad Tawfiq's feud with those who called him by a Christian name.

I am confused, torn between my love for all I see, even the crumbling ruins and the delicate stonework almost buried in the dust of the past, and a yearning for the comfort of the hotel which is like an extension of the European country where I live. I hear the familiar conflicting voices in my head. Where do I belong? In the East or the West?

We take the advice of the serious female student, of a novelist friend, of the driver of a Lebanese acquaintance who has lived in Cairo for years, all of whom have assured us that we will only find what we are looking for in the abattoir.

On our way to the abattoir in Sayyida Zaynab, I notice that my eyes are no longer merely quivering, but would be screaming by now if they could. The buildings and alleyways are covered in rubble, and the children seem to be walking on nothing but mud and dust. Only the flies pay them any attention. But my nose intervenes now and my nostril hairs fight my sense of smell, keen to suppress it before these odours rise to my brain and it stops telling my feet to keep walking forward and makes them return to the oasis of the hotel.

A fetid smell permeates the air where the car drops us. We are standing in some wetness, water mixed with other fluids from the animals' flesh and entrails. A few steps and we're in a world too terrible even for a nightmare, unless someone had eaten a whole camel and fallen into a deep sleep straight afterwards. There's a vast area like a roofed-in yard, broken up only by the women surrounded by open drains of dirty, discoloured water, and occasional pillars supporting the roof. The women, enormous black shapes, tower over their surroundings, seemingly detached from the shouting and the containers full of animals' organs: livers, lungs, guts, and sheep's heads with bulging eyes. They sit cross-legged on wooden benches as if in howdahs riding camels in a festive parade, and nothing escapes them. They observe the young women, who must be either servants or relations, as they pour water, scrub the innards. There is a hierarchy of duties in the slaughterhouse just like in any other job: sluicing the floor, various stages of washing and preparing the viscera, making the tea. We are given this information by a woman who seems to have some difficulty with her breathing and tells us that she has worked in the abattoir for forty years and can't bear to be away from it for too long, even though her health is not good. When I ask her what led her to work there in the first place, she answers with a laugh, "What? Circumstances. My father was the boss here and I helped him, and now I've taken over from him."

"What about your husband?"

"I never married."

Then, as if suddenly deeply suspicious, she asks, "Do you want to buy into the abattoir?"

At the start of our conversation she'd asked me if I wanted some tripe.

Resignation is carved into the women's features as if they've given up on life, but their expressions are transformed when they start cutting up the entrails. They become like birds of prey. They frown, purse their lips, screw up their eyes and swoop down on the prey, tearing it apart with the help of their teeth, which they use like a third claw. I see their mouths closing round the flesh and realize these women riding in their howdahs inhabit a bloody desert, empty of beauty, which is so far remote from them that they do not even picture it in images of blue seas, flowers, sparkling brooks. I understand their harsh, penetrating gaze; it is as if they have had so much contact with the organs of slaughtered animals that to them a heart is just a bit of flesh resembling some kind of fruit, the brains a loofah or some unthinkable greasy lump. We hurry out. My friend is clearly trying to thrust away the picture of a woman with her prey clenched firmly between her teeth, and so she chatters on about it with great agitation.

Meanwhile I try to understand why they work in this trade, which is generally assumed to be for men. I have a vivid memory of the big metal containers, one standing beside each woman. As a kind of bonus they are given the leftovers, the bits that aren't worth much, to sell.

We have to round off our research on the miallima in the City of the Dead in the quarter called Migawreen near the Azhar. In a novel I'd read there was a female character who worked from her house in the cemetery as an impresario managing female singers and dancers who performed at weddings. She had lost her real home in one of the wars.

The tombs, pink and earth-coloured, come into sight. Children run along behind us, and women pick over rice and joke together in the doorways of their tomb-houses. A woman invites us in and shows us the beautiful graves of upper-class women, built of white Italian marble and with inscriptions and flowers of gold. They look on to a wall, and judging from the nature of the images painted there, and the colours, which we see in the light of a match our hostess holds up for us, whoever conceived this tomb must have had the Pharaohs in mind. Then her daughter calls to her from another room. We glance surreptitiously through the door and see what looks like an ordinary room in a modest home. "My children are embarrassed that they live in a cemetery," remarks the mother, "but this tomb's produced a son of mine who's an army officer and my daughter who's a lawyer."

In another graveyard in another street the tombs are not as beautiful; in fact, there are no buildings identifiable as tombs. An old woman invites us in and shows us photos of herself as a young woman in the style of actresses of the period, which she has hung around the walls. At the same time she is trying to calm her wild grandchildren, she points to a patch of earth in the middle of the cement floor, remarking, "See. We sleep with the dead. They come and open up the grave, bury the corpse and fill it in again."

We leave the cemetery, which is teeming with life, the streets busy with children and traders, and to my surprise I notice a woman cleaning the windows. We leave the City of the Dead, inhabited by the living.

We are to end our journey by visiting a Lebanese friend who lives on the fourteenth floor of a highrise in a high-class residential area.

She has been trying to arrange for us to meet an Egyptian film-maker in connection with our project on the miallima. We've told her in detail about the difficulties we've encountered, how we've come to realize that Cairo really does need someone to unlock it for visitors like us, and how we're going to have to send out fieldworkers to penetrate the popular quarters, tap the vein of daily life there, and find us a miallima who roars like a lion and flirts like a girl. But now we inform her that there's no such thing as a miallima these days and recount the story of the taxi driver who took us to the Sultan Hassan Mosque.

Our visit there was to be the culmination of our trip to Cairo because of the beauty of its proportions, which are almost the ultimate in aesthetic pleasure. Its vast interior courtyard gathers in the skies of Cairo and joins them overhead, so that if you stand or sit there you're convinced life doesn't exist beyond the still calm of its huge confines. There you are oblivious to the decay which has eaten into the city, as if the condition of this one ancient building is enough to make you forget the poor state of repair of the others: broken wooden latticework discarded in a corner, a broken wooden table in the middle of the Musafir Khana Palace with a layer of dust more than ten centimetres thick on it, not to mention the worn and crumbling plasterwork.

To return to the taxi driver who was waiting for us while we toured Sultan Hassan: he told us a lot about the mosque, about Egyptian history, and about the history of the city itself as we drove through its streets and past its historical monuments. Then we came to Muhammad Ali Street, famous for the Citadel, and he started talking about the prostitutes who used to frequent the street, pointing out the café where they gathered in the twenties with female dancers and singers and musicians whose bands performed at weddings and soirées. He drew our attention to a heavily veiled woman approaching the café. "She had a lot of power. Everybody wanted to please her. She used to be a concert agent in the old days."

My heart beating in anticipation, I asked him for his views on the character of the miallima and how I could go about finding one. He fixed us in the driving mirror, forcing our eyes to meet his, and gave us the facts.

"A miallima? Don't waste your time. They don't exist any more. That was in the old days when people didn't know any better. They became extinct with the arrival of TV, modern civilization, pocket calculators. Now any man can keep a woman like that in her place. People learn quickly these days. You don't get those types from out in the country nowadays, the ones that used to arrive from Upper Egypt and not have a clue, couldn't handle things so they got bled dry, grew old and ill before their time. Anyone who works for these women has to use a calculator and be able to type, and that's shut them up. They used to take over when their husbands died and they were sole heirs. Now that's all finished. People are trying to manufacture human beings in test tubes."

We laughed. He was the first to make us realize that we were still so influenced by the old Arabic films.

Our hostess rises to go and make the tea and I follow her. I catch my breath at the sight of the roofs of other apartment blocks visible just below our level. They are strewn with objects of different shapes and sizes, outlines of familiar and unfamiliar things which I can't distinguish at first. I stare, move closer to the window, then realize that they are refuse: heaps of broken-down furniture and other articles discarded over the years which have been thrown out onto the flat roofs and left there to rot further. It is a horrifying sight, like wrecks on the seabed or rocks which have risen to the surface and set the sea in turmoil. The colours are brown, black, the colour of rust which has formed a layer even on the wood. These abandoned objects are exposed to the burning rays of the sun and the buffeting of the winds like landing stations for extra-terrestrials. They should have been cleared away long ago; instead, they've been forgotten and left to multiply and engendered fearsome creatures so no one dares approach them any more and people try to forget they exist. The sight frightens me. It's not only the thought of people's laziness or forgetfulness or their reluctance or inability to pay for having their junk transported to the tip. My fear of these disturbing shapes scattered over the roofs like running sores on diseased skin is a fear that one day the whole planet will be given over to ruins, castoffs, flight, death. I hurry back to my friend with my ideas for a film on degeneration and decay and find that she's already up to the fifth shot.

Translated from Arabic by Catherine Cobham

Islands
of the Mind

Looking back on this trip has been a great pleasure, as it was the last one I took with my parents with both of them intact: several months after we returned from the Galápagos, my father had the first of several strokes, and would not have been able to make such a taxing voyage. Despite the physical discomforts, I'm very glad that we managed to do this with him, as it was always one of his dreams to see Darwin's famous stomping grounds. The Trip was worth every itch, scratch, heat rash, and cockroach, and right now we're figuring out how to do it again.

I AM NOT THE WORLD'S MOST INTREPID TRAVELLER. I don't like planes or airports. The sun fries me. If there are insects to be had, they bite me. Bacteria invade me. I get seasick and am susceptible to bad smells. I live in terror of the day when someone, somewhere, will dish me out an eyeball, and in the cause of international relations I will feel compelled to choke it down. Insatiable curiosity propels me around the globe, but I travel with a mini-drugstore of ointments, bandages, sun creams, disinfectants, and pain-killers.

The point is that if I can make it to the Galápagos and back, almost anyone else not actually in a wheelchair probably can too. But for the usual delights of a tropical vacation — working on your tan, poolside romance, piña coladas under the palms — go elsewhere. One of my acquaintances asked me in all innocence if there were any tennis courts. There aren't.

This is how it all came about. I hang out, some of the time, with birders. (Some people refer to them as bird-watchers, but to a birder that is like what being called a lady painter is to a female artist.) Birders take birds seriously, and among them the Galápagos Islands rate high. One of our chief birding connections, Marylee (*Canada's National Parks: A Visitor's Guide*) Stephenson, had been there the year before and had been longing to get back ever since; but birders are often short of cash, since they spend it all on scopes and binoculars. Marylee decided to charter a boat, fill it, and go along as a sort of summer camp counsellor.

When my father heard we were on our way to cruise among the islands where Darwin had cruised, gawk where Darwin had gawked, and throw up where Darwin had thrown up (the great man never got over his seasickness, which makes him, for me, even greater), he did not say, "Why do you want to go *there?*" as he had when informed about previous expeditions of ours. Instead, his eyes began to glitter, and he went to the bookshelf and began pulling out book after book, a sure sign of interest and even approval. My father is a zoologist. Darwin and the Galápagos rank for him as the Mohammed and Mecca, respectively, of any true biological believer.

It struck Graeme and me that possibly he might like to come with us. After a remarkably short period of deliberation, he accepted. "It's about time a reputable zoologist got down there and discovered the theory of evolution," he said. The one hitch was the fact that my mother gets motion sickness in just about anything other than streetcars, and we all knew he'd never go without her. But she gamely opted for medication, and Marylee filled in two more blanks on her list.

We had signed in blood by January; the trip was to start in mid-May. In the interim, we studied up.

The Galápagos are a group of islands in the Pacific Ocean west of

Ecuador. There are sixteen main islands; all are volcanic in origin, and all are geologically recent. All things living on them have come from the mainland, and, isolated from other influences, they have evolved, often into something distinct from parent stock. Thus Darwin's interest: for him the islands were a living laboratory, where birds and animals could be caught in the very act of adapting themselves through natural selection to conditions new to them. This is what makes the islands unique, and this is their attraction for naturalists.

The Galápagos, we learned, could be expected to yield numerous bird species found elsewhere: there are three kinds of boobies and many sea and shore birds such as petrels, oyster catchers, pelicans, shearwaters, frigate birds and tropic birds; there are flamingos and yellow warblers, great blue herons and ospreys. But what gives the Galápagos five stars among birders are the species unlikely to be found anywhere else: the flightless cormorant, with its vestigial wings; the exquisite Galápagos penguin; the lava gull, with its amazing red-lined beak; and the thirteen varieties of Darwin's finch, most prized of which is the woodpecker finch, which uses cactus spines as tools.

As a birder, I'm a good botanist; I prefer things that stay still long enough for me to actually see them. Secretly, I was focussing my hopes on the volcanic formations, the cacti as big as trees, the sluggish marine and land iguanas, and the sea lions and fur seals that were supposed to be fearless enough to allow you to play out any fantasies you might have retained from reading *The Jungle Book* as a child. (This fearlessness, not to be confused with tameness, results from the fact that there were no large predators on the Galápagos for most of the islands' history. In this respect the Galápagos fauna are unique. Mockingbirds sit on your hat; sea lions swim with you and nuzzle your legs. Frigate birds stay on their nests and let you photograph them. You have to take care not to trip over the land iguanas.) I was also yearning for some porpoises, up close, and a hammerhead shark, at a discreet distance.

As the date approached, we began receiving sheets of printed material from Marylee, who, never having organized such a trip before, was determined to leave nothing to chance. We were ordered to get polarizing filters for our cameras, to buy our film in Canada before leaving (Marylee had an in-bulk deal), to supply ourselves with waterproof camera bags and with a plastic bag for carrying our film unharmed past the X-ray machines in airports.

On the appointed day we assembled at the Toronto airport, twelve of us, the oldest of whom was seventy-seven and the youngest seven. We flew to Guayaquil in Ecuador, via Miami.

We spent the day in Guayaquil to recover from our jet lag, catch up on our culture shock. And to hold Marylee's hand because our tickets to the Galápagos proper had not yet arrived at our hotel as promised. But many phone calls were made, and next day we were headed for the islands, 600 miles off the coast in the middle of the Pacific Ocean.

I had expected the plane to be a bit like a flying boxcar, but it was an ordinary, full-size plane. Stuffed with tourists, half of them Ecuadorian, half of them perspiring foreigners, it flew in the normal way to Baltra, where there is a World War II landing strip, a tiny airport, and a lot of cacti. A bus, which *was* like a boxcar, took us a short distance to the dock; and there we were met by our ship, the *Cachalote*.

You can visit the Galápagos Islands only by ship. You cannot camp on the islands, which are highly protected Ecuadorian national parks: you must eat on the ship, sleep on the ship and confine your garbage to the ship. All ships are licensed by the government parks administration. They come in three sizes, which correspond to three price ranges: small, medium, and large. The small ones are converted fishing boats, usually without sails. They take eight or so, roll around in heavy swells, and are good for the young, the poor, and the adventurous. The large ones, such as the *Santa Cruz*, take eighty or ninety and have waiters and fans for the rooms. You are woken by loudspeaker, taken ashore in groups of twelve to twenty, and treated to slide shows and lectures in the evenings. The big ships go out for only four days, don't make it to the outlying islands as a rule, and are not allowed ashore at certain places, where the trampling of so many feet might damage the wildlife.

The *Cachalote* is in the middle group. It carried twelve of us, though nine would have been optimum, and four crew. It had sails, so it was not at the mercy of its motor — a cheering thought. Because we had chartered it, scheduling was flexible: we could go where we liked, when we liked. Life aboard was informal, to say the least, but not punitive.

However, none of these advantages flashed through our minds as we were ferried out to it, in two nervous bunches, in the *panga*, a small motorized boat we would come to know well. What struck us was that the *Cachalote* was, somehow, smaller than it had looked in the diagram. I began to wonder what we had let ourselves in for.

Our first meeting with the crew made us even jumpier. There were lots of dos and don'ts, many of which had to do with the correct way of working the toilet valves. (This lesson was not properly learned by every-one in our group; several times there were disasters.) The main fea-ture was that if you didn't screw the head down properly, the sea would come in and the ship would sink. The other big items were sand on the feet (frowned on) and getting up the ladder from the panga without stepping on the head of the person behind you or get-ting a leg crushed. I noticed that the ship was equipped with a net that extended from scuppers to railing and went all the way around. It was like a giant floating playpen. Pepé, our guide, was probably just as ner-vous as we were, since he had to make it through two weeks without losing any of us overboard or allowing us to fricassee or mangle our-selves. To him, we must have looked like a challenge.

The rest of the crew — a captain and a cook, both named Hugo, and a blond, curly-headed American motor expert called Matt — were in charge of the running of the ship, but Pepé Salcedo was in charge of us. He was Ecuadorian, twenty-four, and looked like a genial bucca-neer. Some of the naturalist guides in the Galápagos do their job only for money, but it was evident at once that Pepé does his for love. He first came to the Galápagos on a school trip, and fell in love with the is-lands. He opted out of the professional future expected by his social class to become a guide, which involves being able to speak a language other than English and Spanish and completing an intensive three-month course. Pepé also studied at the University of British Columbia for a year, taking courses in geography, geology, ornithology, theory of evolution, and entomology. Every evening he went over the next day with us, telling us what we were going to see and why it was the way it was. There wasn't much he didn't know, and when we would encounter other groups ashore, they'd creep around to listen to Pepé as he held forth on why flamingos are pink (it's the brine shrimp; deprive them and they bleach), why the flightless cormorants stretch out their wing stubs (vestigial behaviour, from when they had real wings and dried them that way), or why the large flying thing somebody saw was not a hummingbird (there aren't any; it was a hawk moth). He could make noises like sea lions and many other things as well, and never wore shoes, as the soles of his feet were like bedroom slippers. He was astoundingly good-natured. Jess, our daughter, fell in love with him at once; everyone else took a little longer. My father, having heard him expound on grasshoppers, concluded that he was "a good man," by which he meant scientifically acceptable, a phrase he does not bestow lightly.

My father approved of Pepé for many reasons. Like my father, and indeed like Darwin himself, he had defied convention and expectations in order to go adventuring in search of natural truths and wonders. Like my father (and Darwin) as well, he was initially self-taught and irrepressibly curious. Again like the two of them, he had a healthy respect for bees and beetles.

And then there were what one might call his literary abilities. At one point, Pepé told us he wasn't too fond of what he called "life listers," birders who are interested only in adding to their collection of names, to the exclusion of the birds themselves, their environment, and their welfare. One such man was going too far, in Pepé's opinion: seeing things that weren't there and whining to Pepé on days when he hadn't logged any new species.

"But I got him back," said Pepé. "One day I said, 'Look! A flightless cormorant!' I pointed up into the sky. 'Where?' the guy said, swinging up his binoculars."

Since this was exactly the kind of deadpan prank my father himself was quite capable of playing, he referred to Pepé after that as "quite a boy."

The first afternoon on board, Pepé wisely steered us to a mangrove swamp within easy sail. We racked up ten species of birds, including the lava gull and the large-billed flycatcher, and began to feel a little more confident. After dinner, we crammed ourselves into our respective bunks in an optimistic mood, only to encounter what was to remain a major problem on board: sleeping.

There were, altogether, ten bunks, and eleven of us, plus our daughter, who could not in fact sleep on the floor as we had thought. The six people below deck sometimes found it hot and stuffy (since the ports had to be closed when the ship was moving), and noisy because of the motor. Twice someone forgot to close a port, and waves came in on sleepers, drenching them and their bedding. The four above also found it hot when the engine was on. The best place to sleep was outside, on top of the cabin, or (second choice) on the deck itself; but some nights it rained. In any case, there wasn't room on deck for all. Graeme staked out the chart table, and there was sometimes a territorial scramble for the saloon table. Bad nights resembled a giant slumber party, with people in nightgowns bumping into each other in the dark. On good nights, however, the *Cachalote* rocked gently at anchor, the ports were open, and you were lulled to sleep by the sound of sea lions hunting fish, blowing and wheezing two feet from your head.

This is the place to mention that all boats in tropical latitudes have cockroaches. They are large, live under the floors, are impossible to exterminate, and come out in the darkness, when they sometimes walk on you. Apart from an experimental nibble or two to see whether you're a moldy crumb, they don't bite. You can't expect zero cockroaches. All you can hope for is an acceptable passenger–cockroach ratio, and this the *Cachalote* had. The acceptable ratio may vary with the passenger, however. My father was likely to greet any new cockroach discovery with "Ha!" The reaction of some of the others was less gleeful.

The routine during the days varied, depending on where we were and what the weather was like. Mostly we staggered up early, ate breakfast, which often included papaya and eggs (served separately, not together; there was some growling over the first platterful of eggs until people realized there would be more), were briefed by Pepé, slathered ourselves with sun block, and were taken ashore early to avoid the heat of noon. After being stunned by natural wonders (this is not meant ironically), we were brought back for lunch.

The food on the *Cachalote* was excellent by local standards, and the cook knocked himself out for us, whipping up two impromptu birth-day cakes and serving up tasty hors d'oeuvres of rock lobster the crew had caught. The fish was fresh caught too: we'd often trail a line be-hind the boat and pull in something: wahoo, mahimahi, tuna. But there were several occasions when we didn't feel much like eating it.

For it must be admitted that although none of the sailing was bad by *Cachalote* standards, some of it *was*, by those of nonsailors. Also, the distances between the islands were a lot greater than they looked on the map. During the worst weather we held singsongs to distract peo-ple, and things got more like summer camp than ever. Even in moder-ate winds we found that the best thing to do was climb to the cabin roof and stay as close to the exact centre of the boat as possible, since it moved the least.

I had, I confess, times of doubt: during the roughish sail back from Hood Island, for instance, when I stood on the deck gobbling down the Gravol and trying to focus on the horizon, while the rain poured down the neck of my jacket and my mother turned a delicate Life-saver green on the bench inside the cabin. (My father, having come from a long line of privateers and other forms of salt, did not get sea-sick, exactly; he merely went to sleep. But even excessive sleep can be anxiety-producing in the guilty.) Had I shown total wisdom in sug-gesting this trip? Would my parents get damaged? In the event, they did not: the sprains, falls off the cabin roof, infected feet, and peeling sunburns were all suffered by other, younger people.

("The thing is," Marylee said to me, when we had returned from a jungle stroll on mainland Ecuador that included an unexpected and, for me, hair-straightening tiptoe along the slippery edge of a washed-out dam, with a rocky precipice on one side and a mountain stream on the other, "most people, when they're in danger of losing their balance, slow down. Your mother speeds up.")

In fourteen days we covered the major islands, from Tower in the north, where the frigate birds were mating, to Hood in the south, almost the only spot where the waved albatrosses breed, launching themselves from the cliff there because they don't take off from flat ground. A list of what we saw would read like a list; or, if better written, like Tui De Roy Moore's *Galápagos: Islands Lost in Time*, which I recommend. My favourite things were the eight-mile lava flow on James Island, which was moonlike and, when explained in detail by Pepé, totally engrossing; the land iguanas of Plaza Sur, eating yellow portulaca flowers in an idyllic prehuman torpor; swimming in a grotto with the fur seals; swimming anywhere with the sea lions; and watching the Sally Lightfoot crabs, which are bright red and spectacular against the black rocks.

The highlight for Jess was our snorkelling expedition to the Devil's Crown, an extinct volcano in the sea that has eroded to a jagged rocky rim surrounding a placid centre, home of many bright tropical fish. At first she was dismayed by the name and the ominous look of the rocks and the lack of a beach to climb out on; she held onto the panga and wouldn't let either of her parents float off with her. But Pepé, indispensable as ever, swam to the rescue and took her with him. He dove down to the bottom and broke open a sea urchin, so that all the fish within smelling distance came to eat out of his hands.

"This is my cathedral," Pepé said to Graeme. This was what he wished to convey to his flock: that the Galápagos should be viewed not as a vacation but as a privilege.

For my father, the Galápagos were disappointing in only one respect: there were not enough insects. Wingless grasshoppers, true, and fire ants, and an indigenous bee, and a hawk moth; but not an entomological proliferation. However, this relative scarcity did explain one troublesome fact. Darwin, as is well known, began his scientific career as an amateur beetle collector, which was, in my father's opinion, right and proper. But the actual theory of evolution was deduced from finches and other lesser species, not from beetles. Why had Darwin strayed from the path? Now all was clear.

The deficiency was made up for during the four-day excursion into the cloud forest of Ecuador that we made on our way back. Here there were more insects than birds, and many never before scrutinized by my father's eye: giant crème de menthe–coloured katydids, enormous blue morphos and exquisite clear-winged butterflies, a parade of leaf-cutter ants, a red-spotted beetle that remains a mystery to this day, and many kinds of moths, which fell nightly into the soup. Happiness may be a warm blanket for some, but for others it is a large arboreal termite nest. Luckily, we were able to locate one. "Hmm," said my father, inserting a stick into it so that the termites would come out to be viewed. This is the sound all male Atwoods make when profoundly interested.

Midway through our time in the Galápagos, we anchored at Puerto Ayora on Santa Cruz to restock. We visited the Charles Darwin Research Station, where the various species of giant Galápagos tortoises — are raised to a good age and then put back where they belong. Several species are already extinct; they were heavily used by early sailors, who would stockpile them upside down in the holds of ships, where they would stay alive for months.

Pepé arranged a meeting for me with one of the young scientists. We talked about conservation — the difficulties involved in trying to keep the Galápagos the way they are, or, in the case of some islands, in trying to restore them to what they were. The big problems are caused by species introduced by man, against which the indigenous birds and animals and even plants often have no natural defences. Pirates and fishermen deliberately introduced goats and pigs so they would be able to kill them for meat; rats, burros, dogs, and cats were accidental. The cats eat the marine iguanas and their eggs and are threatening the Galápagos doves; rats, dogs, and pigs have decimated several species of giant tortoise; goats have been devastating to plant life. Because of the climate, animals such as goats breed much faster than they do farther north: a few left on Pinta by local fishermen in the 1960s rapidly became a population of 30,000, now reduced by feral-animal control programs to a few hundred.

Controlling these animals, which are pests in their context, costs about $72,000 per species per year. The money goes for transport — all supplies, including water, have to be taken by boat to the islands — and for equipment: tents, guns, and provisioning for the crew of twenty hunters. The Darwin station, which employs a feral-mammal specialist, a botanist, a herpetologist, a marine biologist, an entomologist, and a human ecologist, costs $600,000 a year. Some comes from foreign zoological associations, the rest from donations (you can contribute through the World Wildlife Fund, earmarking the money).

Later I talked with Pepé about the same problem. I had the usual anxieties about being a tourist: was I, by my mere presence, helping to further threaten a natural balance that was already under siege? But according to Pepé, the Galápagos are one example of tourism actually encouraging conservation. Since the development of tourism as a major industry — which has exploded only since the mid-seventies — the local people have realized that if they wipe out the indigenous animals and plants, nobody will want to come any more. Most of the fishermen have become tour operators, and local inhabitants are themselves helping to stamp out feral pigs and goats. Many mainland Ecuadorians are now visiting their own natural treasure; in Pepé's view, this is how they may first encounter the idea that nature is fragile and will not support infinite exploitation.

Pepé had yet another example of human–animal harmony in his bag of tricks. He took us to visit the Iguana Man, a kindly painter who had been living in the Galápagos since the thirties, having had a difference of opinion with Hitler. His house was visible from the *Cachalote*'s mooring, identifiable by the marine iguanas that covered its tin roof. They went up there to sun, said the Iguana Man, who also told us that, since the iguanas had had the site first, he'd made a deal with them. In return for their land, he would trade them roof basking and food. This seemed fair enough.

Their names were all Annie, he said, after the first one with whom it had been his pleasure to become acquainted. Toward sunset he brought out a large metal dish full of what looked like oatmeal porridge, and banged against it with a spoon, calling, "Annie, Annie, Annie!" Quick as cats, the iguanas slithered and plopped down from the roof and into the dish of oatmeal, where they swiftly became covered with porridge and proceeded to lick each other clean. Their benefactor looked on proudly, noting correctly that this was something we'd be unlikely to see anywhere else. "Who says they are stupid?" he beamed.

"Quite a boy," was my father's comment. You can be quite a boy without being a good man, and vice versa. Possibly he was thinking that, deprived of the chickadees that festoon his hat at certain locations farther north, he might not be entirely averse to iguanas.

Pepé saved the most idyllic location for last: the haunting and indeed haunted island of Floreana. He spent the evening before our landing on it getting us into the right mood with some history and legend. In suitably hushed tones, he told us about the German dentist who, equipped with steel teeth and his wife, had arrived more than half a century before in search of a noble-savage Eden; of the gun-toting baroness who had disembarked with her two lovers and a large supply of bubble bath soon afterward; of the rivalry between the two factions; of mysterious disappearances, possible murders, unexplained deaths. . . .

On some of the islands, black with lava flows, smelly with sea lion dung, or white with guano, it would not have been possible to imagine this romantic saga. But on Floreana, with its gentle hills covered with palo santo trees, its tender inland lagoon, and the most beautiful white-sand beach we'd been on yet, the search for paradise, however doomed, was plausible.

On the last night, we slept on deck, where, in the morning, we found ourselves covered with small black smuts disgorged from the motor when it was started up. It was the *Cachalote's* way of telling us our time was up. Somewhat melancholy, we cruised toward Baltra; as port was sighted, I looked down into the clear bow wave and there, hanging suspended for a moment almost beneath the bow, was a hammerhead shark.

We disembarked at the dock and, dragging our by now pullulating luggage behind us, made our anticlimactic way up to the little airport. Pepé, dressed in a set of spotless whites he'd dredged up from somewhere, saw us off. At the same time he was locating the incoming group, sizing them up for potentially hazardous quirks. We spotted them too: washed, whey-faced, immaculate. We knew they would not remain that way for long, but we envied them anyway. They were about to experience something unique on the planet, and every lurch and dry heave would, we knew, be worth it. We wished we were going too.

A Journey
with My Mother

Every journey is a voyage of discovery. When I think of earning money it is always in terms of the places it will take me because nothing else in life gives me the "fix" to which I became addicted in childhood — the delight of discovering a totally new thing in the world. Coming from an island dogged by the past and by violent nationalism, I am convinced that physical travel advances our intellectual journeys too and attracts us to an unknown future, whereas stasis ties us to an idealized past. When I took my mother to London, I borrowed her authority and she became a child. The short trip turned into an epic voyage and became perhaps my most memorable journey, although my mother now purports only to recall that part of it that pleased her — her single experience of flight.

M Y MOTHER WANTED TO GO TO CHINA OR INDIA. Her father (dead before I was born and fictionalized in two of my novels) served with the cavalry in India, had come home with some monstrous secret which the whole family had to group and grow around, never knowing what it was; a family of women bowed around a botched male supremacy. Its legacy was a summons to adventure to my mother, but here she was well into her thirties and she had never been anywhere except to Blackpool on her honeymoon and three times to the maternity ward.

"I'll go with you," I said. I was about five. We were washing clothes in a big metal tub in the kitchen of the big, grim terraced house in Terenure, in the suburbs of Dublin, where I grew up. We did everything together until I went to school. We were twin souls. I was the youngest, her consolation for everything.

Someone said that happiness is like a butterfly in the hand. You either set it free or it dies. Of course they were talking about love. By the time I was grown up my shoulders were sagging under the weight of my mother's love, her sorrow, her determination that I would live the life that had been denied to her. I cleared out and turned my back on her. She made excuses for me. She remade me into a mythic creation, ever young, ever beautiful, always virtuous: as if I had died.

My sisters used to tease me about this when I was in my thirties. Whenever I regaled them with some frightful episode from my life, they would say, "And she still looks seventeen!"

"Maybe eighteen?"

"Eighteen-and-a-very-hard-life," they would chorus in unison.

"You were like a sugarplum fairy," my mother insisted. "You could have had anything you wanted." She meant that I could have had everything she wanted. It broke her heart that I had wanted (or settled for) different things. I sat opposite her, edgily formal and impatient. I was in my thirties by this stage, much the same age, it one day occurred to me, my mother had been when we pounded washing in the metal tub and discussed places only imaginable in terms of dragons and rajahs. I was married, I was editing a magazine, I had written a novel. The mad notion suddenly struck me, that I could remove the mask she had imposed on me. I could introduce myself and hope she liked whoever she found. But not here — not where she guarded the shrine of an imprisoning nursery and where she was watched over by an obsessive husband. "Let's go away somewhere," I said.

"Where?" she looked desperately uneasy.

"Anywhere you like," I said.

"You mean a holiday?" Where do our mothers go to on us, the girls transformed by bawling burdens into capable young women, every one a pioneer of maternity, making a nest for us and a world for us, creating a happiness that can never be recreated? The Irish women of her generation — poorly educated, jobless after marriage and repressed by the Catholic church, seemed to me the bravest, the funniest, the most generous people in the world, but middle age left them sad and self-effacing.

The exotic destinations I mentioned frightened her. Romantic places made her feel guilty ("Without your father. . . ?"). I suggested places of pilgrimage, Rome and Lourdes, since she is a devout Catholic, but oddly, these evinced no interest. "London?" I said, and for once she looked genuinely pleased and excited. "Do you think we could?" she said. "We can do anything we like," I told her.

Cities mean different things to different people. People's favourite destinations are the places where they have found escape, acceptance, or peace, or have fallen in love. London is where I made myself, escaped from my background, realized my ambition. The happiest hour of my life was spent in a traffic jam in central London in a taxi en route to the publishing house of Hamish Hamilton to sign my first book contract. I love the air, which is crisper than soft, damp Irish air, and the assortment of nationalities on the underground from Heathrow airport. I love the little doll's teaset sized cups of glamour you can have   breakfast in the Ritz or the Savoy, which have an atmosphere of soft intimacy even at nine in the morning; the specialist shops for chocolate or perfume or paper where you can walk in and be almost embalmed in mushy or musky or waxy essences. I love the exotic pockets of imported culture — a perfect cappuccino, a wind-dried duck. I love the brave and sparky humour of English people — quite different from harsh Irish irony. Even the homeless teenagers claim their squares of pavement in Camden Town with a spirited jocularity.

There was also a sneaky pleasure in showing off the life I had made. I wanted to impress her. We would travel everywhere by taxi, eat in the best restaurants, meet my important new friends.

We flew out over Dublin's north coast. My mother's head was pinned to the window. Cobwebs of cloud snatched away a little view of everything she had known all her life. Her fingers, curled around a cigarette, were like a child's fingers, except that they shook a little. I had been wrong when I said we could do anything we liked. My father, in the week or so preceding our departure, brewed up a frenzy of resentment. This began as a silent sulk and grew into a roaring rage. There was no substance to his anger. It was the challenge to his domination, an impotence at her independent flight, the terror that she might never return. She would happily have cancelled the whole trip to placate him but I had arranged and paid for it. She was a child being torn asunder by two adults simply because they had some money and she had none. By the time we left for London she had a crouched look as if she had been punched in the stomach. She had not eaten for days. Her face was white and shocked. She seemed bewildered as a child evacuee in the war, with a label pinned to its overcoat. She had said nothing at all since we left home. "Would you like a drink?" I asked her. "Can you get a drink up here?" she said in amazement, as if she had encountered a bootlegger in heaven.

We stayed in my pet hotel in London, Number Sixteen in Sumner Place, South Kensington. It is a gorgeous little bed-and-breakfast hotel in a pretty Regency terrace, full of flowers and run with gentle charm. I always stay there if I have enough money. I could sense at once that my mother was disappointed. She had expected a proper hotel with a piano bar and restaurant. I found that I did not really like sharing a room with her, this elderly woman with her lack of outward sophistication, slow gait, numerous underclothes, and her older woman's smell. She used to tell me how when I was an infant and she kissed me in the morning, I would back away politely and whisper, "I don't like the smell of your nose." I undressed as quickly as possible and scurried to the bathroom. "You've got a figure like a fifteen-year-old," she called out determinedly.

We went to Harrods, to Claridge's, drank champagne in the Cafe Royale, dined with my literary friends. In the evenings we went to the theatre. Our days (and nights) together had the enforced celebration, the exhausting formality, the overhanging threat of intimacy, of a Victorian honeymoon. I found out that I had lost track of her as much as she had lost touch with me. I became familiar with her frailty (I had not known that stairs cost her her breath, that she walked at a crawl); her fears (she would not, under any circumstances, step on an escalator); her strength of purpose; and, most movingly, her own desires. One morning, on our way somewhere in a taxi, she suddenly scrabbled round in the car, the way my dog does when he has spotted out of the corner of his eye another dog on the pavement. "What's the matter?" I asked her. She said nothing, just tensely clutched the seat back. After some minutes she sat back in her seat again. "Are you all right?" I said. She still said nothing. Watching her, I could see it was excitement that had silenced her. After a few minutes she got her voice back. "They're changing the guards," she said, "at Buckingham Palace!" I suddenly realized she had visualized a different London when she eagerly agreed to my invitation, one of a tourist brochure, with royal ceremonies, beer taverns, chorus girls, beefeaters.

I don't think she much liked my friends. They refused to admire me as she did (and I was all her own work). She thought them too knowing and sophisticated. As always with our mothers, there was the competition to redeem the person she knew from the different one who responded to adult influences. We drank champagne out of long, fluted glasses with a writer friend in the Menage a Trois (alas, now defunct), a pioneer of nouvelle cuisine where all the courses were starters. They were tiny ornaments on enormous plates. My mother loved the look of them, although she did not eat them. "Wasn't she nice?" I said to my mother afterwards about my friend. "I don't know," she said defensively. "She kept calling me darling. I never met her in my life before."

We went to a Harold Pinter play that neither of us could understand, but we both thought it was drab. "There used to be wonderful shows in Blackpool," she sighed. "What sort of shows?" I asked her. "Variety shows, singers, dancers, comedians. They were real professionals," she sighed wistfully.

She liked the lights on Picadilly Circus. The only other thing that made her eyes open wide was a meeting with Beryl Bainbridge. We ate dinner in a Greek restaurant with the wonderful Liverpool novelist. Cigarette smoke blurred the candle flame and wreathed the stuffed vine leaves. Beryl took us back to her house, where we sidled past Eric, the stuffed water buffalo in the hall, and in the living room were introduced to a suited plaster model who is variously Adolf Hitler or Neville Chamberlain. "Tell me, Evelyn," Beryl seized my startled mother in the gloom. "How do you feel about sex?" Beryl was writing a novel with an older woman heroine and was interested to know about the marriages of a previous generation. My mother was delighted to find a woman who had no small talk, whose conversation got to the heart of things.

I don't think she ate anything at all in the week we were away. Tiny forkfuls got pushed about her plate, went into her mouth, and were chewed endlessly. She drank a lot, though. One night when we had got through half a bottle of whiskey, I said, "I want to talk to you."

She sat patient and burdened as someone receiving news of a death while I filled her glass and filled in my history — not a very interesting story but one that showed me up as flawed and greedy and *trivial*. When I finally finished she made no comment at all, just said, "I'm tired now. I think I'll go to bed."

In the morning she said very little over breakfast, just smoked her cigarettes and drank coffee. We met up with friends of mine for lunch and they watched with mildly sardonic smiles while she told them how wonderful I was, how *good*. I sat by in astonishment. It made me think of a cartoon by Ronald Searle, in which two old ladies shear a sheep and then knit a jumper to keep it warm. Overnight, she had unpicked my confessions and woven them up into something pretty.

The following evening I started all over again (we had been to see a dull musical show called *Barnum* and were both exhausted). She tried very hard not to listen. "I'm not a saint," I said, "not a child, not a virgin — not even when I got married." At this point she looked up

38

alertly. "You rotten little hypocrite!" she said. "Why?" I wondered, since I had never lied to her, merely allowed her, up to now, her version. "Going round with that nice little face!" she said crossly.

She did not much enjoy her journey. She was like a child who is promised an outing by her father but then finds that he is really working and she has to spend her time in waiting rooms. She would have liked to see the Queen and Danny la Rue. All the time she was away she was afraid of what my father would say when she got home, and she missed him too and was anxious to get home to him. Several years after that he went mad, a late diagnosis of manic depression, untreatable because of a geriatric condition which would be exacerbated by lithium, so they put him in the locked ward of an asylum and she waited in dread and hope for his return until he died.

We have become great pals. She still tries to paint me up a bit, rather like a mother trying to dress up a daughter who she finally realizes is very plain, but mostly she accepts me as a woman pushing up to middle age, who has made her own life, her own bed, and pretty much likes it. I treasure her forgiving love and her mad, wise sayings. "Any woman can get a man or a child if she wants one badly enough. She only has to compromise." That's one. Another is this: "The downfall of most men is not pretty women but beautiful boys." (She is not referring to gay men, but to the manner in which older men hand down the baton of power to younger men as the possessors of sexual potency.) And recently she said: "You know, all my life I never really understood men, and I didn't all that much like them. Now, finally, I do understand them. And I hate them."

We could go anywhere now. There is no one to stop us; there are few barriers between us, but she won't go away any more. She has learnt her lesson. The trip, the treat, turned out to be a trick. She was promised a visit to Santa and taken instead to hospital. Those late-night talks were radical surgery. They had to be done. They saved a relationship that I badly needed. But they hurt. That night in London, at a stage in life when she had spent almost everything on compromise, she had to take in the fact that the people we love most rarely live up to our ideals.

"Well," she said, when I had told my tale. "Tomorrow we go home." Her voice was a mixture of apprehension, resignation, and relief.

This week I am travelling for the first time in my life to China. I am mad with excitement. It is as if I am about to begin my life again. When I told my mother she looked at me in amazement. "China? Why would you want to go to China?" It seems to me now that parents do pass on their dreams to their children, but only when they themselves have no more use for them.

She has not wholly abandoned her sense of adventure. Her eye is on a different journey now. She believes in reincarnation and is anxious to get shut of this life, convinced that next time it will be different. She talks about her plans for the return journey in a leisurely, self-indulgent way, much as if it were a holiday. "I don't think I'll have any children next time," she says. "I'll be out in the world where I can do some good. Children tie you down too much, they get in the way."

I asked her once what she had liked best about her trip to London and she answered, without any hesitation, "Drinking gin and tonic up in the clouds." If there is anybody up there, I hope they'll have a large one waiting.

WENDY LAW-YONE

The Year of the Pigeon

*Running away from home is one of those projects that help us get through
childhood, whether we actually do it, or just threaten, or plot. In my case, there
came a time when I knew I had to run away, run for my life, if life was to
have any sort of meaning. The great problem was that by doing so, I was taking on not only family and society, but a state which looked on such acts of defiance as amounting to treason. It was a journey I'll never forget because, as
the American writer Ed Sheehan once said, "No voyage outshines the first
one — the one that takes you forever from childhood and home. Other journeys, no matter how far, are side trips by comparison."*

THE TRIP WAS A MISTAKE FROM THE WORD GO, BUT
a necessary mistake. To make it was unwise, but not to make it
was unthinkable. After the fiasco, I wrote: "Even as I prepared and
told myself that it would be a success, I never really believed it would
come off, that it would turn out the way we wished it to . . . and yet, I
could not turn back."

I was running away from home, though not for the usual reasons.
The reason was my recent marriage — a forbidden marriage, call it. I

41

had married a foreigner at a time when foreign visitors were not permitted to remain in the country for longer than twenty-four hours, and we nationals were not permitted to leave — not *even* for twenty-four hours. This was Rangoon, Burma, May 1967.

I had met Sterling, my husband, two years earlier at a concert featuring a Hungarian pianist. It turned out we had family connections (Sterling and I, not the Hungarian and I).

Sterling's father, Gordon Seagrave, was the famous medical missionary and World War II hero known as the Burma Surgeon — the title of his best-selling autobiography. During the war, when my mother was stricken with rheumatoid arthritis, Dr. Seagrave had given her a cholera shot that magically put her back on her feet. Years later, caught in the turmoil of nationalist politics, Dr. Seagrave found himself in a Rangoon jail, charged with treason for giving medical aid to the rebels. My father, by then the outspoken editor of the liberal, English-language daily, the Rangoon *Nation,* came to Seagrave's defence with an editorial titled "Send Seagrave Home" (meaning home to northern Burma, where he had lived and worked most of his life).

That night of the concert, my conversation with Sterling, Dr. Seagrave's youngest son, lasted all of twenty minutes. The next day, Sterling left Rangoon for his trip upcountry to visit his ailing father — just in time to see the old man die. Forbidden, as a foreign citizen, from remaining in Burma, Sterling returned to the United States, where he was living at the time, and I remained in Rangoon, where I was dying — of boredom and frustration. To add to the usual woes of life in a fascist regime, my father was in jail — a common destination for men like him in a state like the one we were locked into. A quote from Thomas Jefferson had graced the masthead of his editorial page: *Let me make the newspapers of a country and I do not care who makes its laws.* The men who made the laws after 1962, the new military junta, were the ones who arrested him. It was under the pall of their reign that Sterling and I first met. I was eighteen, Sterling ten years older.

When next I saw Sterling, it was two years later. We hoped to be married on that very day — our second date, so to speak. True, we had met only once before and only for twenty minutes; true, I scarcely remembered what he looked like ("Perhaps this may sound a bit incredible and rude, maybe, but I didn't pay much attention to your face," I confessed in a letter); but we had been engaged in a most intense correspondence.

For an entire year, we had written to each other almost daily. The infamous postal system came through with surprising efficiency in our case. (One post office clerk on my end even took the liberty of readdressing an envelope I had absent-mindedly addressed to myself. Under the neatly scratched out Rangoon address was Sterling's correct California address — well known to the entire Rangoon post office apparatus by then, no doubt.)

But the mail, true to police state paranoia, was censored. This created the need for pigeons. Pigeon was the code word for our illicit letters, the ones that managed to fly past the normal postal channels. Ours was a romance made for pigeons, a romance of secrecy and danger.

The pigeons flew thick and fast that year. They flew through the diplomatic pouches of half a dozen embassies, or per kind favour — as envelopes were addressed in that era — of foreign friends (and sometimes strangers) who hand-carried our letters back and forth between me, inside Burma, and Sterling, who waited on the outside. Sometimes the pigeons contained more than a missive. Once, Sterling cunningly hid a ring inside a toy, which he then mailed to the son of an American couple posted in Rangoon. Those were known as stuffed pigeons.

But rereading these pigeons now, I wonder why we bothered. We should have stuck to the good old GPO. As I wrote early on: "I must say that so far they have been very efficient in delivering your letters; they reach me within five days of your mailing them, and happily, there are no longer any traces of local glue on the flaps. Apparently, our declarations of love are not spicy enough to be considered worth the reading."

Of course I didn't really think that. At heart, I hoped the gnomes (another one of our codes, for "censors") were spellbound by our epistolary affair. I imagined them poring over our paeans, reading word for word *and* between the lines of our air letters, thick letters, letters on foolscap and onionskin, and the telegrams too: crooked alphabets spelling garbled messages on newsprint that already looked ancient. The truth is that after a sampling of my prose — so purple and breathless it resembled strangulation — the gnomes probably saw that not only was I no threat to national security, I was a bore. At some point they clearly stopped reading.

By contrast, the poor pigeons, those special deliveries, ended up on the dissecting table. In the sordid way of minor diplomatic intrigue, one of the embassy types who offered regularly to pigeon our mail turned out to be with — what else? — the CIA. Another, a junior political officer, later admitted to me that he had read every letter relayed through him, and with utmost care, because he didn't want to abuse the pouch.

But there comes a point in every romance when pigeons are not enough. When that point came for us, Sterling flew into Rangoon on a twenty-four-hour visa — the only kind permitted foreigners at the time — and on Friday May 12, 1967, at four in the afternoon, we were married by the district magistrate.

The wedding — an oddly subdued and surreal affair — went more or less as planned. But not the honeymoon. For that, the groom had to fly in and out of Rangoon on a circuit of half a dozen consecutive transit visas, each one of twenty-four-hour duration or less. The route was Bangkok-Rangoon-Calcutta-Rangoon-Bangkok-Rangoon, and so on. Bangkok-Rangoon-Bangkok was not an option; the operating rule was *transit*, and to be in transit, one had to be *en route* to a different destination from the point of departure. A simple round trip would not do.

I had not foreseen this particular idiocy, hoping that by marrying a foreign citizen, I would be entitled to leave. Not so. In those days getting out of the country was sometimes trickier than getting out of jail. The same arbitrariness that got you behind bars could also get you released. For no good reason you might be thrown into jail; for no better reason you could be set free. But not free to leave the country.

Those were the memorable years of the mid-sixties, when no Burmese citizen — barring a select few on official business — could leave. Not even those ready to forfeit everything just to get out: life savings, properties, families. The only exit left was through the back door and across the border (to Thailand, usually), under escort of a smuggler or trader. One had to rely on those frequent pliers of escape routes with their insider knowledge of checkpoints, rebel outposts, and such.

I opted for this route, finally, when it became apparent that marriage was not going to improve my chances of getting out legally. As things stood, my chances were way below average, and the average was already nil. After a costly merry-go-round of "transits" following our wedding, we decided the time had come for me to take the back door.

Right there was my first mistake: the failure to find the right back door. Taking leave of Sterling, my husband, in our room at the old Strand Hotel (he had flown in for a farewell visit, to see me off), it never occurred to me to seek out a back door. Instead I took the elevator, thereby announcing my departure to the lift operator (in all likelihood a Military Intelligence Service man). Then I walked past the front desk, in full view of the hotel personnel, state employees every last one of them. They were familiar with the comings and goings of our odd marriage by then. It didn't concern me much at the time that they would be curious about why I was leaving the hotel alone while my husband remained in the room upstairs.

I was leaving, as anyone could plainly see, to hail a taxi. How else would I get to the train station? Much later, Sterling pointed out that there were probably only two taxis in Rangoon at the time, both driven by MIS men. I had chosen a state vehicle for the first leg of my cloak-and-dagger mission.

In the back seat of the cab, I worried about other things instead. I had left a note to my mother with my friend M. She was under strict orders to deliver it, but only at a specified time, when Sterling would be safely on the plane back to Calcutta (or was it Bangkok?) and I would be miles away from Rangoon, on a train. Not a minute before was she to deliver the note. Now I worried about M's capacity for intrigue. The honesty I had admired in her was suddenly a flaw. How could someone like her be counted on for subterfuge? She had probably told all, and the police dogs quite likely were after me already, sniffing the trails at that very moment.

(The note itself was a lie: *By the time you get this, I will be safely in Bangkok.* But how could I say the truth: *By the time you get this I'll be on a train with a gem smuggler who has promised to show me the way to the Thai border. The trip should take several days through jungle and rebel territory on foot, although we may have to cross a stream or two on elephant back.*)

I worried about the gem smuggler, a man I knew next to nothing about, save that he had done business with a diplomat friend of mine and was said to know the illicit route to Thailand. (I'll call him TM; those were his initials, and apt, given his meditative streak, which came to light only much later.) I had met TM just once before, at the diplomat's home, where he, TM, assured me of his familiarity with the secret paths and trails that would lead me to freedom. First I would have to take a train to the southern terminus on the coast at Moulmein, thence by shank's mare over hills, across bridges, through thorn and thicket and maybe a rebel stronghold or two, and on to the final crossing at Three Pagodas Pass marking the border with Thailand. (Three Pagodas Pass! The romance of it! I almost swooned.) He offered his services as a guide, told me what it would take (250 U.S. dollars), and we shook hands on the deal, leaving the particulars of time and place for the final rendezvous till later. That was that. I couldn't think of a way to get more out of him, for how do you ask a gem smuggler for references? But he smoked a stylish pipe, and that impressed me.

Would TM show up as promised at the train station, I wondered. Without him there would be no trip, and I knew a moment's panic at the thought of arriving home, tail between my legs, just after my mother had received my farewell note.

Especially I worried about my brother Alban. He had decided in the last hurried stages of planning to make the trip with me. Alban was a free spirit: ever open to the call of adventure, and unemployed. Like me, he was fed up with life in Rangoon, and we had often fantasized about escape. It pleased but did not surprise me that he would want to come along for the ride. But it wouldn't have surprised me, either, if I had got to the station to find he wasn't there.

He was there, all right — arriving in an open jeep, with a contingent. His friends' rousing send-off lacked only the impedimenta of balloons, banners, and kazoos. At last we boarded the train, Alban and I, saving a seat for TM (whom we'd seen on the platform, earnestly pretending — and by then perhaps also wishing — not to know us).

The train pulled out. TM slid nonchalantly into the seat next to Alban, who was still waving to his fans from the window. I sat across from the two men, thinking something like "It's happening, it's actually happening." The thrill of an outing was upon me. Alban and TM had met once before and seemed disposed to getting along. So much to look forward to on the road to Moulmein — station food, for a start: sticky rice, lentil fritters, fried sparrows.

The next thing I knew, Alban was asleep. The farewell partying had caught up with him and knocked him out cold. TM, looking remote and prim, began the elaborate ritual of preparing his pipe. He had a superior air I wouldn't have associated with his trade. He was smallish, darkish, of indeterminate age and personality. I didn't know what to make of him.

I decided to change. Finding a fairly decent toilet (no mean feat on a Burma Railways train), I remade myself into a likeness of the anonymous bumpkin I thought I should become. I can't remember the disguise — only that it was inspired by Viola in *Twelfth Night*, as staged by a school production. I had played Olivia — but Viola, the boy in disguise, was the role I had coveted.

Here at last was my moment for androgyny. I did a pin-up job on my hair to make it look cropped. But some last-minute doubt made me try for a peasant-girl look on top of the Viola guise, and so I smeared on each cheek a chalky patch of sandalwood paste.

When I returned to my seat — incognito, I hoped — Alban was awake. "What the *hell* is *that*?" he said. TM kept his own counsel. Puffing meditatively, he looked determined to rise above some private misfortune. I ignored them both, serene in the logic that my masquerade would be essential once we got off the train. Why I thought we were safe until then I cannot say.

I remember almost nothing of our arrival in Moulmein, except that boats were involved — or perhaps we just went by a jetty or port — and gharry horses. I'd never seen such outrageously tarted up beasts of burden. Flowers and tassels and bells and beads were literally coming out of their ears.

We were in Moulmein to make connections. A local family, friends of TM, were putting us up for a day or two, as I understood, before we pushed on to the more rugged stretch of our journey.

Here my memory is unreliable. I recollect being in a troika. Time has apparently transformed the picture of the three of us, in a horse-drawn vehicle of some sort, into a troika image. But — I don't care what anyone says — I'll always think of riding into Moulmein in a troika.

I am ungrateful to TM's friends, the family that fed and housed us. I cannot remember them. I know there was a couple, a small child, and a cast of peripheral characters including a teenage nephew who seemed important in some way, perhaps because he brought news. There was a great deal of waiting around for news — that I remember. And increasingly, with the dragging days, the news was not good. Again and again some unforeseen hitch, some freak occurrence, would conspire to delay our trip. Enough messengers vanished, bridges collapsed, and roads got washed away in those few days, it seemed to me, to create a national emergency. Meanwhile it rained. And rained. And rained. Trapped indoors, TM paced in one direction and Alban in the other, while I watched them in a stupor from the floor, laid low (as it were) by overeating.

The host family fed us as if each meal was our last. Maybe they felt they had a reputation to maintain: Moulmein cooks were supposed to be the best in the country. Maybe it was the only entertainment they knew to provide. I cannot fathom the feeding frenzy. I may not remember the cook's face, but I'll never forget those dishes. A giant omelet of exquisite complexity, laced with chopped onions, tomatoes, and little green chilies, and fried in just the right amount of oil to frill the edges. Salted duck eggs with lovely grainy yolks. Tender squashes and nutty greens I've never tasted before or since. And sublime little fragments of chicken — more bone than meat — in a sauce described only as "cooked in the jungle style."

I felt like a stuffed goose — and a sitting duck. There was a police station directly across the street. It didn't seem the ideal spot for us to be hiding. But TM insisted that the unsuitability was exactly what made it perfect. It was better, of course, to stay indoors — just in case.

But on the third day or so, I had to go out. It was clear from the unrelenting stream of bad news that we were going to be stuck in our hidey-hole indefinitely. I had to get a message to Sterling before he left Bangkok (or was it Calcutta?) to meet me at the designated place — a village on the Thai side of a river that marked a border crossing. It was not easy, but I managed to persuade both TM and Alban about the necessity of heading out, in a wicked downpour, to the Post and Telegraph office, to telephone my friend M in Rangoon.

Umbrellas were useless against the rain we had to brave to get to the public telephone in Moulmein. Drenched and shivering, I waited while the operator placed the call.

M, being the only co-conspirator who was stationary, was supposed to be the taker and conveyor of messages. We had worked out a code and a password. The password was "darling," while the code for my flight to the border was "wedding." (Have I said we were addicts of code?)

At last — the miracle of M's voice at the other end: a small, scared voice confirming that, yes, she had delivered my note.

"Darling," I said. "Tell everyone the wedding is delayed."

"What?" squeaked M, through a surge of static.

"Darling!" I screamed. "The wedding is delayed! Tell everyone!"

"Oh my God, delayed!" she screamed back.

"I have to go!" I shouted.

"Okay, okay. But darling . . ." came the last frightened yell, ". . . please do *not* call *any more!*"

I was something of an old hand at long-distance calls by then. How many times in the past year had I sprinted to the home of one neighbour or another to take Sterling's telephone calls, which invariably came just when the phone lines in my own house were down. Here the human element cheerfully sabotaged the political. The Rangoon operators would simply put the calls through to the nearest working telephone in my neighbourhood, and the neighbours would come for me. Those transatlantic exchanges over the static of wiretaps and bad connections were taxing enough to leave me hoarse. But again the operators were helpful. Often they would translate or repeat our exchanges. After my screaming repetitions of "What?! What did you say?" they sometimes calmly broke in: "He says he loves you!"

Hoping these calls would soon be a thing of the past, I skulked back in the rain to the safety of our interim home in Moulmein — to continue to wait for news from the front. TM disappeared from time to time to confer *sub rosa* with informants, but returned always with good reasons why we should keep the faith.

At last, on about the fifth day, it stopped raining. All day long we resisted the urge to go outside, but by dusk we had reached the consensus that it was safe for a stroll. Still half-heartedly disguised as part Elizabethan castrato, part Burmese folk maiden, I figured we could pass for three innocent men taking the air.

We were all in high spirits. Maybe that explains our insouciance while walking back and forth in front of the police station. TM and Alban were talking religion, philosophy, meditation, and God. What an enigma TM continued to be! A pipe-smoking smuggler drawn to the mysteries of the universe.

He was saying something about Christianity — I remember this clearly — when we noticed the men waiting by the black car across the street. And they were waiting for us.

One of them called out to TM by name, asking if that was he.

"Yes," TM owned up, in a hedging way, as if to say *not necessarily*.

My first thought at this point went something like, "Oh good, it's him they want. Not me." Hoping to slink away, I took about two steps in the other direction before someone stopped me with a sound, the equivalent of "ah-ah, not so fast." That was the moment I knew all was lost.

One of the men had a pistol. Bad enough he brandished it, he also used it broadside to shove TM into the back seat of the car. TM's only offence was a brief stab at bravado. What, he had asked, was the meaning of all this? The same pistol motioned me in, next to TM. I complied. Alban came in last.

The driver and the man with the gun got in front — and off we went into the night. We drove for either ten minutes or ten hours. After a while, TM whispered in my ear, reminding me that we'd done nothing wrong, had broken no law by coming to Moulmein. Technically we were innocent. "Just remember the story," he hissed. "Remember the story."

The story, the alibi we'd prepared for just such an eventuality, was as follows: Simple folk from Rangoon desirous of a simple outing, we had come to Moulmein to shop. I forget the aliases assigned to Alban and TM, but mine was the Burmese equivalent of Brownie. Not Brownie as in dessert, but Brownie as in dark-skinned — as befit a peasant, I guess.

I passed on the whispered message to Alban, who acknowledged it by squeezing my hand quite painfully.

I expected — and rather hoped — at any moment to pass out from fear. A peculiar urge seized me. I was sensible enough not to give in to it — mainly, I think, because I wasn't sure whether the urge was to giggle or cry. But — vanity, vanity! — my thoughts turned to another concern. Now that the gig was up, I felt mortified by my disguise. How *embarrassing*! A two-bit magician being caught out in a shabby trick. The one twist I was unprepared for was what to answer when they asked me — as they surely would do — which buffoon I was impersonating and why.

We arrived at a building, a barracks of some sort. Following the compass of the gun's barrel, we entered a large waiting room. Immediately, one of our captors set about closing and locking every window and shutter in sight. TM was the first to be led upstairs, leaving Alban and me to wait in the locked and shuttered room. There was no guard — at least not that we could see — so we were free to speak; but I remember saying very little. Dumb with fright, we sat.

Hours passed — or perhaps only minutes — during which I noticed, then became obsessed with, a large stain on the ceiling. The stain was brown — the color of old blood — and had seeped through, I was sure, from the torture chamber directly above. It was very quiet up there. I imagined exotic ways in which they were putting the screws to TM while preventing him from uttering a peep.

TM reappeared at last, only to be led outside under guard. Then it was Alban's turn to go upstairs, leaving me — all alone now — for a fresh agony of waiting.

I returned to my fixation with the bloodstained ceiling. In my list of phobias, torture was paramount. As a child I had a horror of being tied down and tickled to death. Later, a more cultivated sense of cruelty led to an insane fear of being locked in a room with lizards. Then of course there was the matter of pain. *Under pain of torture* was a phrase that raised my hackles. My capacity for pain was limited, very limited.

By the time I was led upstairs, fear had created a kind of atmosphere, a new weather condition. A fog had settled on everything — especially on the room I entered. I could barely find my way to the far end, where I sensed, rather than saw, a desk. Behind that desk sat an army officer, a great glowering buffalo of a man. Him I saw clearly. His forehead was lowered, ready to charge. He did not offer me a seat. I stood in front of his desk, quailing, while he busied himself with the usual scare tactics of looking through papers in a file.

"What is your name?"

"Brownie," I said.

"Brownie, eh? Where do you live, Brownie?"

I realized I had no idea where I was staying.

"I live in Rangoon," I said. "I have come to Moulmein to shop."

The buffalo shook his big head up and down. "You're lying," he said wearily.

"That's true," I lost no time in admitting. "My name is really Wendy Law-Yone and I'm trying to get across the border, to be with my husband."

The buffalo snorted. I think it was a stifled laugh. "Then why don't you just apply for a passport?"

Apply for a passport! The better part of my adult life had been devoted to passport applications. Eagerly, I poured out my heart. I told about how I had been trying to leave the country for years, even before my marriage, even before the romance, even before my father's arrest. About how his arrest had taken place on the eve of my departure for college in California. About how my suitcase was already packed — new comb, new clothes, new pen, new toothbrush . . . all for naught. In a rush of self-pity, I went on to recount how, with the scrapping of my plans for travel and such, I had sought to get on with my life, only to be met with a dead end or barricade with every step I took, every corner I turned. How a music scholarship I won had been awarded to the boy who had placed second. How several months into my studies at Rangoon University, the registrar himself informed me that he was denying me admission. Throughout it all, how I had applied and reapplied for permission to leave, writing letters to ministries, personal appeals to the General himself — even as I went about. . . .

The officer cut me off. "Good, good. My God. That's enough." He'd had all he could take of my little hopes and regrets. Hastily, and with obvious relief, he dismissed me.

I have mostly pleasant memories of the next three days, even though we were behind bars. For one thing, Alban and I were together, in the same cell. Further, we had been told, soon after our "interrogation," that we were going to be released. After a day or two to allow for "arrangements," we would be escorted back to Rangoon. There, we'd be free to go.

The news made us euphoric. Reclining on the bunks in our cell, we told thigh-slapping jokes, scratched our initials into the wood with a stone, and generally carried on like morons. And — to add to the feeling that we were not really prisoners — we discovered we could order out for meals. The jailers brought packets of noodles wrapped in banana leaf, still warm from the noodle shop, and passed them to us through the bars. We paid them out of our cash supply, which we'd been allowed to retain. Oh, the stories we could tell back in Rangoon!

On the morning of our departure from the Moulmein jail came the first bad shock in days. TM, whom we hadn't set eyes on since the night of the arrest, came stumbling out into the courtyard where we had been made to wait before leaving for the train station. Behind him was a soldier who kept pushing him forward rudely. TM was a wreck. They had not treated him well. Uncombed, unshaven, dark circles around his eyes, he looked broken and sullen as he bent down to get a sip of water from a standpipe. I called out to him, but he pointedly refused to look at us. That was the last we ever saw of him.

Later, I heard it suggested more than once that TM was probably in the pay of the MIS and had turned us in. I don't believe so. I think we met as equals, TM, Alban, and I. It was adventure that drove us — that and our abundant ignorance. Maybe he thought *we* were in the pay of the MIS and had turned *him* in. Wherever he is, I hope he has recovered his style, puffing on his meerschaum while pondering the meaning of life.

On the train to Rangoon came the second big shock. No sooner had we taken our seats — Alban and his "escort" facing me and mine — than out came a pair of handcuffs to fetter Alban to his man. "What's that for?" I asked, aghast.

"Security." The cuffer used the English word, pronouncing it *sitjoority*. Our two plainclothes companions had seemed affable enough till then. But something told me at that moment not to inquire further about the security measures. At least they had the delicacy to place something, some jacket or cloth — I forget what — over the handcuffs, to conceal the indignity from the other passengers in the train. And at least I was spared (no threat to sitjoority, I suppose). Thus we sat, waiting for our train to leave, speechless in our new mood of foreboding. Then, as we gazed out our window, we saw an astonishing thing.

A train had just pulled in on the track next to ours. And on that train, hanging out a window, was none other than the teenage nephew of our recent hosts, from whom we had so abruptly taken leave. We saw him, he saw us. His mouth hung open as he semaphored disbelief. I watched him trying to hurry off the train, while stopping at every other window to poke his head out and signal us to wait.

The boy of course had no idea we were being "accompanied." I prayed for a speedy departure, before he could make it on to our train. But no, there he was in a flash, red-faced and breathless from the race, demanding to know what in the world we were doing there, and where was TM, and why had we not come back that night, leaving them to think the worst. . . .

I looked at Alban, who, like me, was trying to convey all manner of warning while basically remaining poker-faced. Alban's escort was staring straight ahead with the detached look of one peeing in a pool. The handcuffs remained hidden, but at a sudden point in the midst of his outpouring, the boy caught on that something was amiss; and leaped out of sight as though on sprung feet.

I saw Alban's man frowning with the effort not to laugh, but it was beyond me to control myself. I laughed and laughed — quietly at first, wiping away the tears, covering my face, but with increasing lack of control — till everyone else was laughing too. Just as I was trying, with every remaining ounce of sobriety in me, to pull myself together, I noticed that in the rough and tumble of comedy, Alban's handcuffs had become exposed, and this struck me as the funniest thing I had ever seen. Pointing at the handcuffs — reckless with hysteria — I hooted. I remember coming to my senses in the end — long after the general hilarity had ended, to be replaced with alarm — only when someone force-fed me a drink of water.

Things were not nearly as funny when we reached Rangoon. Army officers appeared on the scene. We were hurried into a van and blindfolded. I began to suspect that letting us go was not part of their immediate plans. Deprived of sight, I noticed my hearing turned acute. We arrived and were offloaded at what sounded like a crisis centre.

Arguments erupted, orders shot back and forth, doors slammed open and shut urgently, while a stampede of boots thundered up and down corridors and stairs.

The crisis centre happened to be secret police headquarters — and here for the next week we remained imprisoned. I tend to speak of that week as time in jail, but in fact I was locked in an empty office. A metal office table and folding chairs had been moved to one end, and two beds brought in: one for my guard, one for me. No Alban to comfort and cheer me here: only a scared woman, the wife of a junior officer, who was charged with keeping watch over me. All night long she insisted on leaving the bright overhead fluorescent lights on, too afraid to remain alone with me in the dark. No one had enlightened her about the nature of my crime. For all she knew I was a multiple murderer too dangerous to be held in a common jail.

The next day, she begged for a transfer. The old woman who replaced her arrived each day bearing her meals in a tiffin-carrier. Heartlessly, she unpacked and arranged each dish on the table, then sat down to eat without offering me a single bite. (I wasn't starving exactly, but my own meals usually consisted of cabbage broth and broken rice.) She also refused to speak to me. Not a single word would she utter to me. A woman who wouldn't share her food and wouldn't speak — I wondered if they'd planted a robot.

The time had come to protest. One morning, when the peon who delivered my meals brought breakfast (a cup of weak tea and a slice of margarine bread), I told him to take it away, announcing that I was on a hunger strike. I made him understand that he was to inform the authorities; I wanted to be sure they grasped the gravity of the situation.

But there he was again at lunchtime, bearing his tray. "I told you I was on a hunger strike," I said, vastly annoyed.

"Oh, but look!" said the boy, uncovering the dish. "It's Friday. Chicken curry."

So it was. Once I looked, I was lost. "Well, then," I said, "leave it here." So much for my hunger strike.

But I continued to protest — by turns demanding and begging, several times during the day, to see the officer in charge (to no avail, naturally); then complaining, during the night, to the ones who conducted the marathon interrogations that lasted from nine p.m. to nine a.m. The thrust of their inquiry, as far as I could see, was to determine whether I was attempting to overthrow the government through an elaborate plot involving my father, my husband, the CIA, or any combination of the three.

My inquisitors worked in shifts: one team of officers from nine at night till two or three; another team to carry on till nine the next morning.

Once, during one of these witching hours, the second team came on and, to my dismay, the major in charge was still finishing his dinner. He was nibbling on dessert, a sweet, sticky rice cake dredged in grated coconut and sesame seeds. He left it on the table in front of him, breaking off pieces during lulls, and munching. Too distracted to concentrate, I came out with it. "Major," I said as matter-of-factly as I could. "I would like some of that."

"Help yourself," he said, after a long, disbelieving stare, pushing the sweet toward me.

"Tell us if you have any complaints," the major said on another occasion. Ruling out as pointless the most obvious complaint — of being locked up — I picked on the old lady still guarding her tiffin-carrier in my room. "She won't speak to me," I tattled. It was really her meanness about food that I held against her, but the gripe about silence sounded more dignified.

Delighted to prove himself a man of action, the major clapped his hands for the old woman. "From now on speak to her," he commanded; then, turning back to me: "What else?"

By the end of the week, somewhere in the guts of the state security machinery, a decision was reached that detaining me served no further purpose. One morning, I was summoned to a downstairs office. I could see out to the driveway — my first glimpse of the outdoors in a week — where an important-looking limousine pulled in. Up the steps trotted a colonel, an obvious big shot, flanked by guards and attendants. I knew him from somewhere, I couldn't think where until he reminded me that we'd once played tennis.

The colonel was all charm and social grace. He lectured me — in a good-natured way — on my foolishness. I was a naughty girl to have done something so reckless, something that could have caused so much grief. Giving my parents such heartache. The rebels could have made mincemeat out of me. Lucky for me I'd been caught and rescued by the government.

I conceded my great good luck, forbearing to express surprise that my parent's heartache was suddenly a matter of concern to them.

Why all the skulduggery anyway? asked the colonel. Why not just apply for a passport?

I had learned my lesson. This time I did not chronicle my history of passport applications. "Just apply again," the colonel was saying. "Send the application addressed to me. I'll have it approved in ten days." Then he snapped his fingers for a lackey, instructed him to drive me home, and said I was free to leave. Once again I was witness to the whims of a police state — locked up one minute, set free the next — all for no discernible reason.

Alban was led into the office while I was signing the last of the release forms. It was the first time we'd seen each other since Rangoon station. He was so pale he seemed to me to have been locked away for ten years rather than ten days. "Are you okay?" I said. He nodded, but kept his mouth shut in a bitter line, and I wondered how he could help but blame the whole escapade on me.

It was only in the army jeep, on our way home, that we discovered who the big shot was. He was the secret police chief, the head of the MIS.

We asked the army officer behind the wheel to drop us off at the turnoff to our street, to spare my mother the shock of seeing us come up the driveway in a military vehicle.

It was late morning. I walked in the front door and straight into my mother's bedroom, where she was sitting on her bed. She stared at me as if I had risen from the dead. She thought I had long since reached

Bangkok. "Hi, Ma, I'm okay, Alban's with me, we didn't make it to Bangkok, we got caught, they put us in jail for a while, but nothing bad happened, it was fine, we're fine, everything's okay," I reported concisely for once in my life, propelled by the fear of seeing my mother pass out.

Then we went outside to tell the rest of the family, and there was M's little sister, who happened to be my little sister's best friend, hopping around and wringing her hands, insisting she call her mother and sister to let them know I was home.

All the time I was gone, my mother and *their* mother had exchanged news over the telephone — need I say in code? For reasons best known to them, the code they had chosen for the crisis we had caused was "balachaung" — a condiment consisting of dried shrimp, onions, garlic, and hot peppers. "Is the balachaung ready?" meant, "Have you had any news?" Every day they had called each other to ask if the balachaung was ready.

M's little sister picked up the telephone in our living room. Soon she was shrieking, "Ma! the balachaung's ready, Ma! Yes, it's ready! Just now!"

Standing next to the telephone, I could hear the shouting and crying at the other end as her mother broke the news to M in the background. "The balachaung's ready! Oh my God, the balachaung's ready!"

The secret police chief had said my papers would be approved in ten days. On the ninth day after I filed the application, fate thumbed its nose yet again. Riots broke out all over Rangoon. These were the anti-Chinese riots, sparked by events in China across the border, where the Cultural Revolution was in full flame. Allegedly fearing its spread to Burma, a repressed Burmese populace seized this opportunity to vent its ample frustrations by violently attacking the Chinese community. In the mounting riots and brutalities in Rangoon, martial law was declared, offices were closed, and hope — I now knew — was forever lost. "I absolutely refuse to sink into total despair at this point," I wrote to Sterling, even as I sank into despair.

Some two months later, when order was finally restored, offices re-opened, and the mail resumed, the day came when a messenger bicy-cled up to my door and actually handed me those much-delayed, near-mythical papers granting me permission to leave.

I placed my last long-distance call to Bangkok, where Sterling was still waiting. The operators came on, one by one, to wish me goodbye and good luck. "You're leaving? We'll miss you!" said the voices that had become our interpreters and allies.

My departure — another sombre and surreal event — was the first of its kind in years. It set a precedent and signalled the opening of the borders. After that, more and more Burmese citizens were al-lowed to leave — among them the rest of my family, who were let out in stages a year later, following my father's release from five years of imprisonment.

But that night of July 15, 1967, when I arrived at Mingaladon Air-port alone (because of the curfew still in effect, no one could come to see me off), I was not only the first to leave; I was the *only* passenger on Thai International flight TG 304 from Rangoon to Bangkok.

There was one last little fright I had to weather before final take-off, when I heard an announcement that the flight was being can-celled. (Just a practical joke played by one of my good friends, who happened to be part of the ground crew on duty at the airport that night!)

Finally I was really on my way; and it was only then, alone in that empty cabin, safely off in the night skies past the international air traf-fic point of no recall, that I could be sure of it: the expensive honey-moon at last was over.

The year of the pigeon had ended.

The Occidental Tourist

"The Occidental Tourist," named by a good headline writer, not by me, amused me for many reasons when I first saw it in print. Bob Adelman, a photographer friend from New York days, heard that the large majority of visitors to San Francisco were Japanese, and that many of them were on their honeymoon. "Can you believe that?" Bob said to me, which is his way of lighting a fire so I'll go exploring with him.

It's great fun, being a visually oriented writer, to work with a photographer. As Bob would also tell you, he's always overhearing conversations and saying, "Did you hear that?" and I'm always pointing to the corners of buildings where cats are considering suicide and saying, "Look! Quick!" Anyway: we set off for San Francisco, having no idea what to expect. The Japanese were tired, and shy. They had no idea that a photographer and inquisitive writer didn't come with every tour. They put up with us. Finally, they liked us. We liked them, and fell all over ourselves trying to describe the America they weren't seeing.

I am still in touch with Mr. Iida. I have visited him at his home outside Tokyo, and he and his oldest son came from New York, on a later trip, to visit us for part of a day in Maine. Every Christmas, they send a beautiful card on handmade

paper, with gorgeous stamp and sealing wax, and urge us to visit. We send
back the annual photo Christmas card, which features us kissing in various
odd places, such as while peeking through gaps in the stone in castles in Wales.

W HAT DOES MR. IIDA FIND MOST SURPRISING ABOUT
the United States? That he is the only person on the tour who
is not a honeymooner. It was a mistake. This happened, somehow.
Twenty-four young Japanese honeymooners, and Mr. Iida. For two
days he said nothing. Not a flicker of an expression crossed his face.
From scenic overlook to group luncheons (where the Japanese were
given the same sort of food Americans are served when they are recov-
ering from an appendectomy), Mr. Iida looked, but he did not react.

On the third day of the tour (ours was called Mach, and I soon wondered if the Japanese realized that it was Mach as in Mach number —
a reference, of course, to speed), after we had flown from San Francisco to Los Angeles, I finally got up the courage to approach Mr. Iida
as we were led through a patch of grass in Santa Monica. I hoped that
he might understand my good intentions, if not the words I was speaking. I began to talk about Santa Monica. It was a fairly liberal place, I
told him. *Tom Hayden* and *rent control*, I found myself saying. I pointed
to the Shangri-La, identifying it as the hotel where people connected
with the movie industry often stay — a hotel so chic that it has a
Power Gazebo in the courtyard instead of a pool. As we continued our
walk, I pointed in the direction of the Santa Monica pier, giving an im-
passioned description of it pre- and post-storm. Keeping my finger
pointed in the same direction, I tried to characterize Venice Beach: the
skaters, musicians, bodybuilders, and dealers in used Hawaiian shirts
(the bus had not stopped there, but on Wilshire Boulevard a block
past the Shangri-La, where there was nothing to see but grass and
palm trees and some people eating lunch at a picnic table). By this
time I figured what the hell: two days of asking diplomatic questions
and being fed white food — go ahead and talk bodies.

This worked, but not right away. Certainly Mr. Iida could have no idea why the tour guide was marching him in one direction, down a sidewalk winding through a completely inconspicuous park, while another person was gesturing to the distance and talking about muscles. Nor could he know why any of this was of interest to a magazine photographer whose activity would make Mick Jagger in performance seem comatose. I had to sympathize. The group had been in almost constant motion from the time it had left Tokyo two days before. For most, the thirteen-hour flight had been their honeymoon night. In San Francisco, they had cleared customs and joined up with a guide who boarded them onto a bus that immediately began crisscrossing the city. They had arrived on a beautiful day in San Francisco, and there had been a lot to see.

The terms of the trip were clearly set — complied with, if not desired, by the honeymooners: whatever was seen (a conservatory vaguely resembling Kew Gardens; a statue of Joseph B. Strauss, the chief engineer of the Golden Gate Bridge) would only be seen briefly. And it would be seen through a camera lens. Most often, the husband or wife stood alongside whatever was being photographed. One man had brought a tripod and stood beside his wife as the camera's auto-timer did its trick. Many of the women wore lace stockings and pretty patent-leather shoes. None of them wore running shoes. There was certainly no occasion to run: the group sat on the bus, gathering information from the tour guide between stops about everything from the price of California real estate to how much it was customary to tip, while Greg Fetherolf, our bus driver the first two days, chatted with us about where Houdini lived, where Clint Eastwood filmed a famous car chase, where Joe DiMaggio and O.J. Simpson went to high school. It was a San Francisco I'd never seen before — or at least not this way. We looked either at things, or at the land, and when the bus stopped, the Japanese looked at each other through their cameras.

On the second day, I asked Greg whether he had any curiosity about going to Japan, after working nearly one-hundred-hour weeks during the busy season. "Sure, that might be interesting," he said. "I'd like to spend a little more time in places than they do, though." (By the second day, some of the Japanese had gotten up the courage to ask him to step into the picture; all over Japan, there are sure to be pictures of Greg Fetherolf, standing at an overlook or smiling with his arm around somebody's wife while seagulls swirl.) Driving past Silicon Valley, past the redwoods (but not the biggest redwoods), past farm stands advertising FARM FRESH PRODUCE/COLD BEER. Greg pointed out Fort Ord (it wasn't night, so the war games weren't going on), supplied the name of the plants glowing along the highway (*ice plants* — to a Californian, this is like finding out that someone doesn't know what a Christmas tree is), predicted that because the water was still so choppy the seals would not be on the rocks (correct), and slowed down so we could peer at the roof of Clint Eastwood's house.

Wherever we went, there were other buses filled with Japanese tourists. Cameras seemed to be clicking everywhere. Whether it was a valley or a park, Pebble Beach or the shopping mall in Carmel, all of America was a photo opportunity, with bridges as backdrops and sea gulls as special effects. It was quite possible to see the cameras as having a life of their own, with hands controlling them that happened to be attached to the arms of people. Soon I began to feel frustrated about missed photo opportunities: no one got to stand below Arnold Schwarzenegger, running for his life on a billboard above Sunset Boulevard. As we sped on, Tower Records was pointed out, but Spago was not. Perhaps they were not the best photo opportunities, but I began to feel that the places didn't really exist if we didn't stop. Why were we passing Famous Amos without a cookie for everyone? Why were we just looking out the bus window at Ted Lapidus and Hermès and Gucci on Rodeo Drive? There were Christmas decorations in Beverly Hills we went by too fast to study, billboards of John Wayne's orange-tinted face rising above us, and surely the sea gulls from Seal Rock were still swirling, and here we were on the bus, with every other car that cut in front of us a Nissan or a Subaru.

Signs of home were everywhere for the Japanese. The Bank of Tokyo rose high up to the sky. Restaurant after restaurant offered sushi, every chance for *anago* and Sapporo if only we weren't hurtling past — slightly behind schedule but we'd make up the time — to Mann's Chinese Theatre, where patent-leather shoes could settle into indentations made by Eddie Murphy's shoes (BE FREE!), where John Travolta's square of cement got quite a lot of attention and George Jessel's drew none. And look: when Burt Reynolds drew in the wet cement, he wrote PUDLIC instead of PUBLIO the first time around, and changed the D to a B. That near-mistake wasn't going to draw anyone's attention when there was the gaudy theatre itself in the background, when the photograph of the loved one's hand had to be taken next to the imprint made by Elizabeth Taylor. The area around Mann's Chinese looks like Center City anywhere. Boring backdrop material. But earlier in the day it had been glorious at Marina del Rey — so much blue sky and blue water were sure to look vibrant surrounding everyone's beloved — and then there had been lunch at Benihana (America's concept of what a Japanese restaurant is), where shrimp were deveined, de-tailed, and set sputtering on the plates faster than you could say Where's-the-camera?

Duty free! It was a chance to buy gifts for friends and relatives in Japan (it is a custom to return the favour when the recently gifted newlyweds return home). Golf balls were a big favourite. Also cigarettes and liquor. In the outer store, the shelves of merchandise were identified by markers at the top that read: SALMON, NUTS, TOP GUN, PEBBLE BEACH, TEAM SPORTS, MICKEY MOUSE CLUB. Giddy with living in a cornucopia, the yellow Big Birds had toppled in the corner.

Out of duty-free and on to Olvera Street. Pigeons on the roof of La Luz del Día, musicians playing to customers eating outside, and sombreros that appeared from nowhere to help the honeymooners look even more fetching as they sat on top of a stuffed mule to have their pictures taken. Back in San Francisco, the guide's English translation of dinner instructions to the honeymooners had read, "You will have honeymoon steak dinners at the 'One Up' restaurant at Hyatt on Union Square. Please dress up and go to the restaurant. . ." The honeymooners may not have been sure about correct dinner attire without being told, but they did pack everyday clothes that were preppy conservative. They already seemed to know that everything would be a potential prop.

On the fourth day of the tour we went to Disneyland. By the time the honeymooners saw Michael Jackson looking earnest in his bejewelled white suit as Captain EO in 3-D, it probably made as much sense as anything else. Michael's spaceship whirled through the galaxy much the way our tour bus hit the highways. Shy about talking, most of the people on the tour were reluctant to speak English but could understand quite well what was being said. I can only imagine that there was a moment of empathy with Michael, whose problem in the movie was that he had lost the map. What if the tour guide disappeared? If there were no instructions about how to dress for dinner? If somehow things went out of control?

When I had this thought (while shaking hands with Mickey Mouse, I believe), I began to think of the cameras as mechanical pieces of luck, worry beads that might be held to the eye. If one person looked through the camera and located the other person, then the experience was real — there was documentation — even if nothing was felt or really experienced. And for all I know, many things may have been deeply felt. Standing alongside the statues may have seemed like being part of an important tribute. Seen in context, the Golden Gate Bridge may have changed the whole world around it. It was quite apparent that some smiles were triggered by happiness, others as automatic a reflex as a camera lens clicking. The honeymooners said that they were interested in seeing how much the United States was like the movies and the TV shows they had seen. They were looking for similarities instead of differences. They were in the mood to appreciate what they saw because they had just gone through exhausting wedding ceremonies and celebrations, and they had time off (long vacations — with the exception of a honeymoon — are unusual in Japan), and they were young and on an adventure in a land that they could afford. "Cheap," we kept hearing over and over. No one ever seemed to run out of film.

In Tomorrowland, Mr. Iida and I climbed into a car together to ride on Space Mountain. I tried to make sure that he knew what he was letting himself in for. By this time it was apparent to me that Mr. Iida spoke English very well and understood almost everything. This was not his first trip to the United States. He had come before (though not on his honeymoon then either), and back home in Japan he was trying to teach his eldest son English. Mr. Iida understood that I both loved and feared Space Mountain and that I thought riding on it was like being *in* 3-D. Waiting in line, he asked how so many children could be at Disneyland on a school day. I had no idea. He made the observation that the children seemed always to be laughing. I pointed out that kids of a certain age either slugged each other or fussed with each other's jewelry. "Very physical. Very good," Mr. Iida said. As we were whirled around the dark interior of Space Mountain, Mr. Iida made a few slight sounds, but my own screams drowned him out. "Very much scary run," he said when we got off. I staggered out the exit, tears shaken from my eyes.

After this, while the group scattered in all directions, I had coffee and tried to observe, without being observed, a trembling mother picking through a roast beef sandwich for the second time to make sure that all fat was removed before she handed it back to her son. Her other son wouldn't eat anything. Her husband made eye contact with no one. The mother kept saying to the son who had nothing in front of him, "Tell me what you want." He squirmed and wanted to know what the restaurant had. "Tell me what you want," the mother hissed. I thought it was going to turn violent any second. The Royal Street Bachelors sang merrily and played their instruments. "Tell me what you want," the mother hissed again, her hands trembling over a pile of meat.

That night we were at the observatory, looking at the night lights of Los Angeles, then off to the show at Louis Paciocco's La Cage aux Folles on La Cienega. Here, as the honeymooners stepped over pink feathers, a transvestite barked orders about where they were to sit. We were given roast beef dinners, which were actually quite good.

The white food (ice cream) didn't come until later. The Fabulous Gypsy (so introduced) presided over the show. Gypsy had his hair cropped short and looked quite sedate compared with Captain EO. Soon men in drag began doing impersonations of everyone from Julie Andrews to Tina Turner (seeing such a show without a Tina Turner imitator would be like omitting the turkey from Thanksgiving dinner). In the audience, sitting with a group of women called "The Forty Karats Club," was a columnist who, coiffed, dressed, and decolletaged, was a dead ringer for Joan Collins. On the walls were soft sculptures — at least, I think that's what they were — of women's torsos, horizontal to the floor: legs kicking out from under ruffly skirts. A round of applause was asked for the visiting Japanese ("They won't understand what's going on," the Fabulous Gypsy said). Wrong. They had it figured in two seconds. But what *I* was thinking was that after a day at Disneyland filled with illusion and confusion, this sort of parody and hype was like a chaser of grain alcohol after a shot of 100-proof tequila. Fiddling while Rome burns has become commonplace to us, but what could the performers have felt camping it up like this in the midst of the AIDS epidemic? I admit it: at this point in the tour I had begun to feel not so much worn out as worn down, as if I had convincingly been made to see that the world I lived in was so vast and so complicated that it was *properly* experienced in grabbed moments and that the jumble of Disneyland and La Cage aux Folles did indeed make some peculiar, if not cosmic, sense. For days and days I had boarded planes and hopped on and off buses and onto and off rides, looked down at cities from on high when that was where the bus stopped at scenic overlooks or when the plane descended. I had appeared as the person tagging along in my sensible shoes asking questions, while moments later the tables would be turned and I'd be the one being scrutinized. ("My boyfriend," I said, pointing to the smiling face of the man I lived with — a picture taken in a friend's pool in the Hollywood Hills the summer before, when we were in particularly good spirits. Heaven knows why I had that picture, and only that picture, with me. At the mere sight of it, one honeymooner dove into his carrying bag and produced a faded picture of his new wife as a five-year-old, in a kimono with a big bow in her hair, and another honeymooner announced that she would send me her wedding picture. Mr. Iida had the best reaction, however. "California wine?" he asked, pointing to the glasses of red wine at the rim of the pool.)

What the Japanese honeymooners and Mr. Iida were seeing was California as an Impressionist painting. Considering how quickly we moved through every day, I can only assume that the presumption about tours is that by having the tourists essentially removed from the action, it is possible to get the whole picture, while close involvement and examination would only reveal the chaotic bits and pieces that make up the whole. I found myself backing up, squinting, half mesmerized by the light show of the world that California can appear to be, half on simple sensory overload. It seemed sometimes maddening that wherever we looked, there was an illusion. The huge pastel-lit waterfall outside the Sheraton Grande, where we stayed in Los Angeles, was a perfect example. Water bubbles up through the clear vertical tubes, while at the same time a thin stream of water washes down from above so that the waterfall appears to be rising and falling at the same time.

When you take in a vast amount — when there are strong visual stimuli and when the world is full of strange sounds and when context isn't clear — it's very disorienting, to say the least. But while the things I saw often might have seemed, on the surface, like other things (the aerial view of nighttime L.A. was similar to the interior of Space Mountain, for example), there was, finally, no common denominator. Visually they had something in common, but experientially, nothing. There seems every possibility that the Japanese honeymooners will go home and say that California is a vast carnival. I'd like to see the odd game of solitaire that the laying out of the pictures will be when, inevitably, the album is opened and things are put in place. At Mann's Chinese, Burt Reynolds gives his thanks TO THE PUBLIC WHO MADE THIS ALL POSSIBLE. That's it, all right: the land of possibility. And as long as the tourists are willing to come to us, California will never have to take its act on the road. The Japanese — in fact, all tourists — validate us and endorse us by their presence. Every click of the camera is analogous to applause. And we return the favour. With film in the camera and the right moment presenting itself (more helpful, still, if those right moments are declared as such, and the tour bus stops), anyone can be a part of the show. It may not be true, except for the particularly lucky, that the world is your oyster, but this was an experience that certainly proved it *can* be your backdrop. Against it, you can be a star.

Through
a Barren Land

I fell in love with America, as many well-brought-up English girls do, in my mid-twenties. Through my American cousins, the hyphenated Maxtone-Grahams, I met a delightful man of my age called William Petty, who, three days after I met him, began to show me the America he knew and loved. We started, safely enough, with the Staten Island Ferry, and, a year or so later, graduated to the Grand Canyon in all its ruggedness. There we had a proper life-threatening adventure.

The "John and Mary" I am writing to are my cousins in New York, John and Mary Maxtone-Graham, John is the writer on ocean liners. I needed to set down the story in order to preserve the small but horrifying details, which might otherwise be lost in a fog of vague memories. I happened to write it as a letter, and in fact the letter form helped. You can't be too pseudy or purple in a letter — it won't wash, and your cousins will fall asleep. The thought that they would read it, handwritten, over tea in their Manhattan drawing room kept my lyrical urges in check. I managed not to mention God or Eternity once.

DEAR JOHN AND MARY,
I am writing to tell you what happened in the Grand Canyon, as you asked me to. Before I start, I beg you not to think of Bill Petty

as the baddy in the story, the man who took Ysenda down the Grand Canyon and had no idea how to get her out again. He had planned the journey carefully, and had followed our difficult trail, "Tonto East," two years before, in August. He knew exactly how far we had to walk each day, where we could look for shade and water, and how to find routes when they were not clear. His rucksack was twice as heavy as mine, and he was endlessly optimistic, saying things like, "I think our camping ground's just round the corner. Not far now."

And please don't think we shouldn't have gone down the Grand Canyon at all, knowing how hot it was going to be. We were looking forward to it. If you have been sitting in a magazine office in London for months, putting hyphens between "twentieth" and "century" (if it is adjectival), and dreaming of the somethingth wonder of the world which is a mile deep and teaches you all about Time, when you actually arrive at the South Rim you are bursting to go down. Bill had got us reservations on this particular back-country trail, and had booked a table for dinner at the bottom of the Grand Canyon at five o'clock on Thursday evening. We confirmed it when we arrived at the Grand Canyon Village: "Two steak dinners," the piece of paper said. It was heartening. Today was Monday: this time in three days, I thought, we will have joined the main trail and will be having our "steak dinner," surrounded by jolly Germans again.

I will tell you what we had done the day or two before, because it is part of the story. Bill and I converged in his parents' family kitchen in Denver in the middle of the night of the 1st July. I had flown from London and Bill had driven from his brother's wedding in Nebraska. I arrived first, and there was no one at home except a poodle. I looked through the brochures on the kitchen table about the Grand Canyon. They were riveting. Descriptions of beauty beyond your wildest dreams — of the drama of mesas, the shock of the gorge, the timelessness of creeks — were interspersed with small warning paragraphs in italics:

Body, 26, female, found under a rock in Grapevine Creek. Full canteen lying next to her. The victim had obviously tried to call for help . . . but . . .

Bill arrived and we listened to William Byrd on CD.

The next morning, feeling light-headed as you do on the first day of a hot holiday, we put our stuff into Bill's father's beautiful old Mercedes sports car and drove off, southwards. Very soon, we realised two things: first, that the car wasn't air-conditioned, and second, that the sun bore down on one in a monstrous way. All we could do was cower beneath it. Opening the windows didn't help. We decided to take the roof off — better a scorching breeze, we thought, than no breeze at all — so we covered ourselves in sun block factor 30 and drove along like merry people do in old films, shouting above the noise. It was great fun, but at the border of New Mexico, while ringing up my sister to ask how to find her house in Santa Fe, I had to rush into the oily garage and sit down. A few seconds later I fell off the chair, crashing my head on to the floor, and came round with the shock of it, saying "Where am I?" Bill nursed me with an ice-pack.

So we had a glimpse of the sun's power before going down the Grand Canyon. Arriving at Santa Fe was bliss. Livia had made a picnic to take to the opera; we sat under the poplars in the early evening, watching the sun disappear.

On Grand Canyon day, we left Santa Fe at dawn and drove all day through the bleached landscape of New Mexico and Arizona. We drove straight to the back-country office to confirm our reservations on the Tonto trail.

"No one's been on your trail for a month now," the ranger-in-uniform said.

"Is there any water in Cottonwood Creek?" Bill asked.

"It's pretty dry down there. There was a trickle three or four weeks ago. It's probably dried up by now. Take a lot of water."

I sat sullenly in the back of the office, letting the coolness of the room seep into my hot body, while Bill and the ranger talked deeply and slowly about possible water sources.

"We don't have a checking service any more," the ranger said. "You'd better tell a member of your family when to start worrying."

If it had been me talking to the ranger, I would have made high-pitched exclamations such as "Gosh. How frightening. I suppose we'd better." But Bill just stood still, hiding whatever reaction he might be having. "OK," he said, occasionally.

To the Grand Canyon General Store next. It is fun being in America because you take a trolley rather than a basket. Basking, again, in the coolness of the huge aisles, we wandered up and down, picking things off shelves and crossing them off our list: iodine pills, snake-bite kit, first-aid kit, canteens, nuts, beef jerky, freeze-dried vegetables (Bill insisted that these would be useful), torches, batteries, zip-lock bags, pink energy-giving powder to put in our water, and Power Bars with zestful zig-zags on the wrappers.

Then, supper. We went to the Bright Angel Lodge and drank two jugs of iced water. We had soup, roast beef, and apple crumble — nursery food — to set us up. We felt we were beginning to procrastinate, so we paid the bill and drove, via a tap where we collected four gallons of water, to Grandview Point, twelve smooth miles away. In a frenzy of concentration, we pared down our luggage and put it into rucksacks. Mine was small, Bill's was manly. He carried the tent with its nine metal poles; I carried the mats. He carried a huge and potentially leaky water container, as well as his own gallon canteen; I carried my canteen and one of those pretty Spanish water pouches which you squeeze and which stink of fresh leather. We were in a car park. Everyone else was about to go home.

"Let's split out of here," Bill said.

"Yes, let's. How d'you put this thing on? Can you help me?"

My role as weed had started. We took our first step downwards. There it was, the Grand Canyon itself, pinkish and impossible to understand. An eagle was flying over it. We were full of descending energy and had no qualms at all.

It was a stony and rough path, and quite steep. The weight of rucksack bore down on us from behind and we had to use our hands to hold us back. It was seven o'clock and we knew we had to walk for three hours to get to the Horseshoe Mesa, our first camp ground.

"I love the Grand Canyon. I want to *be* the Grand Canyon," I said. It sounds a pretentious remark now, but it did mean something then. Perhaps being in a place like that makes one speak like a hippy.

We had brought twice as much water as we expected to. So when we started sucking on the leather pouch, we felt we were making no impression at all on our supply. But two slightly serious things happened now; first, we passed three people who were coming in the opposite direction. The difference between their mood and ours was sinister. We were in a skipping, light-hearted mood, tripping from stone to stone and agreeing about things. These people, though blond and sporty, were hanging their heads and not smiling at all — not even to be polite to us. They looked exhausted.

"We're out of water," they said. "Can you lend us some?"

"We can't give you much, because this might have to last us for days, but you can have a gulp each."

They fell on the Spanish leather pouch, and each went into a momentary state of bliss, instantly cut short.

"How much further is it to the top?"

"About an hour."

"An *hour*! We thought we were nearly there. I can't go on for another hour."

"It's really not very far," Bill said. "The water will help you."

"Thanks very much. Bye."

They stomped on upwards and we skipped on downwards. The second serious thing was that it grew dark. You always hope that twilight will last for ever, but it doesn't. We wondered whether to pitch our tent there, or to try to get our torches working and walk on in the dark. Bill decided on the torches. We rummaged for them in our side-pockets. We had to find the batteries as well. Bill sat on a rock and got out the quarter-dollar coin he had brought to undo the screw of the torch, but it didn't fit. This mattered terribly; a small thing like a coin not fitting into a screw does matter in a place like this, I realised. But Bill didn't curse or panic; he just felt about patiently for a spoon. The end of the spoon worked. It was too dark to read the "positive" and "negative" signs, but he got it right, and with the light of the first torch assembled the second.

On we walked, feeling proud with our beams of light showing us the way. We arrived at the Horseshoe Mesa at ten, and found a group of people there, chatting and rustling their sleeping bags.

"Is there any water down in Cottonwood Creek?" Bill asked.

"There's tadpole water, so we drank that. It's disgusting!"

Bill set up our tent — the tent he had been setting up since he was seven; a sturdy, trusty tent which does not need to be attached to the ground. We put on our smart flannel pyjamas (we had brought them instead of blankets), brushed our teeth and got inside.

"We got here!" Bill said. "We now know two things: we can walk in the dark, and there's water in Cottonwood. Those people are so ignorant. They came down with two quarts of water each. And they don't seem to realise that tadpole water is what you always drink down here. Look at the Milky Way. Have you ever seen it before?"

We used our trousers for pillows. In the middle of the night I woke up shivering but hot. I put Bill's pyjama top, which he had taken off, over my shoulders and went back to sleep, shuddering slightly.

We woke to the sound of people leaving. It was half-past five. I got out of the tent and talked to a girl in shorts.

"I don't advise going down there," she said.

"Why not?"

"It's very hot, and very dry."

"But we've got lots of water, and we can walk in the dark."

At six o'clock we started walking down the dusty, slippery path to Cottonwood Creek. The expression "route-finding ability" was at the front of my mind, "route" pronounced as "rout" is in England. Our hikers' guide said that you needed it for this path. Bill had it, thank goodness. I just followed. We passed yucca plants, dead-looking and solitary, sticking out of the ground and taller than anything else.

"That's a barrel cactus," Bill said. "If you are dying of thirst you can take all the prickles off and find water inside." The poor cactus was guarding its water, hugging its prickles so that thirsty animals wouldn't try to tear it apart.

"Look. D'you see down there, the pale green trees? They're cotton-woods. That's where we're spending the day." It was before eight o'clock when we reached the creek but the heat was already unbear-able. We sat on a rock and shared a Power Bar. Bill said we should walk up the creek to find water; we *could* make do with tadpole water, of course, but it would be better to go further up and find fresh spring water which had not had time to be bred in. So we left our rucksacks and started scrambling through the confusing, choked creek, hoping that water might appear, but it didn't. I grew cross and demoralized.

"Let's just have tadpole water," I said. "Come on. Please. Tadpole water's fine. You said so last night."

"You wait here and I'll go further up on my own."

I waited.

"Ysenda! Found some!"

It was true. He was standing on a blanket of bright green grass, and the weight of his body was forming a small lake of water.

"Desert water," he said. "Let's have a drinking party."

We took gulp after gulp of our clean tap water, so that we could have an empty canteen to fill with desert water.

Until this moment I had never been at all interested in a zip-lock bag. But when Bill pulled one out of his pocket, tore a hole in one cor-ner, put his hand inside, pressed it into the grass, watched it fill up with pink water (the colour of the water at the dentist's when the man says, "Have a good rinse now. It's all over") and let the water trickle into the canteen, I suddenly took notice of one. It was not a thankless task, this water-collecting. The canteen filled fairly quickly. I had a few goes of pressing with the zip-lock bag, but was not as good at it as Bill. We took uneven turns.

We walked victoriously back to our rucksacks and carried them to a hiding-place for the day.

"When are we going to stop?" I asked Bill.

"Very soon. There's a bit more shade further on."

We tried lying under some squat, dark trees, but they weren't shady enough: shafts of sunlight forced their way through the dense branches. So we took our mats, a book, some beef jerky and nuts, and our water, to a great slab of shade among some Indian ruins. It was becoming absurdly hot — so hot that we couldn't move. We lay in our slab of shade, unable to talk, eat or think "How pretty this is." I tried to read the beginning of *Huckleberry Finn* but was too jealous of the characters because they were not in the Grand Canyon. My one thought was "If only it were this time tomorrow. By this time tomorrow I will be so much happier. But it isn't. It's still this time today."

Bill had warned me that our walk to Grapevine Creek this evening was the hardest part of our journey, and would take a long time. We knew that this meant leaving at five. Between noon and two o'clock the heat was at its height; I know now that it was 125 degrees. But by five o'clock it didn't seem much cooler. We trudged back to our rucksacks and forced ourselves to roll up our mats. We searched for the vital iodine pills in endless side-pockets before finding them. I started to cry with the heat.

"I hate the Grand Canyon's guts," I said.

"Oh, Ysenda, I'm terribly sorry. It's all been a great mistake. I should never have brought you."

"No, it's all right. I love it really. But if only it were this time tomorrow, Bill."

Once we had started walking, it wasn't as bad as all that. Every step brought us nearer to our steak dinner. This walk was not steep, so we made good progress and could walk almost at a normal pace. We wound our way through miniature orchards of cactus plants, and every now and then came across a small heap of three stones, which meant that a human being had been here before. We drank as we walked. Bill drank much more than me, but he was a big man. We longed for the shady sides of creeks.

We had still not seen the geological reason for the Grand Canyon. But now we saw it, and for the first time I made touristy remarks:

"Golly. The actual Colorado River! But it's green. You said it was hot-chocolate-coloured. Shall we take a photograph?"

As it grew darker, the canyons towards Grapevine Creek grew strangely threatening. I had never seen an evil landscape before. Until now, the place had merely seemed indifferent to us; now it seemed to be against us. We couldn't understand it, but we both felt it. We kept not being nearly there. Our destination was a small, round camp ground at the end of a creek: Bill began to take on the shape of one of those statues of the Virgin and Child made of an ivory tusk, which curves inwards. On our right was a drop-off which it was better not to think about. Its sides were horribly smooth.

"Think of Frodo Baggins, Ysenda. *He* went through much worse things than this."

"But he was fictional," I said, grumpily.

Just before needing to use a torch, we arrived, and dropped on to the ground. It was comforting to be surrounded by a circle of stones laid by a human being.

"Let's sleep under the stars," I said. I couldn't bear the idea of sorting out the metal poles.

"I'd feel happier in a tent," Bill said. "You never know what animals might come."

So we put it up, in silence, much too hot to think of eating and too worried to brush our teeth. We wanted to keep a gallon of water each for the next day. But our thirst was great.

I got inside the tent. Bill was lying on his back, thinking hard and staring at the ceiling.

"This is the plan," he said. "We'll wake up at four. We'll look for water in the creek, and if we don't find any in a half-hour we'll go back to Cottonwood."

"Back to Cottonwood! No, we simply can't go back to Cottonwood. We've just come all the way from there. We're on our way to the bottom. I'm not going back."

"But we need water, Ysenda. We know we can find it at Cottonwood."

"You just drink too much."

"We'll go back the way we came, back up to Horseshoe Mesa and Grandview Point. It's the sensible plan."

So our longed-for arrival at the bottom, our easy descent on the last morning, and our steak dinner, were not going to take place after all. Instead, we would have to climb out the difficult way — the way we knew all too well, having come down it.

"Also," Bill said, "there's no proper shade to hide in tomorrow if we carry on going down. We know there's shade in Cottonwood. We'll spend all day there, and climb out in the evening. Now drink: drink as much as you like."

The night was like a night in hell. A vicious, fiery wind blew hard at us, and it was so hot that you had to lie on your side in order to sweat as little as possible. We had no difficulty in waking at four. Bill folded up the tent and went to look for water. I felt for our bags of nuts and dried fruit, and found that they had toothmarks in them: a desert rat or ringtail cat had come in the night and eaten everything except for the beef jerky and a few nuts. It had tried to force its way into the freeze-dried vegetables, but had not managed.

Bill came back, without water, so we put our rucksacks on and walked back the way we had come last night, treading on our old footprints. Stomping English hymns such as "Onward, Christian soldiers" and "Guide me, O, thou great Redeemer, pilgrim through this barren land" helped me along: I marched in rhythm. By eight o'clock we were approaching our dear Cottonwood Creek. It was almost homely compared with Grapevine.

We had memorized where our spring was by looking hard at a large, round rock above it. But it was much harder to find than we expected. It was getting absurdly hot again, and I couldn't believe we were scrambling about, not finding our spring.

"Let's leave our rucksacks and come back for them when we've found it. Take the beef jerky and nuts, and the canteens."

A few minutes later, we found our darling spring. We took our shirts off, trod them into the wet grass, and put them on again. It was delicious.

Our minds were at rest. We lay down, snuggled up as close as possible to the bamboo copse, and fell asleep.

We spent the whole day by the spring, drinking all the water we already had: we had left the iodine pills in our rucksacks and couldn't contemplate going to collect them. The heat above the creek was deadly and it would have exhausted us to walk in it even for a minute. Bill had been sick as soon as we arrived at Cottonwood, but he didn't mind. He just kept drinking. The water was hot and disgusting, of course, tasting of a mixture of earth, leather or plastic (depending on the canteen), pink powder and iodine pills. But I loved it. A yard or so above us, a black and white snake writhed about in a bamboo tree, showing off. We didn't have the energy to worry about it. "It's not poisonous," Bill said. "It's not a rattlesnake, and rattlesnakes are the only poisonous snakes in the Grand Canyon."

Time passed peacefully and slowly. We looked at our little world of spring, grass, bamboo trees and zip-lock bag and felt satisfied and happy. The sun passed over us and we had to move to the other side of the bamboo copse. While Bill slept, I beat a bamboo tree with a twig, in order to frighten off the snakes. "The sun shines bright on my old Kentucky home," I tapped, because my choir had sung it a few weeks ago at a concert in Cambridgeshire.

At five o'clock we decided it was just about cool enough to start the hard work of filling a canteen with spring water. Bill pressed his fingers into the grass and discovered to his horror that it had dried up.

"It can't have," I said. "It's a spring."

But it had. If Bill pressed with all his might, he could form a tiny, dark-brown pool of thick mud.

"This isn't funny," I said.

"No, it's not funny."

"It's the most stupid thing we've ever done."

"We'll have to make do with drinking mud. Muddy water's better than no water."

So Bill started pressing. It was a cruel task, especially since we could remember how easy it had been yesterday, and how we had squandered water today, dipping our shirts into it. Bill yanked clods of mud out of the ground and squeezed them as hard as he could, so that drips would trickle into the bag. He shook with the effort, and needed to drink almost as much water as he was collecting. In an hour or so, with a few gestures of demoralized help from me, he had put two inches of mud into our transparent canteen. It settled, leaving a thick residue. We poured the top layer of brown liquid into our own canteens and went back to our rucksacks to find the iodine pills.

We decided (after wondering whether we ought to stay here till morning in the hope that the spring would fill up again — but what if it didn't?) to leave at eight, which would give us half an hour of daylight to find our way back to the trail. At eight o'clock it was still sweltering; but my spirits were high because I so desperately wanted to get out, and now we were on our way OUT of this terrifying place. We started climbing up the steep, parched path towards the Horseshoe Mesa. We used a code — "Mmm?" "Mmm," meaning, "Are you all right?" "Yes," in order to save energy. We took tiny sips of water. Bill took his shirt off, and advised me to: "It's so much cooler," he said. So I did; and walked on in a Marks & Spencer's bra which had become pink with days of Grand Canyon grime.

After two hours of dogged climbing, Bill said, "OK, we're going to abandon our rucksacks."

"What? Leave them here?"

"I don't mind if I never see mine again."

So we left them, taking only our bag of passports, tickets and money, and one or two sentimental things such as *The Grand Canyon Songbook*, a book I had made for Bill which contained psalms, chants, Bach chorales and the words of "Sumer is icumen in."

Our burden was lightened, and we felt better. And much sooner than we expected, we saw the wooden signpost which meant we were at the Horseshoe Mesa, where we had spent our first night. It was ten o'clock at night, and there was no one at the camp ground. "Only three or four hours to go," I thought.

Then Bill was sick again. The water he had been drinking all day had not been going into his system at all, just sitting there, uselessly.

"But I feel a whole man again now," he said. "Let's go on."

So we did. The joy of being on the home stretch was so great that I could have skipped, even in my state of thirst. I just prayed that Bill would be all right, and he seemed to be at the moment. He told me there was a bottle of sparkling cranberry juice in the car on the rim of the Canyon.

My torch went out. Bill tried to mend it, taking it apart and wiggling a small piece of wire.

"It's broken," he said.

"I'll just have to walk close behind you, and use the light of yours."

That worked all right. But our minute-long rests became two-minute ones, then five-minute ones. Bill was not feeling at all well. Soon he lay down on the path, so dehydrated that he couldn't move.

"We'll lie here for ten minutes," he said, "and if I'm not better by then, will you go to the rim on your own and bring me down the bottle of sparkling cranberry juice?"

"Oh, Bill, please be well enough. I couldn't go up there on my own. Just be well enough for three more hours."

"Ysenda," he said, ten minutes later, "I've stopped sweating. Will you pour some of that mud over me?"

I rubbed the brown gunge from Cottonwood Creek, the smell of which was what Bill's body was revolting against, on to his tummy and his forehead.

"Do you think you could go to the top alone, Ysenda, and find a ranger to come and rescue me?"

"No. I really couldn't. I don't know how to find the path. I'd get lost."

"But I might die. If you're as dehydrated as I am you really can die."

"OK, then." I grabbed the torch, the car keys, the spoon to open the torch with, some more batteries and a 20-dollar note. I felt furious rather than pitying. This reversal of roles was absurd. In five minutes I was lost. I had gone off the path and scrambled up a bank of stones which led to nowhere. Then I thought, "Of course. This is a nightmare. I'm going to wake up in bed in London."

I found my way back to Bill. "I got lost," I said. "Please can I stay here with you? I'd rather die with you than die alone."

So we lay there, looking up at the indifferent stars.

"Ysenda," Bill said. "I really *might* die, you know. Will you try going to the top again? The way to find the path is to shine the torch on to the ground in front and look for old footprints."

"All right. I'll go. Bye."

The footprint method worked. I leaped from stone to stone in a kind of frenzy, taking tiny sips from the muddy dregs of my water. That walk has contracted in my memory so that I can't describe how long or far it was; all I can remember are moments of it: sitting, panting on a stone, looking into the dark wastes and thinking of Bill lying there; tipping my head back to take sips from the bottom of the canteen, and only then seeing the rim which was still far above me; worrying that if and when I reached the car, I wouldn't be able to start it (it had been difficult recently) or actually drive it, never having driven an automatic car. And where would I drive to? I had no idea what time it was. The walk went on and on and didn't change character for two or three hours; every steep, dry footstep just led to another one. My lips tasted as salty as crisps. Every now and then I allowed a minute drop of water to escape on to the outside of my mouth rather than be swallowed. All I thought about was sparkling cranberry juice. It seemed impossible to believe that a world existed where you could come across a whole bottle of liquid.

When I pointed my torch at a wooden step for the first time, I was encouraged: I remembered from our journey down that some of the steps in the first half-hour were wooden and level. Then (oh the joy of it) I saw a wooden signpost: "To go beyond this point you must make a reservation at the back-country office." So now I really was within lazy-tourist walking distance of the car park.

Then — the beloved wall. I have never been so excited to see a wall before. There I was, on the Tarmac, shining my torch round the empty parking lots. The beam shone onto something which looked like a useful map but it turned out to be one of those pretty National Park weatherproof signs which told me all about the interesting trees which grow near Grandview Point.

I looked for the car and couldn't find it immediately. Then I did. I ran towards it and opened the boot. I knew exactly where the bottle was. Like a drunkard, I tore off the gold wrapper, prized open the lid and took gulp after gulp of strange fizzy juice. Then I put one of Bill's shirts on, and got into the driving seat. The car started. I worked out what "P", "R" and "D" must mean, and in a minute was driving along the deserted road. No one passed me. I drove for twelve miles, into the village, and swung into a petrol station but it was closed, so I swung out again. Then I saw a light on in what looked like a hotel reception room. I parked the car and ran in.

There was a large woman behind the desk.

"Hello. I've just come out of the Grand Canyon and I've left my friend down there, who's dying. Can you send someone to rescue him?"

"Yes, Ma'am."

She rang the Park Ranger service. For an hour a man asked me questions: when did I leave Mr. Petty? What colour was he? "Mud-coloured." What had he been drinking? "Mud." Where was he exactly? How did you spell Ysenda? I answered every question as promptly and desperately as someone in an oral exam.

"Stay by the phone," the man said. So I collapsed into a chair in the lounge, having gone to the car to collect a jersey: suddenly I felt rather cold. I went to the ladies' "restroom" and saw my reflection for the first time for days: apart from having white, dried-out lips and the old bruises from fainting, I looked fine. I splashed my face with tap water.

The telephone rang again. This time it was the young ranger who was going down to find Bill. It was four in the morning. I told him I

85

would be in the Yavapai Lodge (that was the hotel) until Bill came to find me. Then I sat on the chair again and a night-time ash-tray cleaner came to talk to me and brought me some cold coffee. At five o'clock I started to cry.

"Is there a room here?" I asked the woman behind the desk.

"No, Ma'am. We're all booked up."

"I've got a sleeping bag. Could I possibly sleep on the floor somewhere?"

She put me behind the Grand Canyon Flights and Tours desk. With my bottle beside me, like a tramp, I got inside and shuddered to think what might happen. For the first time I realised that Bill's dead body might be hauled out of the Grand Canyon; that I would tell his parents the story and we would stand round a coffin at a quiet funeral in Denver, with an electronic organ playing slow, vibrating chords. The terrible sadness of it overwhelmed me and I turned away from the Flights and Tours desk towards the skirting board.

When I woke up the room was loud with bustle. People were checking in and checking out. The large woman was standing over me.

"Your friend's doing fine," she said. "The ranger's with him now and they'll be hiking out later this morning."

I spent the morning in the cafeteria and the lounge, drinking and dozing. I worked my way through glass after glass of iced orange juice, basking in relief and watching American families having breakfast. On my chair in the lounge I felt like an exhibit: there should have been a notice beside me saying, "This sleeping girl has just been down the Grand Canyon and has not seen a human being (except her companion, who nearly died last night) or a running tap for days. Notice her pinkish shoes and sore lips. Don't let this happen to you. Take a flight or tour."

In the middle of the morning I drifted across the road to the general store to buy a new hat (the old one was in the abandoned rucksack) and two litres of water. At lunch-time I went back to the cafeteria and ate a plate of tomatoes. I wished Bill would come in.

Then he did. I turned and saw a dazed, muddy figure walking towards me.

"You're alive," I said.

"Have you got us a room?"

"Yes. Let's go there now."

We drove: it was in a motel-ish wing.

"Let's have baths."

The inside of the bath was brown and encrusted; I had always longed to need to wash as badly as medieval people must have, just to see what it was like.

We didn't stop smiling for two days. Bill told me his story: he had lain on the path, not sleeping but obsessed with sparkling cranberry juice. Dawn broke at five o'clock and he began to worry, because the monster sun would come and kill him. He thought I might not have got to the top. At half-past five he decided he had better pull himself upwards as a last gesture. He felt his heart might burst, so weak and dehydrated was he. He was worried for me; and says now that he frankly was resigned to die. But he heaved himself upwards at a snail's pace, as the air grew hotter. Then he heard a voice.

"William?"

It was Barry the ranger. Bill says he couldn't believe how quickly he was brought back from death's door to the jolly world of American chat about this and that. Barry had a huge rucksack and gave Bill three litres of water, very slowly. He told him he had lost half his body fluid. By the time he was ready to walk, it was too hot to climb out, so Bill had the choice of waiting till evening, or ordering a helicopter to come and collect him from the Horseshoe Mesa, the nearest flat place. He chose the helicopter.

He loved his helicopter ride and promised to take me on one the next day. We spent two nights in the Grand Canyon village, convalescing — drinking, sleeping, having scrambled eggs and bacon for breakfast and writing letters. We drove everywhere and arranged for our rucksacks to be collected by a young ranger who was saving up for a truck. We stood on the rim in the evening, gazing at our desert.

87

We had our helicopter ride, "a complete sight and sound experience," with headphones and the *Water Music* playing. I loved it. But I turned round and saw Bill quietly being sick into the bag provided.

Love from Ysenda.

KATHERINE GOVIER

In Fez
Without a Guide

*Sometimes the apparatus of travel overwhelms the event. There are trips when
I feel that everything set in place to facilitate tourists is in fact preventing me
from seeing the place the way I want to see it. The journey becomes a game of
fox and hounds as I try to escape the tour operators, translators, souvenir sellers, crowds, staged events, and advice givers of all kinds to discover the "real"
Japan, Hong Kong, or, in this case, Morocco.*

*Such tension almost always exists in travel today. There is a form of arro-
gance in the notion that we, alone among tourists and on a two-week package,
can cut through the commercialism and find the heart of a strange land. Here
was a trip when I learned the folly of flight. Morocco I found to be like the pro-
verbial onion: remove the layers of hucksters intervening between oneself and
the experience and you have nothing left. Though they brought tears of rage to
my eyes, guides* were *Morocco.*

AS WE STAND ON THE STATION PLATFORM IN RABAT
waiting for the train to Fez, a young man admonishes me about
the open zipper on my bag. Never mind that the exposed compartment contains only a large bottle of mineral water, he fingerwags, in

French, I must close it: there are thieves about. When the train arrives he rushes with us to the first-class cars. He vanishes just long enough for the conductor to arrive and check our tickets. Once we are settled, and take cognizance of the other travellers in our compartment, we notice, lo and behold, that the young man has returned and has taken a seat.

This is Abdul. He is a student, he says, with seasonal employment as security on the train. Fez is his city; he is going home for several days off work. He is a student of German literature, certainly not a guide. Nonetheless, he would like to show us around Fez. It's good you're not a guide, says my husband, because we really don't want a guide.

We'd been in Morocco two days. We landed in Casablanca and took a bus to Rabat, stopping only to have a glass of superb freshly squeezed orange juice. Our hotel was vast, cool, and marble-floored: the elevator was flanked with photographs of the King and his sons. I wanted to stay by the pool forever, but John convinced me we should see the town.

We escaped the hotel unescorted, and walked for twenty minutes alongside the walls of the Royal Palace on a road crazy with motorbikes, trucks, Renaults, bicycles, and donkeys. We were aiming for the ruins of Chellah, described in our guidebook as "wistful," with an "intangible sense of antiquity." The exquisite site is a walled enclosure which likely flourished from the time of the Phoenicians and was ruined by the tenth century, after which it was used as a necropolis. We passed under the huge crenellated gateway at the entrance. Inside, a spring watered a jungle of bamboo, banana, hibiscus, begonia, date trees, and a garden arranged in squares, for meditative walks, continually coming back upon itself.

On the pathway, two men had set up a child's table, which looked as if it had been lifted from a fifties schoolroom, upon it a small piece of plastic-covered cardboard on which was written TEN DINAR. We began by energetically declining to purchase a ticket because our guidebook said we didn't need one, but soon gave in; it wasn't worth ruining the atmosphere. Next, we deflected a young man with a Canadian flag sewn on the knee of his jeans who wanted to be our guide. We succeeded in getting partway down the hill in the silence and magical ambience of the Merenid sanctuary, where hibiscus and morning glories swarmed the collapsing walls and giant, dying palms.

But there, beside the burial grounds, a more subtle fellow in a purple windbreaker lay in wait. He began, uninvited, to deliver us his wisdom on the grave of the Black Sultan. Here were the pools for purifying the dead bodies, here the room for wrapping the corpse in draperies. He told us he couldn't take us to the sacred pool (it didn't seem to be his territory), so we paid him another ten dinars to leave, and moved on.

Our goal was the sacred pool, where women were said to come to feed hard-boiled eggs to black eels, as a remedy for infertility. And here it was. Around its edges a family had taken up residence, but there were no women, no eggs, and a small boy was only able (for a price) to show us one thin, lonely eel swimming above the stone floor. We took a taxi back to the hotel, paying the driver the exorbitant price he demanded, because he did not turn on his meter.

The next morning I saw eggs, in the Rue des Consuls. An old man pulled them in a deep cart; half of those he had for sale were already broken. When he could do no more business he tipped the cart up on its front wheels and went to sleep under it, against the shaft. We were on our way to explore Oudaia, a casbah at the top of a cliff overlooking the Atlantic. This was the heart of the original pirate town. Salé, across the Delta, and new Salé, had mainly concerned themselves with robbing ships and trying to win back Iberia from the Spaniards. Robinson Crusoe fell prey to the pirates of Salé, in fact.

The casbah was the fortified home of the wild Oudaia tribe, mercenaries hired to quell the Berber tribes. We walked under the famous gateway of red sandstone with its Kufic decorations, the entrance to a palace hall of which nothing remained. Immediately we were descended upon by a guide.

"No thank you," we said.

Undeterred, he walked with us.

We attempted reason. "Nous voulons là visiter seule."

This statement enraged the man. He followed us for a hundred feet or more, shouting. "You can't go in without me, I live here."

We turned, thinking to defeat him by taking a footpath that seemed to be beyond his purview. We found a beautiful garden in the Andalusian style, rich with begonias, roses, and little pathways all marked out like a maze. Thinking ourselves very clever, we walked through the casbah from this direction. As schoolchildren skipped past, home for lunch with their backpacks, we happened upon the tiny perfect Café Maure, with its blue-painted tables and chairs, on what had been the semaphore terrace, a dizzy-making perch over the Atlantic. The Coke, served in old-fashioned Coke bottles with Arabic script, tasted absolutely marvellous.

Elated, we walked on. I bought a toy camel made out of wound wool from one of the only female hawkers I was to see in the entire country. We were managing Oudaia without a guide, but wondered about our stubbornness: had we missed something? Were we trying to be too independent? The guide's voice haunted me: "I live here!" On departure we had a minor altercation with a fellow who tried to direct us up the hill to "very good fish restaurant" when we wanted to go back down the hill and into the medina. We felt nervous about turning our backs on the man; his eyes seemed to throw knives.

In the medina, we played a stone-and-pebbles version of "Hi-Q" with a friendly craftsman. He was amazed that John could repeatedly jump all the stones and leave only one in the middle. We were amazed that he sold the game and had never learned how to win. John taught him "le système" and we left with a wood-framed mirror which I had admired, at a reduced price. We were proud we'd gone it all alone. Little did we know: the guides of Rabat were triflers compared with those to come.

And now the train ride to Fez. In the first-class compartment the three Moroccan men and John talked. The conductor came again; again Abdul disappeared, reappearing after tickets had been taken. On return he inspected us carefully, as property he had been forced to leave un-attended on a bench. His offer to escort us through his city of Fez caused the eyelids of the other Moroccans to flicker, but (did I imagine this?) out of national solidarity they did not blow his cover. John agreed that we would meet him outside the door of our hotel at ten the next morning. We were to tell the patron that we were going out with "un cousin Marocean."

I offered mute resistance to this plan. I knew Abdul wanted something, although he insisted he'd take no pay. But it was hopeless. Abdul and John were now onto German literature. I asked what it was Abdul loved about it; he answered something to the effect that each author was so different. Then he studiedly returned his gaze to the men.

Perhaps he suspected I was on to his game. Perhaps Moroccans really do prefer not to engage in discussion with women. I thought of Naguib Mahfouz's patriarch in *Palace Walk*, who raged when his beautiful daughter's hand was requested in marriage: "Has someone *seen* my daughter?" The possibility that a man might desire marriage into his family for reasons other than "a sincere desire to be related to *him*" infuriated the tyrant.

But the veil not only hides the face: it covers the mouth. Giving up on talking, I looked at the scenery. En route to Fez we were travelling south and west through arid brown hills with occasional green valleys. Sometimes grey and white horses with prominent ribs could be seen, often lethal-looking clumps of spiny grey cactus. Trees grew in straight lines alongside elevated troughs on tawny soil. Here water determined all. The original Fassis (inhabitants of Fez) had created such an intricate system of pipes and sewers and streams that it nearly destroyed them: conquerors were obliged only to block the outflow of the dam until it burst, and the water broke down all the walls and flooded the town. Then they rode freely in.

Evening drew in. Suddenly the ancient town of Fez was all around us, on hills. It was fabulous, mystical. And the guides, like a plague of locusts darkening the plain, fell upon us as we exited the cab. We had to fight our way through their numbers.

The Palais Jamai loomed as a refuge. We entered it as dusk was falling, and did not have the nerve to venture out again for dinner. Its Old World decor was heavy, tiled everywhere with the Morocco green of hope, with the usual squared garden drooping with blossoms, enormous peach-coloured roses watered by means of delicate, turquoise-painted aerial troughs.

The brothers Jamai who built this palace were favourites with the sultan; however, at his death they ran afoul of the jealousy of his relations and were sent to prison, where they were chained together. One died and the other had to endure a prolonged close relationship with the corpse in hot weather — so our guidebook says. However, he did survive to be liberated.

The restaurant had intricate red-plaster ceilings and tassled cushions for reclining. Our feeling of having died and gone to heaven was accentuated by the fact that the waiters (male) appeared dressed as angels, with little white bands around their heads and long white dresses.

We peeked out after dinner: in the courtyard waited scores of would-be guides. We were prisoners ourselves. The hotel was built right into the medina walls; five times a day the call to prayer blared from a loudspeaker in the *katoubia* (tower) only metres away. At four-thirty in the morning it was particularly effective, this long, keening howl which was joined by other howls from the some 350 mosques in the medina.

I lay awake, thinking of Abdul, the new addition to our company of two. It seemed that relations with the various mafias of local males were overshadowing our trip. People had warned us, but warnings are always useless. Why was Abdul so keen to spend time with us? Why should I tell a lie to the hotel patron? Why did Abdul's presence invoke my silence? I practised French, the better to dispense with him come morning. "Cesser de me dire qu'est que je doit faire!" Et cetera.

94

As we stepped outside the hotel at the appointed hour, the standing gentry all nodded and pointed: your friend is waiting *à gauche*. Somewhat unnerved, we found Abdul with dark glasses, sitting on a wall out of sight of the hotel. A handshake, and questions about Madam's health, took only minutes, and then we were plunged into the narrow, winding, medieval reaches of the medina. Assaulted by the smell (fetid, rank, putrid, fragrant, rich, unnameable), by the hooded crowds, by the strangeness, confused by a thousand turns and forks and slopes and cul-de-sacs, all we could do was follow like the sheep we were.

Abdul's tour began auspiciously with a visit to the medersa, the first university in the world, which was founded by a woman, Fatima, one of two wealthy sisters. No, women did not attend; they went elsewhere to study embroidery. Abdul was up on Arab innovations: he asserted that his people discovered the number zero. (Before that, there were only positives and negatives.) We saw a public library and peeked inside various mosques, from the portals: in Morocco, non-Muslims are not allowed to enter mosques.

Nor are women. they sit in separate outer chambers. An exception has been made at the tomb of the founder of Fez, where women are allowed to enter as far as the tomb, in order to sit and touch it and wail. The men greet one another with obvious affection, clap hands to shoulders, hold hands frequently, kiss, and murmur.

We passed a carpenter turning out a handmade wooden plough, an entire *souk* (avenue) of sellers of aphrodisiacs, dates, odd-shaped vegetables, powders, and unguents; a cinema showing *Terminator 2;* kiosks overflowing with skeins of lumpy, grey-white wool — "live wool" as well as "dead wool." There were baskets, chickens, the carcases of lambs, herbs, pottery hats, and computer parts. Donkeys and burros clomped up and down the narrow alleys, burdened with everything from sofas to firewood to sacks of flour. Drivers with sticks cried "Balek!" (make way). We saw the communal ovens where the children brought fresh dough in the morning to be baked over a wood fire, for picking up later from the family shelf.

Everywhere there were wild cats, small and skinny, little boys with balls or metal hoops, and rug sellers. Before long we found ourselves in the Vizier's Palace, a rug emporium. Abdul had slipped discreetly out of sight. We were then in the hands of Sebti, who had a set of burly men throw the rugs out onto the floor, dizzyingly, one after another. He taught us the Arab words for hold — "Hali!" and reject, which sounded like "Ichmal!" Drunk on the power of these two words, we inspected rugs to a two-foot depth on the floor before succumbing, and buying one. We knew we had overpaid when Sebti grandly offered us a free lunch that would have fed ten. But no matter: Abdul was there to help dispatch the couscous and salads and curries. He made no reference to the rug.

The enormous restaurant was empty save for two Englishmen across the room, eating with several young Moroccan boys. The one wearing the white panama and a wry expression watched us eat and made signs as if to say, "Well what did you buy, to deserve that spread?" In our hotel we saw him again: he was Ken of Ken and Colin, and he laughed as we lugged in our sausage-wrapped rug.

We all had a gin fizz at the pool. Ken and Colin had been to Morocco five times before. They sought to enlighten us about guides, about the commissions they got from the merchants. About the fact that they wouldn't leave you alone to have a meal in peace. Or how they will insist, if you want to see the pottery factory, that the pottery factory is closed, when in fact it's not closed at all, it's only that this particular guide gets no commission from that particular factory. Ken had horror stories. If you didn't buy, he said, they'd abandon you in the centre of the medina and you'd be skinned alive before you found your way out.

Guiding practices had sunk to a new low since the drop in tourism caused by the Gulf War, said Ken. In Ken's telling, guides' abilities to keep the scent took on an almost supernatural sharpness. Take their experience yesterday. One had picked them up at the airport. After Ken and Colin arrived at the hotel the guide had telephoned them in their room, this *despite the fact that they'd never given him their names, and besides, they had changed hotel rooms three times*. His call, incidentally, was to say he couldn't meet them the next day but was passing them on to his brother.

We all wanted to know what things were worth. But there was no answer to this question, said Ken. In the medina value is simply what you can get for a thing: it is completely fluid. If a merchant sells one for half of what it cost him, he might sell the next to a "punter" for five times that. All in a day's work.

I began to see what naifs we were. An American couple, Lynn and Arnie, pulled up chairs. This was their first trip to Morocco. Arnie and Lynn were hurt because their guide had promised that at five o'clock, after an exhaustive shopping tour, he would take them to his home for tea. But apparently they did not buy enough, for after the call to prayer, he abruptly escorted them back to their hotel and dropped them.

John had promised to meet Abdul that night at seven, over my grumbles. There he stood, in the shadows, wearing his sunglasses. We went by taxi to the Merenides Hotel to look at the lights of Fez on the hills. There was nothing more to say about German literature. He was even less forthcoming about his job on the railway; he had dropped his pretences and was too insolent to bother inventing new ones. We asked to see the mellah, where the Jewish jewellers were. He didn't want to take us. We insisted, as we paid for his drink. He took us. All the shops were closed.

Now Abdul was angry. We were angry. He marched ahead of us on a very long, very dark walk back through the medina. We had become passive, trapped by the guide who was not a guide; while he, in turn, was hampered in his role by the fact that he denied it. Everything rushed by us in reverse; the bakeries closed their doors, the rear ends of donkeys disappeared into hostels, the little boys ran home slipping on wet stones as water gushed underfoot, sweeping the day's refuse toward the putrid river beneath. Abruptly, halfway through this nightmarish forced march, Abdul stopped, pointed to a window three stories above us looking over the streets, and said, "That is where I live."

In front of our hotel, we told Abdul that we would stay all the next day in the hotel. He did not believe us. You need me, he said, as he left.

Sleep was again dismantled by the call to prayer before dawn. In the morning we breakfasted late, played tennis, sat at the pool. But Fez was out there, rank, raw, centuries in the making, its crooked alleys luring us. Feeling guilty about Abdul, we decided to sneak out.

We ran the gauntlet of guides at the hotel gate and got a cab to the Palais Royal, where we were menaced by a man who wanted to escort us around its paved exterior. As we fled the short two blocks to the mellah we had to send away several other persistent and unsavoury characters. We tried Ken and Colin's advice: ignore them completely, never make eye contact, never respond to such jibes as, "Don't you want to talk to Moroccan people?"

Nevertheless, in front of the jewellers' stores we were bitterly harassed. I was trying to buy a gold camel for my mother's charm bracelet. While we were negotiating with the man behind the counter, a character stepped up from the street and inserted himself in the conversation, clearly intending to partake in the deal. The vendor was unhappy. We were unhappy. The "guide" chatted on. John finally cracked and shouted something like "Ta gueule!" (Shut up!) Our tormentor launched into an affecting speech.

"What does it matter to you if I take a ten percent commission on what you buy? You don't want to give your money to the Third World?"

At this point the vendor, who had previously been on our side, we thought, closed up his shop window. The tirade continued for several minutes, until we had moved across to another shop.

"I hope you die with your money!" shouted the guide. "I hope you lie in your grave with your hands on your chest and your money with you!"

Suddenly, magnified keening broke out over the loudspeakers. It was the call to prayer. And then he delivered his *coup de grâce*. "I am going to go now and pray for the world. It's all we can do, as long as people like you have the money."

We continued through the mellah and into the medina, our reputation spreading like a stain before us. We were as lepers. The street widened and emptied before us. Storekeepers slammed their shutters in our faces. (Actually, it was time for afternoon nap.) Chastened, the rhetoric of the last would-be guide ringing in our ears, we kept our hands on our first-world wallets.

It might have gone on this way forever. But suddenly, the figure of a shy, white-clad young man stepped into our line of vision. His name was Ahmad. He wasn't a guide either; he only wanted to practise his English. He was the seventh in a family of nine. The state only paid for the education of the first two children. We stopped and bought him an English book.

Gentle Ahmad leading, we walked homeward through the medina. At least it felt like homeward: our ultimate direction was impossible to ascertain. Ahmad showed us nothing, but, when we pressed, he agreed to take us to a place where Berber blankets were sold. We chose two we liked. We bargained. We feigned disinterest. The deal was concluded. Out came the mint tea. Then we discovered John had no cash, only credit cards, which they would not take. Somehow it was decided that John and a salesman would go back to the hotel, where he would give the salesman the money while Ahmad and I waited with the blankets. When the salesman came back with the money, I would get the blankets and Ahmad would walk me back to the hotel.

It was getting dark. Even in the inner reaches of the medina I could tell: the skylights gave back a purplish blue. On I waited, in the huge room draped and stacked with woven bags, pillows, blankets, watching over our blankets as if they were in danger. Ahmad giggled and tried to talk to me. I looked up at the skylight: the sky was dark navy now. The other Moroccan men skirted me, courteous, with smiles that were too large. It occurred to me that this had been a very stupid idea. Why had we concluded that the blankets needed protection? Was Ahmad to be trusted? Were these sellers of blankets to be trusted?

Had Abdul been right that we needed him? Would I ever get home again? I pictured Ken and Colin having their gin fizz at the pool. I pictured John trustingly peeling the dinars out of his wallet. If I tried to run, I would be swallowed into the coiling entrails of the medina.

Suddenly it was over. The salesman reappeared with the money, the blankets were skillfully rolled, and Ahmad escorted me to the gateway of the medina, from which I could see the hotel door. Then, waving his English book, he vanished like a ghost.

That night we crept out of our hotel 300 metres down the alley to a restaurant and back, without incident. As we ate, we were entertained by belly dancers and musicians. A red-clad man wriggled on his belly toward us bearing a brass tray of burning candles on his head. He rubbed his thumb and forefinger together salaciously. He wanted money. I was paralyzed with mortification and could not move. He came closer, writhing, grovelling. We shook our heads. He guffawed.

The call to prayer woke me again at four-thirty in the morning.

So what is there to say, then, I wondered, lying awake. We could join with other complaining tourists in asserting that Third World desperation is spoiling "our" tourist sites. Or we could throw up our hands and agree that this system, with its blind alleys, multiple doorways, devious passages, archways within archways, its piracies, its lies within truths and truths within lies was invented here, like the zero, with the specific aim of driving the linear peoples of the world stark raving mad.

We'd both been losing sleep. The next morning, as we were about to leave our hotel, John threw what we would later refer to as a "typical North American shit fit." We wanted a cab to the airport. A *petit taxi* would have done fine. But we were told that because we hadn't ordered it in advance, we would have to take a *grand taxi* (a Mercedes) at four times the price.

"I'm tired of being lied to all the time!" shouted John at the patron.

A stillness overtook the foyer.

"It is the regulation, sir."

"Bullshit!" and so forth. "Get me a god-damned cab to the airport or I'll walk."

I was glad they complied, even if we paid quadruple, because we had four suitcases, a heavy rug, and two blankets. As we struggled into our grand taxi, Ken emerged from the staircase. He was grinning understandingly, as if he recognized our mental state to be a *stage*. This was even more infuriating.

"It *is* a regulation," he said. "Probably the only regulation in the entire tourist industry."

In Marrakech, we were advised to hire an official guide from the hotel, to keep the others at bay. Aziz was an educated man, laconic and superior in his bearing. He met us at the door of our hotel, which was even more palatial than the Palais Jamai, and around which a truly staggering crowd of men lounged. Aziz parted their numbers and led us around the medina. In the great open square of Jemma-el-fna Aziz he gave a few dinars to certain beggars, while others he waved off scornfully, saying, "You know he begs here every day, but he is a very rich man."

Aziz told us that tomorrow was a national holiday and all the shops would be closed. He said there was a rare Berber auction around the corner. But his ruses didn't work. There were all manner of leather bags, djellabas, burnooses, brass trays, bolts of fabric, pottery dishes, giant baskets of pungent spices. There were *babouches* — leather slippers in bright yellow with curled-up toes and no heels, and tables and boxes made of beautiful thuya wood. There were legions of men lounging in gates, along promenades, leaning against palm trees, under doorways, waiting, as Ken and Colin had said, for the "punters."

But we weren't buying. We had become incapable. Although it was apparently our moral obligation to do so, we could not work up any desire. Consumer lust had been defeated by resentment, by our foreknowledge of the inevitable weight of the transaction, by the necessity to bargain, to posture, to fight, to make up, and to drink another cup of mint tea. And by everyone waiting, watching.

Don't they have anything else to do? we ranted inwardly. The answer is no. The Berbers were nomads, the Arab traders middlemen. It's a desert land, so few have a plot for a garden, a sheep, or a field of grain. Buying and selling is their agriculture. We — the tourists — are the main crop. The eighties were good years. But the Gulf War caused a drought. It must have been like this on the prairies in the late 1880s. The buffalo are no longer coming!

Like sulky children, John and I followed Aziz under hanging rows of glowing fabrics in the dyers' souk, past the dangling feathered carcases of chickens. Aziz tossed off bitter asides in Arabic to the disappointed hucksters. Eventually, right in the centre of the medina, he threw up his hands and left us. But Marrakech's secrets were easier to penetrate than those of Fez, or we were learning. We navigated ourselves back through to the square. In the jewellers' souk, a merchant darted out to say he could sell us earrings at a much better price now that we weren't with that bad guide.

"Guides take twenty-five percent, and they have nothing to pay," he said. "I have a shop, I have a family, I have a mortgage . . ." (Did he really say mortgage? Perhaps memory invents, but what he invoked was some moral equivalent.) We bought the earrings. Out of the corner of my eye I saw Aziz descend on the merchant as we walked away.

We didn't do well in Marrakech — in fact, Marrakech defeated us. The last morning we tried to get into the post office to buy stamps. A smirking street kid wanted to guide us to the correct cashier.

"Why do you not like to talk to Moroccan people?"

We avoided his eyes.

"Money is nothing. Only people are important."

We walked around the corner. He followed.

"I want good price for you. Money is no good for you. Why do you try to keep it? It's bad luck, to keep your money."

I lost my cool and stopped, waving my hands madly around my head and yelling, in what may have been an unconscious imitation of the Muslim divorce ceremony, "Fuck off! Fuck off! Fuck off!"

Our final stop was Taroudant, an oasis in the desert. Ours was the ultimate hotel, set in acres of garden, with rows and rows of roses. The dining room was under a great circular tent. A Mick Jagger look-alike across the room, scrapping with his very tall and bored blonde wife, turned out to be the real thing. The others looked like officials from Vichy France.

Opulence in accommodation varied inversely with the local economy: Taroudant was a dusty, poor town. As for guides, we'd moved finally from the A's (Abdul, Ahmad, Aziz) to the M's — Mohammad. He followed us for half a mile, a bad egg, possibly drugged. Then a man with a Berber cap on the back of his head took over, and we were grateful to him for shooing away Mohammad. Our new man led us to "his" shop, where several energetic salesmen cornered John, because he spoke French. What was the meaning of "tabernacle"? they asked. It seemed to be a part of a church, and yet, people said it as if it meant something dirty.

While they discussed French-Canadian obscenities, I was caught by the elbow by two salesmen, who began to roll out kilims. This time I really didn't want a rug. I had a rug, and two blankets. Oh, they understood I was not interested, but if I was, what would I offer?

They started at something near $1,500. I said $300. It was meant to shut them up. But at $400 we were shaking hands. I was congratulated. What a good bargainer I was. Not a Canadian at all, they imagined, but a Berber! It was difficult not to be flattered. All the same, I didn't want the rug.

In the spirit of celebration, mint tea was brought out. Then these young men produced, rather unbelievably, a well-thumbed copy of Fay Weldon's *Darcy's Utopia*. They had all read it. They loved it. She imagines a world taken over by women! So preposterous as to be titillating.

Our last night in Taroudant, and our last in Morocco, we went for a walk outside the hotel gates before sundown. The birds were singing. The flowers bowed, heavy and sweet. Women in cobalt-blue wrappings which clung to their bodies in the dusty wind walked down lanes which wound to some centre we'd never reach. Only a few desultory guides were hanging about the gates.

"Going shopping?"

"Into the medina? Need a guide?"

"No thank you, no thank you."

One recognized us.

"Oh, it's the Canadians!"

They had motorbikes, these fellows. Several clustered around us, revving their engines.

"Yesterday, you go in medina!"

"Buy rug!"

We were speechless.

"It's you who buy the rug," they said, smiling broadly and pointing at me.

"Four hundred dollars!"

That stopped us. "How did you know that?"

They were all laughing. We couldn't tell whether it was because we were fools or brilliant shoppers. Somehow it ceased to matter. That's when I knew I had finally reached Morocco.

"You buy in my brother's shop!"

"We did? Well tell your brother we enjoyed meeting him."

"Thank you. Need a guide?"

Highway to the
Black Mountains

"More and more the Indus cast its spell over her, a formidable attraction beck-oning her down. And, bouncing on her hard seat in the truck, the strangely lu-minous air burnished her vision: the colours around her deepened and intensified. They became three-dimensional. Were she to reach out, she felt she could touch the darkness in the granite, hold the air in her hands, and stain her fingers in the jewelled colours of the river. Trapped between the cliffs of the gorge, the leviathan waters looked like a seething, sapphire snake."

The above passage is from my first novel, The Bride. The novel is based on an actual incident involving a sixteen-year-old Punjabi girl. To my mind the story of the bride, the girl I write about in the novel, is indelibly linked with the journey I took into the region described by the ancient Chinese pilgrim Fa-Hsien as the Black Mountains.

THE MOUNTAINS AT THE KNOTTED HEART OF WHAT is known as the Northern Areas, the 27,000 square miles that are Pakistan's frontier with Afghanistan, Iran, India, and China, constitute an almost impenetrable mass, a natural barrier that has imprisoned its scant population for centuries. Pockets of habitation linger intact, like genetic specimens from a bygone eon. The ice age, the cave era are still tucked away here.

One can look down upon a hamlet in a narrow valley and see only Semitic features crowned by a froth of ginger hair, and from a mud rampart protecting a hive of caves see nothing but straight-haired blondes. A little to the east, near Hunza, a principality known for the longevity of its inhabitants and for its fiery local wine, the handsome tribes display wide cheekbones and faintly tilted Mongol eyes. Hunza, nestled at 8,500 feet, is believed to be the Shangri-La of James Hilton's novel, *Lost Horizon*. The farther east one travels along the Highway, the more pronounced the Mongolian aspect becomes.

There are no metal objects to be found in most of these mountain settlements; plows are nailed with wooden spikes wedged into grooves. It is this diversity of eons, of races and cultures, together with the dramatic topography, that so impressed itself upon my imagination.

It was January 1965. Colonel Safdar Butt, the genial, hazel-eyed Kashmiri engineer in charge of constructing the Karakoram Highway at the time, had invited my husband and me to a remote camp embedded deep in the mountains.

The construction of the road was a joint venture, with the Chinese building the Highway from their end. They had already paved the road through the Khunjrab pass, 16,000 feet above sea level, that provided a gateway through the Chinese frontier into Pakistan.

Toward the end of our month's stay at Dubair we had driven further along the Highway to Pattan, another camp established by the army, to see a bridge constructed by the Chinese. This bridge, an asphalt arrow that spanned the Indus, was ornamented with red-painted Chinese lions: talismans of good luck. They looked to me more like seated bulldogs as they rose tall from the paling on either side like hefty supernatural sentinels guarding the bridge at evenly spaced intervals.

The Karakoram Highway follows the ancient Silk Route of traders from Central Asia. It runs along the Indus gorge and then swerves east from Gilgit to push through the Hunza and Baltistan agencies, where the Hindu Kush to the west, Karakorams to the north and northeast, and the Himalayas to the south interlock with the Pamirs, at the very "Roof of the World."

The Karakorams, the most rugged of all mountain ranges, are also the cradle of some of the world's loftiest peaks: Nanga Parbat, Rakaposhi, and K2, which at 28,000 feet is second only to Everest. (In a recent survey by an American satellite, K2 was in fact higher than Everest.) In any event, with its sheer flanks, treacherous avalanches, and glaciers, K2 is certainly the most formidable: it has claimed more lives than any other mountain. Every summer one hears of European and Japanese mountaineering parties that have lost some members to K2, and sorrowfully called off their assault.

On a day that was bitterly cold even in Lahore, we flew north to Rawalpindi and spent a night with my brother at the Murree Brewery. The next day we drove two hours up a gentle incline to Abbottabad. Named after a British deputy commissioner, Abbottabad was one of the outposts created by the British to guard — and endeavour futilely to advance — the Northwestern Frontier of their Indian Empire.

The colonel had sent a jeep to fetch us. While bumping and winding along the perilous unpaved highway carved from perpendicular bluffs and overhangs, we learned it was to be an "all-weather road." In lay terms, a road negotiable even in winter. The builders would try to maintain it at an altitude of between 5,000 and 6,000 feet. A few hundred feet too high and the Highway would become impassably snowbound. The junior officer who had been assigned to accompany us informed my husband and me of the hazards of building the Highway. They had already lost over a hundred lives to dynamite, avalanches, landslides; to sudden gusts that lifted men clear off ledges, as if they had no more heft than cardboard hoarding, and flung them thousands of feet down into the gorge.

Once we had joined the river at Bisham, the scenery of the Karakorams, already spectacular, became heart-stopping. The Indus, an immense, glacier-gorged cobalt snake churning in its dark canyon, and the frozen rhythm of soaring granite, created a beauty that still graces my life. And there was a pristine quality to the loveliness, the mystique of space unsoiled by man, his technological advance, or his covetous eye.

Every short while we had to stop to clear boulders from our path. At intervals small groups of men, mostly taciturn Kohistani tribesmen wrapped in sheepskins and cloth made out of beaten wool, worked with shovels and pickaxes to clear the debris from recent landslides. We were told that the road, which looked like a worn, low-slung belt strapped to the mountains, would take about sixty years to settle. The light-skinned tribesmen working on the Highway, and the sprinkling of darker-hued army conscripts from the plains who were supervising them, were the only humans we saw.

The road was already opening up the immediate area on either side. Men who had never seen cloth, let alone transistors, jeeps, or money, were being abruptly exposed to some of the artifacts of the twentieth century. Squatting by the roadside, traders from Abbottabad and Swat set up shop out of tin trunks, or conducted transactions from corrugated iron-sheet lean-tos. They offered canvas shoes to men with leather strips molding the sheepskin to their calves and feet. Sewing needles, thread, safety pins, flashlights, were put to ingenious use.

I saw a mountain-man industriously pry out the gravel embedded in his calluses, and then stitch together the thick fissures on the soles of his feet.

Dubair, with its lineup of military three-tonners and regiment of khaki tents that humped over the undulating gravel, was a pleasant surprise. A clamorous stream went hurtling to one side. The clearing had a trim, hewn-stone bungalow with a patch of lawn in front. The bungalow served as the officers' mess and living quarters. It had a sitting room, an elementary kitchen with raised, wood-burning clay pits, bathrooms with chamber pots that were cleaned by an army sweeper, and some bedrooms. I never found out how many, and it is too late to do so now. The camp was destroyed, together with a long stretch of the road, by an earthquake about ten years ago. Earthquakes are common to this region, which is still in the process of geological upheaval. The road was restored sufficiently to allow traffic within a month of the earthquake. It is all taken in stride, allowances being made for a mountain road in the process of "settling."

In a country known for the hospitality of its hosts, we were made to feel extravagantly welcome. Colonel Safdar Butt, the camp doctor, and the junior officers (among them Major Jan, who was a passable palmist) were eager for news and conversation. They were all amateur mountaineers. And Safdar Butt, whom I had not met before, proved to be an inspired and accurate raconteur. He was full of historical references and speculation: "Alexander the Great, they say, stopped at Bisham for a night on his way to plunder India. Of course, I think this route might have been a bit out of his way, but then who knows? There is a lot of forgotten history here." And he would point out this or that pass through which other scourges had swooped down on the Indo-Gangetic plains, and describe the colourful composition of by-gone armies on the march.

Our hosts were also full of the fierce tribal lore, stories culled from the romance, myth, and adventure of their setting. And they were as eager to communicate their discoveries as we were to absorb them.

In the incandescent afternoons, beneath the cloudless deep-blue spread of the skies, we half-slid, half-stumbled down the precipitous gorges to the white sandbank on our side of the Indus. The river, endlessly alluring as its silky mass tumbled and crashed down its course and flew into a million white bubbles over eternally wet stones, had turned us into nature intoxicated pilgrims. The opposite bank, about half a mile away, marked the frontier between Swat Kohistan, where we were situated and which has a semblance of administration, and the "Unadministered Territory."

Although it is a part of Pakistan, the latter area has no law and order as we know it. Secluded by the Karakorams, the isolated tribes that inhabit it live by their own notions of honour and revenge. The bands of cultivated steps, hewn out of the mountains over successive generations, yield only a meagre crop of maize. The communities subsist on an almost unrelieved diet of maize bread softened with water. The harshness of their terrain, so rugged that a man has to trudge thirty days over the mountains to fetch a bag of salt on his back, dictates their severe code of conduct. A trickle of water stolen and directed into the wrong channel, a man's pride slighted, and the price is paid in bloody family feuds.

A sagging rope bridge, a horrendously unstable contraption that looked as if it had been crocheted out of rotting wool and matchsticks, spanned the Indus where it was harnessed by a narrow canyon. A little downstream the cliffs stood away, allowing the sun to ignite the water to turquoise, and the river gentled to form a wide lagoon.

A few days later we discovered how deceptive the relative stillness of the lagoon was when we ventured onto its surface on a log raft navigated by a Kohistani oarsman, and trailed our hands against its powerful, icy current.

That was a most foolhardy excursion. In the flicker of the time it took the eye to sweep across the water, five tribesmen, like pieces of fur strewn on the desolate sand, suddenly materialized on the opposite bank. It was as if they had sprouted, from the grainy whiteness in their supine postures, heads propped up, spread legs communicating contempt, dangerous yellow eyes focussing their disfavour with an intensity that compressed the distance. Like most Kohistani tribesmen, they carried antiquated Lee Enfields and hazardous-looking handmade guns.

An authoritative voice carried a message across the water in tribal dialect. The instant tension on our oarsman's face, as he called back and abruptly changed the course of our skimming raft, made the threat clear.

Another cry, floating shrilly down from somewhere behind us, penetrated the roar of the Indus to sound an eerie warning. Shading our eyes in order to look up, we noticed for the first time a picket of three conscripts, so high in the cliffs that they looked like silhouettes of toy soldiers, guarding us with drawn weapons.

I had already heard the story of the girl from the plains. For some reason this incident triggered in me the reaction that — as if by osmosis from the air or through my heightened senses — fleshed out the tragic occurrence in hitherto unintelligible and invisible detail.

My vision began to register a detached one-room stone hut clinging to a cliff edge like an eagle's nest, almost indecipherable to the unaccustomed eye; and the maverick, contemptuous expressions on the faces of the men whom Sir Bindon Blood and the might of the Raj had failed to subjugate. I could feel their scorn of me: an immodest woman who affected alien ways by wearing trousers, who smiled at and consorted with obviously unrelated men. I was unable to meet their derisive, demeaning eyes. Not because I lacked a commitment to feminist daring but because I was enormously conscious of my intrusion into a land where I was not welcome, my trespass on a time to which I did not belong, a way of life that I affronted with my very presence.

What I represented threatened not only their values but also their survival. They grasped this instinctively; whereas I, sensible of our *civilized* world, knew it to be true. The age I belonged to, the civilization I represented, would destroy not only what they stood for, but also them. Years later, when the Russians invaded Afghanistan to the north, and that neglected, poverty-stricken country became the warm theatre of the Cold War, it did not require any great prescience on my part to predict — as I did in an interview in America — that when the Russians and the CIA finally withdrew, the Old World country would reel into an unsurvivable tailspin of bloody chaos.

The cheerful expressions, the contentment on the faces of children unaware of a world full of electronic toys, took on an added poignancy; as did the wrinkles of strain that aged women in their twenties, and the deprivation of men old at forty. This awareness detonated unfamiliar currents and channels in my mind, and supplied my imagination with an uproar of possibilities that challenged previous assumptions and shaped the new experiences into fresh insights and searing shafts of understanding and empathy.

A couple of months before our arrival, the conscripts working on the road had been astonished to see a lissome young woman from their part of the world in this remote and inaccessible region. The girl, slender and tall, her head modestly covered by a shawl, wore the loose trousers and printed knee-length kameez of the Punjab. There was no mistaking her identity: besides being dressed differently, she was also much darker than the Kohistani women. And yet she was accompanied by an old tribal who had the light, weathered skin and amber eyes of the mountain people.

Filled with curiosity, concerned for the girl, the conscripts presented the strange pair to the colonel.

The old Kohistani told them that he was taking the girl to his ancestral village across the river to marry her to a kinsman. The girl, though painfully embarrassed by the scrutiny of the strangers, did not appear to be under any constraint.

The colonel and the other officers were invited to the wedding a few weeks thereafter. They politely declined. It would not be politic to venture so far into tribal territory, or be beholden to the hostile, demanding, and importunate tribesmen.

A month later they heard that the girl had run away.

In that part of the world, where wives are a scarce commodity and are often bought, a runaway bride is an intolerable insult, an affront that humiliates not only the husband but the whole clan. The husband's family was out hunting her as if she were a wild animal.

The girl had managed to survive in that stark, convoluted wilderness of trackless mountains without food or shelter for almost two weeks. Some instinct had guided her through the maze of canyons and ridges to the white sands, to where she was almost exactly opposite the camp at Dubair. Had the girl managed to cross the rope bridge spanning the river, she would have been safe. But the huntsmen were sure of their terrain and of their quarry, and they are infallible.

A tribal, most likely her husband, located her at night. The conscripts discovered her body, and the severed head with its long inky hair snagged in some rocks in the water, the next morning. Death was the only acceptable punishment for a runaway wife in the highlands of the Unadministered Territory in northern Pakistan.

The girl's story haunted me on my return to Lahore, as did the expressions on the faces of the tribesmen, the incredibly harsh conditions of their lives, and the rules by which they lived. I was obsessed by the need to describe them, to relate the girl's story. The tragedy appeared to reflect the condition of many women on the Indian Sub-continent who have no more control over their destinies than straying cattle or flood-swept insects.

This was what I can only describe as a *mystical* experience. My exposure to the radiance of the Indus secreted away in the granite folds of the Karakorams, to the silence of soaring dark rock communicating only with the skies, to the magically glowing air, combined to release a creative energy in me that craved expression. I realize now that there were other factors that compelled me to become a writer, such as my isolating illness as a child, and my insatiable appetite for reading, but the journey to Kohistan was the catalyst.

I thought I would write a short story depicting the girl's experience. However, without my being conscious of it, my imagination began to create a past for her. After all, the Punjabi girl with her modestly covered head, whose passage had so intrigued the conscripts and the officers, and whose death had so affected them that they could not stop talking about her, had not been conjured out of thin air. She must have had a history of her own before she appeared so improbably on the Karakoram Highway. Where was she born? Who were her parents? Did she have siblings? How had she spent the sixteen years of her life? How did she meet the old Kohistani, and what were the circumstances that brought her to the remote region? In creating her background, in unconsciously fabricating the answers, the short story turned longer, and into *The Bride*.

It took me four years to write the novel. I toyed with it and changed its shape as if it were clay. I juggled various beginnings and spun the scenes around. And during that time of energy and experiment, writing became a habit, an addiction, a labour of love.

Loath to leave the Karakorams at the end of our visit, I promised myself that I would be back. I was. We drove all the way to Hunza, on a more *settled* road. This was in summer, when the Indus is swollen and muddy with melting snow and the air warm.

It is said one cannot repeat an experience of this nature, but I was lucky. Four years ago I was back again with friends. We spent a freezing winter night at the newly built cut-stone rest house at Bisham, where the Indus forms a mile-wide sapphire lagoon — and the spirit of the Black Mountains and the radiant river once again pervaded the air.

SUSAN MUSGRAVE

I Told You When
I Came I Was a Stranger

I spent two years travelling in Panama and Colombia in the early eighties, and I have only begun to write about my experiences. I was hooked up with a smuggler so I dared not take notes and spent a great deal of time waiting in a windowless van at the side of the road while the men sat in the house doing business. Looking back, I realise how preoccupied I was with the relationship, and how I experienced quite a different Colombia from the one my partner did. This quote sums it up for me.

"There we were, riding down the spine of a brand new continent and all I could think about was . . . does he love me today? (Or, for practice ¿Me quiere él hoy?) I still remember what it feels like to miss the world going by because your gaze is fastened on the man up ahead, lost in the arms of the universe, while you wrestle in the grip of the Relationship. We were riding through two different realms; he went to South America and I went to a dark uncharted country with a population of two and a history of wars."

Marni Jackson
The Masculine Mystique

"I AM LOOKING FOR ADVENTURE BECAUSE ACTION raises my blood pressure, giving me enough energy to live," I wrote, the day I stopped attending the trial. Five Americans and eighteen Colombians had been charged with attempting to smuggle thirty tonnes of marijuana into Canada. When they'd run out of rolling papers, they'd brought their ship in for supplies on the west coast of Vancouver Island. A sympathetic jury acquitted. And when Paul walked out of the courthouse, wearing an unbleached linen suit and a T-shirt that said I SCORED, I offered him a ride.

We knew little about each other. I told him I wrote poetry; for me, mystery and unknowing was energy also. We crossed the border with Leonard Cohen singing *It's true that all the men you knew were dealers who said they were through with dealing every time you gave them shelter* on KISS-FM. In Sudden Valley we camped, drinking white rum by a fire in the night. Paul showed me his tattoo — a pair of faded lips, as if a ghost wearing lipstick had kissed him — above his left nipple. I kissed his lips. In the morning we flew the Whisperliner Jet Service to Miami. I'd signed on for the duration.

In Miami Beach we danced in a cabaret where two blond sisters sang other people's songs; then made love, that first night, in a vegetarian hotel. When we checked out, the desk clerk told me some people take a bath every day but you can't wash your heart.

I remember the day so clearly because it was the first turning point in our life together. At the Bounty Hotel in Coconut Grove I overheard Paul on the bathroom telephone talking to his former girlfriend in Texas: he said she was giving him a big erection. As my mother would have said, the honeymoon was over. I thought of turning back as I walked the streets alone, back to the predictable life I'd left, my husband asleep in his overstuffed chair with an empty wine glass in hand and "Emotional Rescue" turning soundlessly on the stereo. When I'd called to say I had left with Paul he accused me of being a "ruiner," said all I'd ever fulfilled were his worst expectations. But I'd wanted the strange and the wild and wasn't ready to turn my back on a world I hadn't explored yet. I wrote postcards to friends, quoting the poet Caesar Vallejo: "What can I do but change my style of weeping?"

My friends, I knew, could not understand why I had abandoned a loyal husband to follow some dealer into some troubled Latin American régime. I finally came up with an answer while watching *Tootsie* on the plane from Miami to Panama. Jessica Lange was explaining a similar predicament: "There are a lot of men out there. I am very selective. I look around to see who can give me the worst time, and I choose him."

In Panama we changed hotels every other day, each time registering under a different name. When we ran out of hotels, Paul found a penthouse with a view of the Panama Canal, overlooking a walled garden filled with orange-blossoming trees, vines that dripped a lavender-scented moss, and bougainvillea. It was paradise, but beyond our means. Paul rented a basement apartment, instead, with a view of the House of Carnage where I could buy meat. Our landlord called his building "The Elite" for reasons that were not apparent. Marisol, his wife, gave us a termite-infested sofa that gave way into a bed, and a desk lamp that gave me electric shocks. But at least we had a mailing address. My mother wrote saying she was "puzzled by our freedom of choice for place of domicile which is usually determined by the husband's place of work."

Paul's work took him south for *negocios delicados*. He came back with the souvenirs he'd bought for me in airport giftshops: a silver llama brooch, a Peruvian devil-dancer, a panama hat. To make up for having stayed away so long, he'd whisk me into the hills to a restaurant called the Godfather, where the river had washed away part of the dining room, then up the coast to Punta Charme, where we'd walk the night beach, black water dragging the shingle back.

Each time he went away he was gone for longer. I explored Panama City on my own, rising early to buy *arepas* on the streets as the bootblacks were opening their stalls under the colonnades. I'd wash the buns down with thick, sweet coffee, sitting in a booth at Manolo's reading about Colombia in the *Miami Herald*, stories of the *sicarios* from the *barrios* who kill for the cocaine cartels for as little as $100 a hit. I took Spanish lessons at the YMCA in the Canal Zone. One taxi driver, his face like polished black hardwood, took me the long way, through the slums. He unzipped his trousers, using sign language to demonstrate his desire to join me for intercourse in the back seat. I told him the only line I'd learned at my lesson: "Mi esposa toca el piano muy bien." ("My wife plays the piano very well.") He got the impression I was a *loca* and drove me straight to the zone without further deviation.

"Esas ollas, que bonitas, cómo brilliantes." At the Y I also learned the words housewives needed in order to communicate with their maids. "These pots, how pretty, how they shine." There were times I wished I were part of their world, with a fixed address and children who took piano lessons after school, and a man who read the stock market quotations over breakfast instead of one who flew stand-by from Bogotá with powder burns on his body and a stomach full of condoms packed with cocaine.

Desperate for someone to talk to, I befriended a Panamanian I'd seen every morning in the booth across from mine at Manolo's. He also read the *Miami Herald*, English edition. John Jesus worked in pharmaceuticals and owned a different-coloured Mercedes for every day of the week. He drove me to the beach at Vera Cruz, where we sat in partially submerged deck chairs under a sign saying WARNING SHARK INFESTED WATERS drinking exotic cocktails that came in a baby's bottle with a nipple. There he confided in me about his difficult but beautiful American girlfriend. He told me you could tell true emotion when someone was weeping because the veins would stand up on their hands. When he'd bought his girlfriend a silver BMW for her birthday, she'd cried, but her veins had stayed submerged. He wondered if he should have given her a gold Mercedes instead.

I couldn't advise him, but I told him, instead, about my own unsettled love life: whenever I asked Paul why I couldn't join him in Colombia, he told me it was too dangerous. As a *gringa* I would be an obvious target for kidnappers.

Jesus said Paul should hire me a bodyguard, my own personal Uzi man. But Colombia remained too dangerous for me right up until the day I discovered a sharp red fingernail clipping (it wasn't mine; I bit my nails) in Paul's trouser pocket. Then he confessed. The danger was Elizabeth.

He described her, over the phone, how her hands felt hot to the touch (he complained that mine were always cold), how she was "something of a poet herself" and had won a prize at high school. That night I packed and booked a flight to Vancouver. But Paul arrived before my plane left and told me, over "Mired Seafood" at the Godfather, that he was trying hard not to fall in love with Elizabeth. I heard, in the back of my pounding head, Leonard Cohen singing *I told you when I came I was a stranger*. I wanted to say it was fair, we had never promised each other everlasting love, but my heart had shrivelled into a fist and I struck him instead.

"I wish you could meet the person who causes you so much unhappiness," Paul said, when we'd both recovered.

I had never thought of myself as a victim; I told Paul I *had* to meet Elizabeth, and that I was willing to accept responsibility for the consequences. The next morning he gave notice on the apartment. He paid Marisol $600 toward the phone bill, which left $500 owing. Marisol kissed me goodbye. I think she had grown fond of me, or perhaps felt sorry for me being mixed up in a life where I was being "dragged about" from continent to continent by a man who didn't pay his phone bills on time.

Paul flew back to Colombia ahead of me. I said goodbye to Jesus, who believed I was going to execute Elizabeth. Colombian prisons were very inhospitable, he said, and gave me the card of a lawyer in Bogotá who would be able to fix things with the judge.

I asked the Avianca agent for an aisle seat over the wing in the non-smoking section of the aircraft. I got the middle seat in the back row between a chain smoker and the Panamanian I'd pinched going through immigration because he'd butted in.

I peered past the Panamanian in the window seat, saying goodbye to the freighters lined up at sea waiting to enter the canal, and to the vultures over the Hilton. On the far side of the steamy runway there were bananas strung out along a clothesline, which reminded me I had forgotten to call home to ask my husband to pick up the dry cleaning

I'd left behind in Sidney two months ago. Beneath the wing a group of baggage handlers hunched together with two men dressed as pilots, sharing a cigarette.

"You see that?" said the Panamanian. "They are smoking drugs. It is probably why we are late."

He introduced himself and gave me his card. Julio was in the "international market." "So the pilot gets drugs and steers us into the Andes," he said. "No problem. They find another pilot. Everyone in Colombia is a pilot." He went on to recommend that I always buy my drugs from the police. "They get them for nothing, so they can sell them cheap."

In Bogotá I had a three-hour stopover and I fell asleep in the Telecom room, the one dimly lit area of the airport. When I opened my eyes a policeman was standing over me, holding an oily lunchbag. He wore his white gun-belt aslant, cowboy-style.

"Está enferma?" he asked. He reached into his bag and pulled out a fistful of greasy pork-scratchings.

I told him I wasn't sick, just sleepy. He munched on his *chicharrónes* for a while and then asked to see my papers.

"You are very far from home. Your husband is not with you?" he asked, in rapid Spanish, his greedy eyes circling my breasts. He stuffed his bag of pork rinds in his trouser pocket as two more officers, one a woman dressed in a bottle-green suit with slits up the side, headed my way. The officer asked his boss for permission to look through my purse; the *jefe* shrugged, and I handed it over to the policewoman. "Hay uno problema?" I asked her. She patted her revolver. It wasn't the answer I'd been hoping for.

The jefe thumbed through my passport. When he smiled he showed two teeth rimmed with gold. "You are a Canadian citizen?" he asked. He spoke English without the trace of an accent.

I felt cold, all of a sudden, and for the first time noticed the bad smell in the terminal, half-diesel, half-human. By the door a *campesina* was selling oranges she had built up into a little pyramid. The jefe walked over and helped himself to one, broke it in half and offered me a section.

"In Canada," he said, applying his mouth to his orange half and sucking the juices out, "I have a brother who is in prison." Then, spitting a seed, he dropped the sucked-dry orange peel on the floor.

The other two officers had taken apart my fountain pen, searching for contraband. Neither of them looked happy about the black ink on their hands. At the bottom of my purse, in a pink plastic case, they found a tampon — one designed by a woman gynecologist, that didn't come with an applicator. They eyed me triumphantly.

Then they began to speak fast, rolling the tampon over in their hands. I looked at the jefe, and tried shrugging. I had "travel insurance," in the form of a U.S. $100 bill in my wallet, but I didn't know if a bribe was necessary yet. The officer with the pork rinds held the tampon in his palm and began unwrapping it. The jefe kept his eyes on me while the woman kept an ink-stained hand on her gun.

The officer had the tampon dangling by its blue thread. I gave the jefe a look so much as to say *he* was a man of the world, *he* understood this business, then I took a risk. I nodded toward the officer who was swinging the tampon around in a slow circle. "Next he'll be wanting to use it," I said.

The jefe had another moment of blankness before his face doubled up into a grin. The others caught on, and began snickering, too, as if they thought some joke had been made at the gringa's expense. The jefe continued to grin, handed me back my tourist card and my passport, and pointed me in the direction of the departure lounge.

"She is not a tourist," I heard him say, as I left.

The Hotel Desaguadero was not what I'd been hoping for, but it was the only one in Cali with vacancies, Paul had explained, as we drove in from the airport.

"Desaguadero" meant "drain": the road down to the hotel was impassable by car. The owner looked surprised to see us and asked Paul how we had chanced upon the place, as if it were impossible that anyone might come to his hotel by choice. In the evening he served chicken necks, rice with gravel, and Coca-Cola on a patio under a crackling bug-zapper; the scorched remains of flying insects fluttered down onto our plates.

Elizabeth was not the femme fatale I'd been expecting, either. I'd pictured her taller than me, full of sophisticated talk about punting in Brazil, cigarette smouldering from an ivory holder. But even in red stilettos she didn't reach my armpits. She wore a Snoopy watch and chewed gum non-stop. "I dream of air conditioning and international cuisine," she repeated, practising "the King's English" on me.

Elizabeth carried my shopping bags when the three of us went to the market where I bought jet-black maize, basil, wild strawberries, and a bouquet of cream-coloured freesias. On a sidewalk two *brujas* had laid out luck charms and magical prescriptions. Paul found a protein powder that was meant for expectant mothers. Elizabeth made a joke about her fat stomach, and said maybe she had a baby inside. I said, rather sternly, "Whose?" "Anonimo," she replied, as I lingered by the monkey fetuses used as ritual abortifacients.

When we'd settled in our apartment I invited Elizabeth for dinner. She asked to read some of my poetry and, to be polite, I asked her what *she* did. Elizabeth worked as a volunteer for MAS — *Muerte a Secuestradores*, literally "Death to Kidnappers." She assured me she was committed to doing only good deeds for the community, like the time she smuggled a grenade in her vagina into Bella Vista prison and blew up forty notorious *secuestradores*. She spoke as casually about killing people as she did about my culinary skills: when I made a pesto sauce she said basil was used in sorcery, never in cooking. I made the further mistake of adding the wrong kind of cheese to my pesto so that the mixture turned into a slimy green ball. Paul tossed the bewitched sauce in the river as we walked to the Avenida Sexta to see a film about French chefs eating themselves to death. Afterwards we stopped at a *churrascaria* for *rachitas*. The shoeshine boys asked for our leftovers, then hunkered down on their shoeboxes in a little circle, feasting on our picked-over ribs.

Elizabeth insisted on repaying us with "Colombian hospitality," and, on a feast day in honour of Our Virgin of Mercy, invited us to her house in the Barrio Popular. In the living room she seated us under a bleeding heart of Jesus and a poster of Pablo Escobar with the slogan I'LL NEVER RUN AWAY. We drank beer she had brewed from maracuya, yeast, bananas, and blackberries. I was on my third glass when Elizabeth began laughing at me and speaking to Paul in Spanish. "Of course it gives you damn diarrhea, but who says an evening of happiness isn't worth a bit of shit?" Paul translated.

After the beer, Elizabeth served *mondongo*, a stew made from rice with tripe. The smell made me sick. I went to the door for fresh air and stood under a horseshoe and an aloe vera sprig (both for good luck). After watching a gang of children firing at each other with imaginary machine guns, I broke off a piece of the aloe plant for Paul; he'd had nothing but bad luck in his business lately. As I went to sit down again I heard him talking to Elizabeth about moving his operation further south again to Bolivia.

When the time came I helped him pack his suitcase, which always smelled of coffee. And then, I don't know why, I started to weep. Paul asked me if I thought something was ending — he was worried, also; he said he saw himself huddled in a corner with the four winds hitting at him, and didn't know how to get out. I drove him to the airport in his linen suit and the T-shirt he always wore when he travelled, but the words I SCORED had faded in the wash and were almost unreadable.

I woke up the next day still feeling ill, and called Elizabeth, who arrived with leftover mondongo, a stomach settler, she tried to convince me. After I'd vomited for twenty-four hours, she drove me on the back of her motor scooter to a clinic, where a doctor diagnosed appendicitis and said he must operate at once. I rolled off the dirty, bloodstained sheet and got dressed to go home. Judging by the streets lined with funeral parlours surrounding the hospitals in Cali, a hospital was a place you went to die.

The doctor gave me an injection which "might help the vomiting" and Elizabeth stayed with me over the next few days. I tried to tell her I'd forgiven her for her love affair with Paul, but she pretended not to understand and rattled on about how nervous she often got, waiting to gun a kidnapper down. She'd found a trick which seemed to help: she got a bullet, took out the lead, and poured the gunpowder into a hot black coffee. She drank the lot and it steadied her nerves, she said.

When I felt better, Elizabeth took me to see her doctor for blood tests. The results were positive: I no longer had to risk carrying tampons around with me in Colombia. Elizabeth wept with happiness and made me promise she could be the godmother.

I didn't know where to reach Paul, though Elizabeth had kept me up to date on his travels. Two of her brothers were in the same business. One week he was in Santa Cruz, Bolivia, waiting for a load to come in a truck full of potatoes; the next week he was in the llanos making payoffs to the army. I didn't ever know what to expect from him. Only one thing was certain: I saw the funeral parlours, their window displays of tiny white coffins with twisted brass handles and crimson satin linings, and I knew I would not have my baby in Colombia. I packed my typewriter, my books, and my few clothes, then wrote a letter to Paul saying I didn't know when I'd be back. In stories, I said, there had to be resolution; not so in life.

I booked a one-way ticket to Vancouver in my own name. Elizabeth offered to drive me to the airport but I had too much luggage for the back of her scooter. I ordered a cab, kissed her, and threatened to send her my recipe for pesto sauce. Elizabeth hugged me, hard, and wept again when I asked her to look after Paul, whenever he made it home.

Her emotions were true — I checked. The veins were standing up on her hot, manicured hands.

Alone Across
the Outback

We must have made an odd sight — a woman, four camels, and a dog — as we travelled some 1,700 miles across Australia's western wilderness. But what better way to cross a desert than by leading or riding a camel? Some times were miserable, like the day of pouring rain when one camel slipped and hurt a leg. Other times were euphoric, days of extraordinary freedom.

———

SOME STRING SOMEWHERE INSIDE ME IS STARTING to unravel. It is an important string, the one that holds down panic. In the solitude of the desert night I feel the patter of rain on my sleeping bag — too light to lay the dust, too heavy for normal sleep. Sometime before midnight I come fully awake, and cannot find myself. There is neither in nor out, up nor down. I do not know where, or who, I am.

Inside me I hear three different voices. The first says, "So this is it, you've finally lost it. Good-bye." The second voice urges, "Hold on, don't let go. Be calm, lie down, and fall asleep. You will find yourself again."

The third voice is screaming.

At dawn my dog, Diggity, licks me awake. The sky is cold and pitiless, like a psychopath's eyes. My four camels stand hobbled nearby — welcome, familiar shapes.

Instinctively I start the morning routine — boil the tea, pack the gear, saddle the camels — and head south once more. It is my seventy-first day of travel across Australia's western desert. Slowly, as we get under way, the strings inside me knit together and I know who I am again.

During the following four months on the trail the voices never returned, and in time I came to enjoy the silence and solitude of the desert. Australia's arid western region, from the town of Alice Springs to the Indian Ocean coast, is a beautiful, haunting, but largely empty land. Dominated by the harsh, almost uninhabited Great Sandy and Gibson deserts, the region is known only to Australian Aborigines, a handful of white settlers, and the relatively few travellers who motor across it.

Why cross it by camel? I have no ready answer. On the other hand, why not? Australia is a vast country, and most of us who live there see only a small fraction of it — the large coastal cities, interior towns, and recreation areas, nearly all of them connected by surfaced roads. Beyond the roads, in the area known to Australians as the Outback, camels are the perfect form of transport. One sees little by car, and horses would never survive the hardships of desert crossings. For me, the only choice was camels.

Three years before my trip, at the age of twenty-five, I gave up my study of Japanese language and culture at the university in Brisbane and moved to the town of Alice Springs. I planned an expedition alone from Alice Springs to the Indian Ocean, a distance of some 1,700 miles. The very first requirement was camels.

For nearly a century, from the 1860s until recent times, camels were commonly used in the Outback. The animals, imported from Afghanistan and India, proved highly successful until cars and trucks began to replace them in the 1920s. Many camels were then simply turned loose to roam the Outback, where I was to find they can present problems for travellers.

Camels are still being trained in Alice Springs for tourist jaunts and for occasional sale to Australia's zoos. Sallay Mahomet, an Australian-born Afghan and a veteran handler, agreed to teach me something about the art of camel training.

I worked with Sallay nearly three months, for camels are not the easiest of beasts to train. To begin with, they can kill or injure you with a well-placed kick, and their bite is as painful as a horse's. Patiently Sallay taught me to understand camel behaviour — how to feed, saddle, doctor, and control the animals, the latter by kindness, discipline, and use of a noseline attached to a wooden peg inserted through the animal's nostril. Camels are similar to dogs; a well-trained one answers best to its accustomed handler. For an expedition such as mine, it was essential that I do most of the training.

Through part-time jobs, loans from friends, and finally with support from the National Geographic Society, I acquired the necessary equipment and four good camels: a mature, gelded male whom I named Dookie; a younger gelding, Bub; a female, Zeleika; and her calf, Goliath. Training and preparations took more than a year, but finally, in early April, I was ready.

My friends were not. Sallay, for one, was concerned about the trip. "Not many people have tried it alone," he said. "You'd do better with a friend along. What if you get sick or break a leg out there?" But gradually he came around, as did other friends, to the idea that I could make it.

On April 8, 1977, Sallay and my father — who had come from Brisbane to see me off — trucked me, the camels, and my dog, Diggity, to Glen Helen Tourist Camp, eighty miles west of Alice Springs. From there I journeyed to nearby Redbank Gorge, pausing long enough to say good-bye to my closest friends and helpers from Alice, who had all gathered there: Toly Sawenko, Jenny Green, Peter and Margaret Latz. Then I was off for Australia's west coast, alone except for the intermittent company of photographer Rick Smolan.

DAY 1   That first full day on the trail was both exhilarating and terrifying. My initial stop was to be the Aborigine settlement of Areyonga, via an old abandoned track that wandered through dry, stony creek beds and gullies and often simply disappeared. A dozen times during the day I was struck by the chilling thought, "Am I lost?" It was to become an altogether too familiar question in the months ahead.

At sundown I camped beside the track and estimated my progress: twenty miles. Not bad for the first day's trek, and only some 1,680 left to go. After hobbling the camels to graze, I built a brushwood fire and cooked a dinner of tinned stew. The blaze was welcome, for nighttime temperatures in the desert can drop to below freezing during Australia's autumn and winter seasons.

Finally I slid into my sleeping bag under an extra blanket or two and spent most of the night alternately dozing and wondering if I would ever see my camels again. But the occasional sound of their bells was reassuring, and at last I drifted off.

The next morning settled one worry; the camels seemed more scared than I was. I awoke to find them huddled as close as possible around the swag and Diggity snoring happily beneath the blankets.

DAY 4   In the afternoon we reached Areyonga, all slightly the worse for wear. My feet were blistered and my muscles were cramped. Diggity, too, was footsore and had to ride for a spell on Dookie's back, an indignity the dog could scarcely bear.

Zeleika was a complete mess. Her hindquarters were weak, her nose was infected, and she had a huge lump in a vein leading to her udder.

Bub was still uncertain about the whole thing. During those first days he had shied in terror not only at rabbits but even at rocks and leaves. He obviously wished he were home safe and sound.

Dookie was the only one without grumbles: he was having a great time. He continually smiled to himself, regarding everything around him with satisfaction, and stepped high when he walked. I suspect he has always wanted to travel.

After four days of total solitude Areyonga came as a shock, though a pleasant one. A mile outside the settlement we were greeted by a welcoming throng of Aborigine children, shouting, giggling, and begging for rides. Seemingly hundreds of small hands reached out to pat Digg-ity when she was allowed down from exile atop Dookie's back, and there was endless tickling of camel legs.

For three days I rested at Areyonga, worrying about Zeleika, Bub, and Goliath. I wondered what the next thirty-mile stretch to the homestead at Tempe Downs would do to us all. Dookie, of course, viewed the whole thing with lofty unconcern.

Sick or well, the camels proved a key to communication with the Aborigines. The people of Areyonga belong to the Pitjantjatjara tribe, who used camels for walkabout until cars and trucks finally replaced the animals. Yet many fond memories and stories of camels survive.

The few stumbling phrases of Pitjantjatjara I had learned in Alice Springs brought gasps and a good deal of laughter from my new friends. I discovered that before I had reached Areyonga, word had spread that "Rama-rama" — a term meaning "crazy person" in a rela-tively kind sense — spoke fluent Pitjantjatjara!

DAY 8   A few Aborigines accompanied us out of Areyonga for the first ten miles toward Tempe Downs. Bidding me good-bye, my compan-ions warned that the route over the mountains was an old one, unused for many years. I promised to call from Tempe Downs over the "flying doctor" radio, the emergency medical network that links Australia's Outback settlements.

My friends didn't exaggerate. After fifteen miles the mountain track occasionally began to peter out, and I spent hours sweating over maps and compass. I took a couple of wrong turns into a dead-end canyon and had to backtrack out.

The strain of uncertainty carries over into the unconscious, and I dreamed continually of being lost. Without the almost human compan-ionship of Diggity and the camels, I'm sure I'd be in those mountains still, muttering and stumbling around in circles.

To complicate matters, Bub chose the mountains to throw an unfor-gettable fit. Shortly after a midday pause he decided to buck the en-tire 500 pounds of assorted swag, tucker, and water drums off his back.

As each article crashed to the ground, the more terrified Bub became and the harder he bucked. Finally he stood petrified, the dislodged saddle hanging under his belly and the items from the pack scattered for miles.

Despite the setbacks, we made it to Tempe Downs in three days and marked our hundredth mile from the starting point at Glen Helen. After a radio call to my friends at Areyonga, I filled my drinking-water bag with rainwater and set off for Ayers Rock, 150 miles to the southwest.

We were entering sandhill country, an expanse of great motionless waves of reddish sand stretching mile after square mile ahead of us. The effect was pleasing, but some of the local inhabitants were not. Flies by the zillions engulfed us in dense clouds, covering every exposed square centimetre of human, dog, or camel flesh. Although they didn't bite, they crawled under eyelids, into ears and nostrils, and when they finally gave up at night, clouds of mosquitoes took over.

The country itself was exquisite. Huge stands of desert oak that lined the valleys among the hills sighed, whispered, and sang me to sleep at night. There were varieties of flowers, plants bearing strange seedpods, and other plants adorned with what looked like feathers.

Two bizarre residents of the sandhills intrigued me. One is a type of ant known as the inch ant, a monstrous thing nearly three centimetres long, with a very aggressive nature, eyes that stare into your own, and fangs that look like spanners.

The other creature, whose name I do not know, is the most endearing little beetle I have ever met. He's an unprepossessing chap to look at, and when he sees something coming toward him (I imagine that four camels, one human, and a dog would be somewhat frightening), he buries his head in that bright red sand, sticks his bottom in the air, and waits till you have either crushed him or missed. I always tried to miss, but Diggity and the camels. . . .

DAY 21   After 250 miles of travel from Glen Helen, we reached Ayers Rock. Among the mass of tourists who fly or drive in to see the great natural wonder, I found Jenny Green, my friend from Alice Springs, who had come to meet me. We talked — or rather, *I* talked — for four straight days. Having travelled for most of three weeks without company, I had undergone considerable change without realizing it. I babbled on to Jenny like a madwoman, and, as is often the case, one makes oneself better by making others sick. Dear Jen. She flew home feeling depressed, and I rode out of Ayers Rock feeling on top of the world!

The next 140 miles, to the settlement of Docker River at the eastern edge of the Gibson Desert, went smoothly until the weather dealt us an almost fatal blow. So far I had not encountered rain and had wondered how the camels would take to the bright orange plastic raincoats I had designed and made to cover their packs.

Just past the area known as Lasseter's Country, heavy clouds began to bustle over the horizon. Down it came. It rained cats and dogs. It rained elephants and whales, and it hailed. Within an hour the track was a running river and we were all drenched, though the camels soon grew accustomed to the flapping of their orange raincoats.

Camels have feet like bald tires. They simply cannot cope with mud, and leading them over precariously slippery patches is painful and exhausting to both driver and animal. In the midst of the storm Dookie, my best boy, my wonder camel, who was last in line, suddenly sat down with a thud and snapped his noseline.

I went back to him and tried to get him up. He refused. I shouted at him and had to kick the poor beast until he groaned to his feet. To my horror I saw that he was limping. It looked as if the trip was over.

We made it to Docker River in painful stages. Each night in camp along the way I cut shrubbery for Dookie and brought it to him. I massaged his shoulder, I cuddled him, kissed him, shed tears, and begged him to get better. To no avail. The thought of perhaps having to shoot my best camel gnawed away at me. Slowly, painfully, miserably, we limped into Docker River.

In the end it took Dookie a month to recover from what probably was a torn muscle in his shoulder. I never really diagnosed it, but at one point I even flew back to Alice Springs to consult with the veterinarian there. For good measure I consulted with a doctor, a dentist, a chiropractor, and some of the Alice Springs hospital staff, but since none of them could examine Dookie, the answer was always the same: "Wait and see."

Docker River is an Aborigine settlement. I was a hero, a celebrity, when I walked into the community of Docker River. Aborigine children were running and jumping and dancing; there was a great tumult. Word was out that a white woman was crossing the desert by camel, and to my surprise the entire population turned out to greet me. I never looked upon what I was doing as anything but a good, yet ordinary, adventure. I wanted to see the desert; I wanted to learn about camels; I wanted to be with the Aborigines. The people were wonderfully hospitable. My few phrases of Pitjantjatjara were put to good use when I joined them in hunting, dancing, and gathering insects and wild plants for food.

DAY 69 At last Dookie had improved enough to travel, and that morning we set off westward into the Gibson Desert. Before we had covered many miles some wild camels suddenly appeared.

I had been warned about these creatures by Sallay. "Make no mistake," he had said, "wild bull camels can kill you when they're in rut. They will try to take a female, and if you are in the way, you'll be attacked. The only thing that will stop them is a rifle bullet. If the time should come, don't hesitate."

And now the time has come. Two hundred yards ahead stand three large wild bulls, obviously in season and aware of Zeleika. Faced with sudden danger, I find myself outside the situation, observing and talking to myself.

Panic and shake, panic and shake, Robbie D. Remember what Sallay said; take it a step at a time. One, tie up Bub, who will surely bolt, and sit him down. Two, carefully take the rifle from its scabbard. Three, load and cock. Four, aim steady and fire.

By now the bulls are only thirty yards away. One of them spurts a small cylinder of blood where his heart should be. He seems to be stopping, thinking. All three come forward again.

Zzzt. This time just at the back of the wounded one's head. It hurts, and he turns and ambles away. The other two seem puzzled at his behaviour.

Zzzt. This time in the heart, I'm sure of it. But he's only down, just sitting there.

Zzzt. At last, in the head, and it's over. The other two bulls trundle off.

Darkness comes too quickly. I hobble the camels and try to keep them close. The campfire flickers on white sand washed with moonlight. All night long I hear the rumble of the two bulls, endlessly circling the camp.

At dawn one of the two, a young and beautiful bull, stands fifty yards away in the scrub. I resolve not to shoot him unless he directly threatens me or my camels.

I round up Dookie, Zeleika, and Goliath, and turn for Bub, good old unreliable Bub. In a flash he is off with the new young bull, galloping despite his hobbles. For an hour I try to catch him and can't; the wild bull stays too close to him. It is Bub or the bull. End of resolve. This time, even through tears, my aim is straight.

DAY 71   It was on this night that I heard the three voices and thought I was going mad — perhaps from a combination of worry over my water supply, the terrible monotony of sandhill country, and the effect of having had to shoot the wild bull camels. But the feeling of madness passed with sunrise, and we journeyed on. My worry over water was real, for we were down to ten gallons — less than one-fifth of capacity. Walk, walk, walk, over one sandy hill, then the next. Somewhere ahead, according to my map, lay an artesian well with an abandoned windmill and storage tank.

Supposing I missed the well, or the water tank was dry? I would simply push the camels on to the next water, five days beyond. They could do it, I told myself. Uncomfortable, but they could do it.

Walk, walk, walk. Would the sandhills never end? How could I once have thought them beautiful? The strain began to tell, and I sobbed as I walked: "God, please, the windmill must be over the next hill. No? All right then, the next. It's *got* to be the next one. No. . . ."

Diggity licked my hand, whining, but I couldn't stop. I raved at the hills. Then we crested the last one, and the land flattened out. A patch of green shone in the distance.

Panic melted and I began to laugh, patting Diggity. No need to find the well and tank that night; they were there by the patch of green. So I camped, and, sure enough, next morning there were the windmill and the water tank. The camels drank, Diggity drank. And I drank. Then I had a freezing, early-morning bath. Laugh, splash, and gurgle, Robbie D. It was good to be alive.

DAY 75   This was a memorable day, for it brought the gift of Mr. Eddie. He is a Pitjantjatjara man, and he arrived at my camp that evening with several carloads of Aborigines from the settlements of Wingelinna and Pipalyatjara. I served them all billies of tea, and as we chatted, he caught my notice: a dwarfish man, little taller than five feet, with a straight back, a beautiful face, the most wonderfully expressive hands, and makeshift shoes on his feet.

My guests spent the night, and next morning they decided that one of them should accompany me to Pipalyatjara, two days' walk ahead. I kept a polite silence and simply started off — to be joined by the little man.

I turned then, and we looked at each other. There was such humour, depth, life, and knowledge in those eyes that somehow we started laughing. We laughed for five minutes, then he pointed to himself and said, "Eddie." I pointed to myself and said, "Robyn," which I think he mistook for "rabbit" since he pronounces that word "rarbin."

No matter. All that day and the next we communicated in pantomime and in broken Pitjantjatjara or English, falling into helpless laughter at each other's antics. I don't think I ever felt so good in my life. And so we came to Pipalyatjara.

Pipalyatjara is one of those rarities in the Outback, an Aborigine settlement where the whites do a really splendid job of helping the Aborigines cope with prejudice, neglect, and government bureaucracy. Glendle Schrader, a friend from Alice Springs, is Pipalyatjara's community adviser, and we spent three days exchanging news. As I began packing for Warburton, 180 miles due west in the Gibson Desert, Mr. Eddie announced that he was coming too.

DAY 80   That morning we set off together, and after a mile or two Mr. Eddie insisted on a detour. He wanted to gather *pituri*, a native, narcotic tobacco plant that Aborigines chew, and we turned into a valley beside the trail. We searched in silence for several hours, and in my "white-fella" preoccupation with time, I began to wonder if we would ever reach Warburton. But Mr. Eddie seemed to flow with time rather than measure it, and eventually I relaxed and began to enjoy my surroundings. It was not the least of lessons he was to teach me.

The following day was either a disaster or a delight, depending on one's viewpoint. By afternoon we had trekked fifteen miles and were tired, hot, dusty, and fly ridden. At three p.m. on the trail I tended to get the blues. They weren't helped this time by a column of red dust that gradually rose on the horizon. Cars on the trail, though rare, frequently meant tourists, and I was in no mood to be gawked at today.

These were worse than usual. The car drew up beside us, and several men in silly hats spilled out, festooned with cameras.

"Hey, Bruce," one yelled, "come look at this gal, she's got a *safety pin* for an earring!"

"Will you look at those crazy sandals? And she's got a boong with her!"

Now "boong" is the white's racist term for an Aborigine, and Mr. Eddie is one of the finest people I have ever known. Temper sizzling, I pushed past the men's battery of lenses, and attention shifted to Mr. Eddie.

"Me take photograph longa you, Jacky-Jacky," one of the tourists announced in ghastly pidgin. "You stand by camel, there's a good boy."

Behind me I caught the multiple click of shutters; then all of a sudden Mr. Eddie seemed to go berserk. Brandishing his walking stick and giggling insanely, he drove the tourists back to their car, alternately raving in Pitjantjatjara and demanding payment for the photographs in broken English.

The startled men beat a hasty retreat, emptying their pockets of bills as they went. Mr. Eddie tucked the money away as the car vanished. Then he walked serenely over to me, and we cracked up.

With tears streaming down my face I thought of the Aborigines, how they had been poisoned, slaughtered, herded into settlements, prodded, photographed, measured, and left to rot with their shattered pride and their cheap liquor. And here was this superb old gentleman, who had lived through it all, who could turn himself into an outrageous parody of the Aborigine, then do an about-face and laugh with the abandon of a child. Reflecting on my own lesser problems and hardships, I thought: If you can do it, old man, me too.

DAY 94   We parted in Warburton, Mr. Eddie and I. I still think of our three weeks together on the trail as the heart of my entire journey. I had already arranged at Pipalyatjara to have a gun similar to mine waiting for Mr. Eddie at Warburton. He had fallen in love with my rifle, and it seemed the perfect gift.

The most dangerous part of the journey now lay ahead of me — the Gunbarrel Highway. We would travel 350 miles of the Gunbarrel's total 900-mile length, taking us across the forbidding Gibson Desert. The camels could not carry enough water to make it all the way, so my friend, Glendle Schrader, from Pipalyatjara would drive a truck with additional water from Warburton to the western part of the Gunbarrel. From Pipalyatjara the round trip comes to 800 hazardous miles, whether on foot or by motor. Such is the quality of friends.

So now, the Gunbarrel. I had been told at Warburton that in an average year only six vehicles pass over it, and I could easily see why.

The track amounts to a pair of shallow ruts that only the sturdiest four-wheel-drive machine can negotiate. On July 15 I set out with Diggity and the camels for the other side of the Gunbarrel.

Diggity was superb, a perfect and loving friend. She was a ball of muscle, covering fifty miles a day scampering back and forth. She had an unfailing sense of direction, always led me back to camp after an evening stroll, and excelled at chasing away creatures like centipedes and snakes.

The country was harsh, though lovely in its way. Sandhills stretched over some of the route, interspersed here and there with great stands of lacy but impenetrable mulga bush. Golden tufts of spinifex grass turned portions of the trail into a giant pincushion that continually jabbed at our feet. The camels strained under loads consisting largely of water, and noselines frequently snapped. Progress was achingly slow.

Yet there were some moments along the Gunbarrel that I will never forget. One morning before sunrise — grey silk sky, Venus aloft — I saw a single crow, carving up wind currents above the hills.

One evening I opened a tin of cherries, the ultimate luxury, ate half, and put the other half beside the swag for breakfast. Woke up the next morning: Bub's great ugly head, asleep on my legs, suspicious crimson stains on his lips. Good-bye breakfast.

DAY 112   Two weeks and 220 miles into the Gunbarrel, I had a wham-bammer of a day. It began like most others, except there were clouds. Rain, I thought as the first light slithered under my eyelids and into the folds of the blankets. But the clouds vanished, and then I realized something was missing: the sound of familiar camel bells!

Zeleika and Bub were gone, and Dookie, it developed, was only around because he had a great hole in his foot and couldn't walk. Where were Zeleika and Bub? How far had they gone? What about Dookie?

Then I recalled what a very wise friend in Alice once said to me:

"When things go wrong on the track, rather than panic, boil the billy, sit down, and think clearly."

So I boiled the billy, sat down with Diggity, and went over the salient points:

You are a hundred miles from anything.

You have lost two camels.

One of the other camels has a hole in his foot so big you could sleep in it.

You have only enough water to last for six days.

Your hip is sore from walking.

This is a god-awful place to spend the rest of your life.

So, having tidied all that up, I panicked. Fortunately, it didn't last, and after four hours I finally managed to get Zeleika and Bub back. Then I doctored Dookie's foot as best I could and set off once more along the Gunbarrel. The water situation was saved shortly afterwards by the arrival of Glendle and his truck.

When he caught up with us, he was so exhausted from the trip he could barely speak. We unloaded two of the three 40-gallon water drums from the truck, then filled my own drums from them with gallons to spare.

"You'll be wanting the other drum down the trail a bit," Glendle said. Wearily we drove some fifty miles to the west, dropped off the drum, and returned to camp. Minutes later Glendle was dead asleep in his blanket.

Next morning Glendle headed back toward Pipalyatjara. When he had become only a dust cloud on the horizon behind us, the silence and solitude closed in again.

I was not in the best of shape. My left hip, sore from endless slogging over sandhills, was barely usable. My skin was dry as dog biscuits, my lips were cracked, I'd run out of toilet paper, and a sun blister was trying to take over my nose. What, I wondered, do you do at a party when your nose drops off into your beer? At times I was so scared of dying that the knocking of my knees woke me up in the morning.

Had it all been worth it? I still thought so.

DAY 118   At the cattle station called Carnegie, at the end of the Gunbarrel, I received another blow: The station was little used because of severe drought, and I could not resupply with food as I had planned. There was nothing to do but trek northwest seventy-five miles to the station at Glenayle and hope for the best. Food ran so low that I once shared Diggity's dog biscuits — not exactly a banquet, but if they could keep her going, they could do the same for me.

By great luck I met two men travelling by car to Carnegie, and they gave me some tucker. One of them kindly made a leather boot for Dookie's sore foot. It didn't last long, so I made another one that lasted even less time. All I could think of was Glenayle and escape from the drought.

We straggled in at last, a miserable sight. I hadn't washed for a month, my face and clothes were covered with red dust, I was exhausted, and I looked like a scarecrow. As I entered the Glenayle homestead, the first thing I saw was a lovely, middle-aged lady watering her flower garden. As I approached her, she smiled and without a lift of the eyebrows said, "How nice to see you, dear. Won't you come in for a cup of tea?"

And so I met the Ward family — Eileen, her husband, Henry, and their sons, Rex and Lou. They would not hear of my pushing on for at least a week and insisted I stay with them. What warm, generous, and utterly charming people, and how little I can ever repay their kindness.

That week gave me a memorable look at western Australia's disastrous years-long drought. Though situated on the edge of the desert, the Ward's cattle station survives on occasional rain and on groundwater from wells. But as we toured the property, I saw what devastation the drought had worked. The horses were skin and bones and the cattle were even worse. Some of the animals died of exhaustion and hunger before our eyes.

Yet never once did I hear a complaint or a harsh word from the Wards. Their entire future was at stake, with no relief in sight. Still, they hung on with courage and hope.

While the horses and cows suffered, my camels — who could browse on trees as well as on ground cover — fared better, and after a week were slightly improved. One morning as I stood talking with Henry and patting Bub, big, jealous Dookie came up behind me. By way of attracting my attention, he opened his great jaws, took my entire head between them, and squeezed gently. Then he opened his mouth and galloped off, immensely pleased with himself.

I don't allow bad manners among my camels, but this once I could only laugh at Dookie's particular form of wit.

Soon afterwards we began packing up to leave Glenayle. The camels seemed pleased to get into their travelling kit again, so I didn't tell them what lay ahead of us: the Canning Stock Route.

The Canning is an Australian legend. It runs nearly one thousand miles, linking the small towns of Halls Creek and Wiluna and, far north of our route, crossing the Great Sandy Desert, one of Australia's worst. The route got its name from the days when cattle were driven along it from well to remote well, though I don't see how they survived.

Fortunately, I had to cover only the most hospitable section of the Canning — 170 miles, from a point near Glenayle to Cunyu. There the Gibson Desert would be far behind us, and the remaining 450 miles to the Indian Ocean would be much easier.

DAY 129   We left Glenayle after a week and headed for the Canning at Well Number 9. This was dingo country, and I was terrified that Diggity would pick up one of the poisoned baits set out to exterminate the wild dogs. I put a muzzle on her, but she whined and scratched at it and was so disconsolate that I finally took it off.

The area was rougher than anything we had crossed before, and at Well Number 6 I called a halt. The setting was lovely, an infinitely extended bowl of pastel-blue haze carpeting the desert, with crescent-shaped hills floating in the bowl and fire-coloured sand dunes lapping at their feet. In the far distance five violet, magical mountains soared above the desert. Have you ever heard mountains roar and beckon?

These did, like a giant lion — a phantom sound meant only for the ears of madmen and deaf mutes. From the pit of my stomach I longed to journey to those mountains. I had found the heart of the world.

Well Number 6 hardly deserved the name. The surface of the water lay nine feet below ground level and could only be reached with a bucket, a rope, and enough effort to cause a hernia. The water tasted foul, but none of us cared, and I camouflaged mine with huge doses of coffee.

The night was incredibly lovely. I made camp in a cathedral of fifty-foot silver ghost gums bordering the well, and built a mattress of fallen leaves that scattered golden jangles of firelight in a million directions.

The camels had more forage than they could possibly eat. In the evening they rolled and played in the white dust, raising puffs of cloud that the fat red sun turned to bronze. For three days it was perfection, and I wanted never to leave. All the good things of the journey seemed to crystallize in this one place, and I felt somehow untouchable.

On the third night Diggity took a dingo bait. I had to shoot her. Before dawn I left that place I had thought so beautiful.

DAY 137 My only thought now was to push on to the end of my route. The country passed unnoticed beneath my feet, and I recall little of that time. I think I reached Cunyu on August 27.

There at last the press caught up with me, and I first learned of interest in "the camel lady." To avoid pestering questions, I left the camels at Cunyu and sneaked away to Wiluna, forty miles to the south. The people of Wiluna asked no questions: They simply took me in and cared for me. Within a week I was setting out for the Indian Ocean coast.

Behind me lay nearly 1,300 miles — five months of travel. Ahead lay only 450 more miles. We made them slowly, for beyond Cunyu Zeleika fell seriously ill. She had nursed Goliath, her calf, throughout the entire six months, and now she suddenly began bleeding internally. I dosed her with everything in my medicine kit, but I was afraid she wouldn't make it. I was wrong.

DAY 180   A month after leaving Cunyu we arrived at Dalgety Downs cattle station, only 156 miles from the sea.

David and Margot Steadman, homesteaders at Dalgety, took us in and proceeded to spoil all five of us. The camels were fed barley, oats, and lollies, an undreamed-of diet. They were praised, patted, stroked, and talked to. With such care even Zeleika began to improve. To help matters along, I tried to wean Goliath from her by putting the two of them in neighbouring yards with a fence between. But clever Zeleika, sick as she was, always managed to manoeuvre her udder within Goliath's eager reach.

For a time I considered leaving Zeleika behind with Dave and Margot and pushing on to the sea with the other three camels. But she continued to improve, and I decided that a dip in the Indian Ocean might do the old girl a power of good.

On that final stretch of 156 miles we rode in style for about thirty. At Woodleigh, thirty-six miles from the coast, two kindly homesteaders, David and Jan Thomson, offered to transport the camels and me on their flatbed truck to a point only a couple of hours' walk from the beach.

I accepted, but the camels had reservations. After the long journey, however, their trust in me was complete, and they finally climbed aboard. Up they went at last — Dookie first, bravely, then Bub, who would follow Dookie's rear end through hell if necessary. Then wise, stubborn Zelly and finally Goliath, that gregarious little pest, who wasn't about to see his milk supply carted off. We trussed them up like plucked chickens, and off we headed.

DAY 195   Six miles short of our goal we unloaded and set out on the final leg. Oh, how my spirits soared! Two hours later I saw it, glinting on the far side of the dunes — the Indian Ocean, end of trail.

An anticlimax? Never. We rode down to the beach toward sunset and stood thunderstruck at the beauty of the sea. The camels simply couldn't comprehend so much water. They would stare at it, walk a few paces, then turn and stare again. Dookie pretended he wasn't scared, but his eyes were popping out and his ears were so erect they pulled his eyelashes back.

I was riding Bub, and when the surf sent globs of foam tumbling over his feet, he danced and bucked and shied and nearly sent me flying. Zeleika would have nothing to do with that freakish ocean, but the others were entranced. They refused to believe it wasn't drinkable. I mean, if it's water, you can drink it, right? Each time they took a mouthful, their expressions broke me up.

We stayed one glorious week, then it was time to go. I had decided to leave all four camels in the care of David and Jan, who loved them dearly and who would give them a perfect home at Woodleigh after I returned to my own home on Australia's east coast, where I could not keep them. On October 27 David and Jan showed up in the truck, and we turned from the beach for the last time. For a second I was tempted to saddle the camels and start over. But no. The trip is not meant to be repeated except in my memory — over and over again.

Dear camels, may you spend your dotage being fed lollies, facing Mecca, and contemplating the growth of your humps.

Many times since the trek I have been asked why I made it, and I answer that the trip speaks for itself. But for those who persist I would add these few thoughts. I love the desert and its incomparable sense of space. I enjoy being with Aborigines and learning from them. I like the freedom inherent in being on my own, and I like the growth and learning processes that develop from taking chances.

And obviously, camels are the best means of getting across deserts. Obvious. Self-explanatory. Simple. What's all the fuss about?

Irene Guilford

The
Cold Sea

When you listen to stories, over and over again, about places you have never been, a landscape starts to grow in your mind. With each retelling, with each new detail, you travel a bit farther. What drew me to making this trip, apart from the tug of family history, was a desire to see how such imaginary travels, and actual physical travel to the real places, would converge. I did not know what to expect, except that there would be a jarring clash. Towns and villages change, memory is faulty at best, and the images in my head were based not on my own memory, but on someone else's. What's the point, other than a respectful acknowledgement of the past? But stories, if they have become alive in the mind of the listener, wrap themselves around the journey like arms and legs, holding the traveller within their embrace, carrying her along.

As I look at the Czech Republic on a map of Europe, the big country touching it on the left throbs, like the pulse inside a thumb. Germany. My mother has spoken of places there, a village where she hid after the Soviets invaded Lithuania, a town where she waited after the war for her new life to begin. Until

145

now, I have known them only through a handful of photographs, casually, infrequently viewed, and the wisps of her memory.

I tell Nigel I will go there first, fly over a few days early, meet him in Prague where he will be speaking at a seminar on computers, and where we will afterwards vacation. I do not ask him to come to Germany. He is a friend, he cares for me, but I do not want him watching. This history is not his, only mine. However, he is also a husband. Intent on goals and itineraries, he will become impatient. I want no plans, no rushing, no need for patience. He says he will only drive, assist, protect. He makes promises.

I have never liked history, nor have I seen war, but I know dates and battles, armies and uprisings. I was born in Toronto, but I know of killings, of deportations to Siberia. I learned it as a child at our dinner table, at Lithuanian school on Saturday mornings, at Lithuanian camp in the summer. It was what my father and mother talked about with friends. *Where were you when it started? How did you get away? What happened to your family?* It was always present, as constant and unremarkable as air.

Let me tell you the history I do know. On June 21, 1941, German soldiers poured into Lithuania on their way to fight the Russians. Hitler called it Operation Barbarossa, after a legend about Frederick I. An ancient king sits sleeping at a stone table, his red beard still growing. When it grows through the stone and wraps itself around the table three times, he will awake to lead his people to world conquest. The battle went on for three years. In 1944, the Russians won and occupied Lithuania. Of three million Lithuanians, eighty thousand fled west, my father and mother among them.

Those are the public events. Let me tell you the private. My father was twenty-one, working as a seaman on a barge on the Nemunas River to evade the press gangs who seized young men for the German army. Dreaming his mother was dying, he set off for home, but arrived to find her already dead. There was only him to bury her, for his father had died long before and his brother was nowhere to be found. He dug her a grave in the forest beneath a birch tree. Then, with the dirt still fresh on his shoes, he jumped a train.

My mother and her parents escaped by horse and wagon. After loading it with three smoked hams, a bucket of lard, and a quilt for a bed, they huddled through the night. Bombs screeched, bullets cracked. The horses reared and clawed the air. Near dawn, they raced — down a hill, along a gravel road, over a bridge across the river that was the border. Now part of a trail of refugees, they covered perhaps three miles a day.

My mother was seventeen. The morning German soldiers came down the line, taking young men and women to dig trenches and graves, she had been walking instead of riding. *Play sick under the quilt,* her mother had hissed, then stalled for time by raising a commotion. My mother clambered to get inside, but the neck of her blouse caught on a nail. Someone — she remembers only that it was a woman — pushed her from behind, and she was free.

Those the Russians overtook, they shipped back. My parents left soon enough, ran fast enough to get away.

The Soviets demolished farms, bulldozed entire villages. My mother has never returned to Lithuania. She says there is nothing left to see. I do not believe this. I have been to Lithuania with my father, but the country I saw was his, not hers. Nor has she ever been back to Germany. She pretends these parts of her life are not important, as if all that matters is her life now, with her second husband in their bungalow in Etobicoke. *Why should I go? What is Lithuania to me? I could have been born in Spain or Africa, for all it matters.*

I prepare for my journey in her kitchen, studying maps and photographs. She tells me how she left Lithuania in 1944, in the fall, and spent the winter in Klingenbrunn, a village near the Czech border. We cannot find it on any map. I begin to wonder if her memory is fading. She is sixty-six. The war has been over for forty-eight years. German place names are confusing, long and dense with syllables. But she points adamantly to the same empty spot on the map.

Nothing there, really. Just a railway track and a sawmill, but she draws her own map, a line that looks like stitching.

When the war ended, there were a million like her, loose and ragged in Europe that summer of 1945. Displaced persons. DPs. The United Nations and the victorious armies organized them into camps, over a hundred of them. We find hers easily. Scheinfeld, just east of Frankfurt, right on the road to Prague.

Drawing the map of the camp, she puts in the cafeteria, the school, the gymnasium they used for basketball and folk dancing. She draws the tailor shop, the doctor's quarters, the barracks, and the showers. She draws orchards. She draws paths. She builds a whole society. *I never went into town,* she tells me.

There are photographs, ten of them, the only evidence of the four years she spent there before she came to Canada in 1949. Yet it is amazing that there are even these, for she had no camera and was travelling only with what she could carry. She would have had to bargain or cajole, perhaps even plead for these photos, each a small proof of her existence, a thin hook holding memory, yet each so slight it could be lifted by a breeze. She marks the spot on the map where each photograph was taken.

She slept on a cot, she says, the only other furniture in her room a table and chair, and worked in the storeroom helping two men distribute parcels of sausage and bread. The day they received butter, they gave her a little extra, and she ran back to her room, the butter hidden between her breasts. In one photo she sits in her room with her elbows on the table, the light of the window behind her. It is impossible to make out the expression on her face.

I decide to take the photos with me, though I dare not tell her. This is all there is of the young woman she once was, a pretty girl who sang in national dress, waving away the American soldiers who called to her along the path as she returned to the barracks from choir practice, arms linked with two other girls. There is nothing else, except her voice, which is still strong and lovely. Though I am by nature careful and not superstitious, it seems to be tempting fate to separate these photos from her, to take them all this distance, to carry them back to the side of the Atlantic from which they came.

We spend hours talking. Night after night, I stay late. It is like a new language for us, and neither of us can get enough. Only when sleep is so close I can fight if off barely long enough to get home, do I edge my way out her doorway.

Nigel and I fly to Frankfurt, then drive east into Bavaria. It is June, and against the green land, the white stucco houses with their square windows and red roofs look solid, safe. We will reach the DP camp first. I would prefer to trace her route as she took it, not go backwards into her history, but this is what happens when you travel west to east.

My mother warned there might be nothing of the camp buildings left. The wooden barracks in which she'd lived had been old in her time and had probably been pulled down by now, or if not, were surely rotted. It is an easy one-hour drive on the Autobahn, and as we pass one exceedingly tidy village after another, I start to prepare myself. I hear her words and my own common sense. *There won't be anything left.* Still, I can't stop hoping.

We turn south onto a good country road through open farmland contoured like the palm of my hand. Our first glimpse of Scheinfeld is suburban; the outskirts are self-confident in their modernity — a fast-food restaurant, a supermarket, a video store. But this is temporary. Soon we are on the main street. Even though there are many shops, here the present does not brazenly shoulder the past aside.

It is early morning in Germany. My eyes are burning, forced open in the bright sunshine after a night with no sleep. My skin and clothes are grimy, and I need to brush my teeth. But before resting, before washing, I want to see the camp.

Of course, she was right. There are no barracks left, not even ruins to stumble over. Instead, there are new houses and an old-age home. Everywhere I look there are hedges and stone walls, too high to see over, too dense to see through. Perhaps there is nothing left from my mother's time, but what there is, I want. I do not like this refusal of my sight. I want to stride into the gardens, peel back their lawns, pull off the stones of their drives to release the earth beneath.

The paths remain. As I follow their curves, it seems they too obey my mother's map. Her photographs lead me, and I stand in the places she stood. I want new photos to lay next to hers, to say to her *Look, look where I have been.* Nigel photographs me, taking great care to position me exactly. I will never be here again.

I don't write good postcards. I want to say something clever, but struggle just to fill the space. Sometimes I cheat and write big. But the words to my mother come immediate and true. *No barracks, but my feet walk the paths you drew.*

The Gasthof where we stay is just built and not quite finished. Wooden beams lean against the walls, waiting, and wood shavings lie in curls on the floor, giving off a sweet, biting scent. As we sit at breakfast, workmen in heavy boots wander through carrying drills and wires, nodding in formal greeting as they pass.

After breakfast, I leave Nigel reading in our room and go to the cemetery. It slopes away from a small church on a rise in the centre of town. One of my mother's photos shows three Lithuanian headstones, not family or friends, just Lithuanians. It is astonishing that out of a camp of one thousand, only three died, almost as if those who survived the war refused absolutely any ordinary death.

A woman tends the graves, coming in and out through the iron gate, silent. As I walk around, holding my photograph before me, looking for the graves over which three birches arc, she watches me without looking. I find them, the graves, the birches, but the valley beyond, which was empty in the photo, is now crowded with orange roofs, and this disturbs me more than I can say, this life cluttering the once wild and silent arena of the dead.

Two of the gravestones are easily legible, but the carving on the third is worn away. My mother told me once about a young woman who had returned to the camp after folk dancing, hot and flushed. She had showered, caught pneumonia, and died. She'd been twenty-one. My mother has a picture of the open casket, one end propped up against the wall so that the dead girl stands almost upright. Lace edges her face, tall candles and biers of flowers crowd the casket. On each side a young woman stands guard, one of them my mother. They wear national dress, vests and long, woven skirts, blouses of white linen, the red embroidery encircling the billowing sleeves like a script passed down from mother to daughter, learned by hand and eye.

She never told me who the dead woman was, and now I feel along the headstone with my fingers, tracing letters, piecing together a name. I want this to be her, this body beneath my feet the same one my mother had once stood by and honoured.

I write her name down — Anele Skimbirauskaite. When I return, I will track down her family, tell them I have been here. I will describe her grave edged with red begonias. But she has been dead forty-seven years. Perhaps there is no one left. Perhaps she is forgotten.

We have to be leaving soon. I want one last walk around the DP camp, and I want it alone. Once more, I leave Nigel at the Gasthof, promising not to be long, promising we will leave as soon as I return.

Although it is Thursday, the shops are closed. It must be some kind of festival. Buckets of gladiola stand in front of the shut doors. Freshly cut birch branches, tall as a grown person, lean against the walls every few feet. I can see the slanting wound of the cut, and it bothers me, this lopping off of young branches for this one day. The streets are deserted, and in this quiet, I take time, stopping every few feet to listen, watch, and wait. It is no different, this last solitary walk, and turning back toward the Gasthof, I realize I would need weeks or months here, not just two days.

In the distance I hear chanting and a sombre brass band. It is a procession, a first communion. First come the priests, then the little girls in white dresses, then the villagers. Everyone in town must be taking part, for the procession fills the paths my mother drew, crowding me aside. Even though they concentrate on their chanting or on the rosaries between their fingers, the villagers' eyes flicker over me as they pass. Later I will learn it is Corpus Christi day. All of Bavaria is closed.

Suddenly, I feel the outsider I am, a lone woman standing on the sidewalk, watching. I want to go back to the Gasthof, but there is no way to get by, nothing to do but wait. The procession moves slowly up the path, then, turning a corner, disappears.

Back at the Gasthof, Nigel is frantic with waiting. I have been gone too long. In his distress, he is helpless before the collapse of promises made before we came. I sit on the bed to help calm him, the tear at my attention like a loose piece of skin pulled away, half-dead, half-alive. It is as I had feared. I am not free to forget him.

We have trouble finding Klingenbrunn, the village where my mother spent the final winter of the war. Not the town, which is easy enough to find on a local map, but the place my mother knew, for when we arrive, there is no village, and no railway.

We drive back and forth, back and forth, until I notice a woman standing in her front garden. She has a trowel in her hand, but her creamy white gloves are still clean. I say to Nigel, *Stop the car, get out please and go ask her.* On my lap, my mother's maps, crisp at the start of this journey, now lie limp from the heat of my hands.

But this is it. Klingenbrunn. He points to the sign. He is frustrated with driving, with pushing against the limits of vocabulary, with the war and DPs, with my mother and me. *Your mother was right. There's nothing here.*

I say nothing, turning instead to stare out the window. He gets out to speak to the woman. His German accent is good, his grammar passable. He has looked up the word for railway. She listens, head tilted intently, then falls to thinking, a finger pressed to her lips. *Aaah*, she finally says, *you want Klingenbrunn Bahnhof.* She gives us directions. Just before we leave, she leans in to me through the car window. She is my mother's age, but her hair is still the colour of wheat.

It is the coldest place in Germany, she tells me. *We call it the cold sea.*

In Klingenbrunn, in February 1945, my mother stood up to her hips in snow, wearing the thin-soled shoes in which she'd left home the previous September. She had no stockings. Her master ran a sawmill. His wife, whispering *Wear it under your own so he won't see,* gave my mother extra clothing. As my mother piled planks of wood in the yard, she could look up and see the Alps in the distance.

In Klingenbrunn, in June 1993, I land up to my hips in grass. Wading through brambles that scratch my bare legs, paying no attention to the houses sprinkled around, I make for an old wooden tower ahead, suddenly sure it was once part of the sawmill. A graveyard surrounds it — cars from East Germany, Wartburgs and Trabants, cars through whose empty windows grasses grow.

I decide to walk the railway track. Panic leaps in Nigel's eyes as I go. We are both beyond words, those that would help him comprehend or allow me to explain. I leave him to wrestle alone with something he does not understand.

I walk to the end of the platform. My mother came by rail, not by the road we took, winding down between thin, tall firs, dropping lower and lower through a silent forest. All the time she was here, she probably didn't know that just above her was a town filled with people. Here is something new I will be able to tell her.

I step down onto the track. It is like dropping into a silent cleft. For a moment, I balance on the rail, staring down at my white cotton runners, feeling through their pliable soles the rigid metal underneath. Then, as she would have done in her descent from the train, I step down into the gravel. I twist my feet deeper, burrowing down between the sharp, grey stones, searching for the place she once stood, for the prints buried beneath. My soles curl and pull at the earth. If I look up, I will cry. Then, breathing deeply, my feet stilled, I make myself. Through air that is extremely clear, my eyes following the taper of the railway track, I look back into the distance toward the place from which she came.

Suddenly, I cannot hold my gaze. I am frightened. I don't expect to see ghosts — part of me wants to — but there is danger here. The air is menacing with long-held pain, with shame and defeat — a cold cup of cries. It makes no difference that I come from a different place and time, that the life I visit here is not my own. With my hands, I cover my ears against the echo of wails. They threaten, threaten so much I must flee.

In the distance, the car sits waiting, and in it, Nigel. I can see him, his face turned to watch for my return, his right arm holding the curve of the steering wheel as if he must not let go. I walk toward him steadily but cautiously, holding my arms in, moving almost sideways as if to slip between drops of rain. I do not dare to disturb, to bruise with my passing what hangs in the air.

When I reach him, the motor is running, the car door is standing open. I have only to step inside, but I turn in one last slow circle, photographing air.

I have photographed everything — the sawmill tower, the railway track, the beige cars dead in the grass. Back in Etobicoke, I sit with my mother around the circle of her kitchen table, the pictures piled like booty in the centre. As she looks, first through Scheinfeld, then through Klingenbrunn — we don't even bother with Prague — I watch closely.

A long-dormant creature rises behind her eyes, rearing like a dragon, slamming into her face so hard she is left almost swaying. She grows hot and flushed, plucking her damp T-shirt free from her chest with thumb and forefinger. It is the certainty of her recognition that is compelling. After all, these pictures show only a curving path, a stretch of railway track. But I know she is seeing more, things I can never see.

She pushes away from the table, opens a window and fans herself, takes a long drink of water. She sits back down, then shuffles through the photos, finding the one she wants. Holding it propped on its edge between two hands, she speaks, but she is somewhere else, no longer with me. "This was a warehouse. We never saw inside all the time we were there. The doors were always shut. They opened it when the war was over. Guess what was inside."

My heart contracts. I remember this building beside the sawmill with its slash of red words painted on the side. Even with the dictionary, Nigel and I could not make out what they said.

"When they opened the doors, it was an avalanche, there were so many. It could have buried me.

"Boots. Warm leather boots, with laces. Hundreds and hundreds."

My mother, standing barelegged, up to her hips in snow.

MICHELENE ADAMS

Where Mih
Navel String Bury

The narrator of this piece, having lived away from her home in Trinidad for several years, considers whether she is something of a stranger to her country, but in recounting disparate experiences she has on a visit to the island, she discovers, happily, that she is a child of Trinidad after all.

I WAS EIGHTEEN WHEN I LEFT MY FAMILY AND MY native Trinidad to attend university in Ontario, Canada. It was August, the tail end of the rainy season. The sky was a heavy blue-grey and the mountains a rich green thick with scent. I remember still. I expected to remain in Canada long enough to finish a B.A., but eleven years later, I'm still here, far from where mih navel string bury.

I've had a recurring dream since I've been living in Canada. I'm in an airport lounge and someone rushes in to tell me that the plane is about to leave but I can't find my passport/ticket/wallet, though I've checked for them over and over before now. Another version: I'm packing when it occurs to me that the flight was scheduled for nine a.m., not p.m., and rather than being four hours early, I'm eight hours late. An anxiety dream about leaving? About staying?

I took Trinidad for granted until I experienced the hollow missing that's reserved for patria. Now when I visit, I breathe in slow, concentrate on absorbing it into my skin by osmosis. I'm coming to know my country in the manner in which a stranger comes to know a foreign land. I'm putting a sense of it together fragment by fragment.

I'm in Trinidad on vacation. My mother and I are sitting on the back porch before dinner. She's happy that I've come home just in time for the Carnival celebrations, since I haven't been here during this season for nine years now. In her indirect fashion she's asking me to join her and her friend Pat for J'ouvert. I remember that the last time I went out into the streets for J'ouvert I was seventeen and didn't enjoy the experience. I've played "pretty mas" in broad daylight, dancing in the streets to steelband music and brass bands under brilliant sun, but the close crush of bodies in the four a.m. blackness unnerved me. "Yuh playin' in costume or jus' trailin' along?" I ask.

"Trailin' along as usual," she says, "i's three days away. Yuh really reach jus' in time."

My mother wakes me at 3:15 on Monday morning already dressed in jeans, a T-shirt, and sneakers. I get out of bed and am ready just in time for Pat's pick-up time of three-thirty. We drive to my grandfather's house in Woodbrook and park the car in his garage. He's centrally located for all the Carnival activities. We walk from Cornelio Street down Tragarete Road in the cool dark. A Rasta wrapped in a loincloth, holding a walking stick, moves past us at a pace. Across the street is a group of five Blue Devils, horns attached to their heads, skin covered in paint. Somebody is blowing a whistle and is accompanied by a rhythmic clanging.

"I wear mih oldes' clothes," says Pat. "Las' year some nasty Jab lolassie rub up on mih an I had to throw away mih blouse." She's chuckling.

"All a'dat in it," my mother responds. I watch her from behind, amazed at how swiftly she's chipping in the dark, in time to the sound of bongo drums that's floating great distances in the night. My godfather tells a story of a Carnival some forty-five odd years ago in the days when steelbands feuded. When two of them ran into each other on Belmont Circular Road there was a brawl. Broken bottle was flying and Uncle John says he began running away from the crowd. Being an athlete, he felt he was moving fast but he watched over his shoulder as a young woman sped past him in a blur. When he met my mother a couple of years later he recognized her and expressed his admiration.

At the corner of Fitt Street the dark tricks me into thinking that Patrick Manning, the prime minister of our island, is approaching sporting the customary dark suit and tie and carrying a briefcase but, of course, it's only some individual wearing a papier-mâché mask made to look like Manning's face. The crowd is growing, so we sit on someone's wall hoping that a group of revellers with their own musical accompaniment will appear. We haven't long to wait. We hear them long before we see them. There are East Indian tassa drums, African drums, and a few whistles. The high pitch of spoon on bottle rings out in cadence with the drumming. The harsher sound of metal on metal is part of the mix.

"Dat soundin' like de real ol'-time J'ouvert bands," my mother says and for an instant she looks several years younger.

"Yes, Michi," Pat adds. "All yuh young people doh know de real J'ouvert. More an' more organize' bands makin' costumes but it didn' use' to be so."

"People use' to wear any ol' thing," my mother chimes in. "Da's what 'ol' mas' mean. It wasn' suppose to compete wid de 'pretty mas' we play later in de day on Monday an' Tuesday."

"I's de slaves, once dey were free, dat take J'ouvert as a time to let out some a deir frustrations." A couple covered in grease, the whites of their eyes stark against the black, walk past holding hands. "Where yuh think de Jab Molassie come from?" she continues, pointing at the couple. "I's molasses dey originally use to paint on. 'All yuh fin' we black? Well, watch black!' It was a kin'a protes'. Molasses made from sugar an' i's because a sugar dey bring de Africans here in de firs' place. 'Jab' is patois fuh 'Diable.' Jab Molassie — Molasses Devil."

159

The band we've been hearing turns on to Tragarete Road from Luis Street. They're a ragtag assembly, though two women hold up a banner at their head indicating they are an organized bunch. BRING BACK DE OL' TIME DAYS it reads. My mother, squinting at the banner, says, "Amen to dat!" and jumps off of the wall. We follow. We fall in with the crowd taking advantage of the swift rhythm of the drums, chipping in time up Tragarete Road. The band seems to be an amalgam of the original Carnival characters. There are Sailors in fake white naval uniforms throwing powder. I spot Jab Molassie covered in black grease, horns on their heads and thick long tails attached to their shorts, which they swing and slap against the surface of the street. They're carrying tins and bottles that they beat with spoons. Robbers are a part of this too. They are dressed in sedate black suits and the absurd Robber headgear towers three or four feet above their heads. They have whistles strung around their necks and they blow on them shrilly and fire their toy guns into the dark. They aren't chanting the poetic litany of their exploits as outlaws; they're saving it for the "pretty mas," when a captive audience will be seated around the stage in the Queen's Park Savannah.

There are Wild Indians in the band as well. They were originally modelled on the groups of South American native Indians who came to Trinidad in the last century to trade. These masqueraders wear elaborate headdresses made of brightly coloured feathers. Though it was the Venezuelan Warao they had in mind when they came up with this character, the costume has clearly been influenced by the Hollywood North American Indian. The East Indian tassa drummers are dressed as Borokits, appropriate since that character is an adaptation of a figure from Indian folklore, a kind of centaur. The man's torso extends out of a donkey made from fabric stretched over wire and decorated with lamé and sequins. The animal rocks with his movements as he attacks the drum strapped to his body. I've been watching one of the Borokits, who is not carrying a drum, drink a full bottle of Carib beer in one long swallow. As though he feels my eyes, he turns and I recognize an old friend. "Twaz!" I laugh and he comes toward me grinning.

"Yuh back wid us," he says, throwing one long, brown arm around my shoulders. "Moms!" he exclaims to my mother and draws her closer. "Come, ladies, we ain' goin' home till Ash Wednesday!" We chip with Twaz and my aunt keeps up, holding one arm above her head at intervals when the rhythm of the drums is especially affecting.

We stay with this ol'-time band all the way into downtown Port of Spain, along Wrightson Road and back onto Woodbrook. The sun is up now and the drums have stopped but the bottle and spoon are passed among us and we keep a rhythm going till we reach Luis Street where the band originated. Somebody runs around the side of the house, which has doubled as a mas camp for the past weeks, and drags out a garden hose. He turns it on the revellers collapsed on the pavement. Some people shriek and run out of the way of the arc of water, but many lie back in surrender or throw their heads back and let it soak their skin and hair. Paint begins to trickle down their bodies and the drummers, in accompaniment to this Old World water ritual, pick up a new rhythm and the ol'-time band rises to the dance once more.

We get to my grandfather's house just after six-thirty and he has coconut bake and buljol waiting for us, the codfish sprinkled with olive oil and seasoned with lemon juice, onion, and sweet pepper. He turned ninety-one last year but this morning he went out at five a.m. and joined the crowd trailing a steelband as it moved past Cornelio Street. We leave him making sandwiches for the crowd that will use his house as a refuge from the sun later today.

The first thing I do when we get home is take a long shower, watching the dust slide off my skin and believing I'm more tired than I've ever been. I crawl into bed and fall asleep almost instantly but at one p.m. I'm leaving for the streets again, ready for "pretty mas."

"I hear yuh get deported."

I laugh, recognizing Nadia's voice on the other end of the line. "Not exactly," I say.

"I was plannin' to take de day off tomorrow. Yuh wanna do de north coas' drive?"

"I' been dreamin' 'bout doin' de north coas' drive."

"I'll pick yuh up around ten."

Nadia arrives on schedule and as always she gets out of the jeep and comes to the door to meet me. She never blows the horn from the street. We carry out the usual ritual. We hug and I lift her effortlessly about six inches off the ground. She's a small woman. Bird is surely her animal spirit. The first time she visited my home we were sitting in the living room when a ground dove flew in. It isn't strange for birds to fly into our home but it is strange for it to happen at night. On another occasion we were on the porch when an owl glided by in plain sight. It was daytime.

The top is down on her Suzuki jeep. "I guess yuh figured I could use de sun," I say and we laugh. We drive through Maraval along Saddle Road. When I was a child, the Saddle was a nightmare full of hairpin curves that I endured only because when the car stopped we would be parked in front of the sea. Once the suburbs of Maraval are behind us, the Saddle is lined on the right by a sheer cliff that rises into forest and on the left is a fertile valley. I look over my left shoulder and see Port of Spain in a haze of blue in the distance. We're directly in line with the village of Paramin, a cluster of houses perched on the side of a mountain.

"I tol' yuh in mih letter I went to Paramin to hear Parang las' Chris'mas?"

"Yuh know how long I want to make it dere? Da's de home a Parang music. De Pañols who use' to live dere brought Parang here. Wha' was it like?"

"Somethin' else. I had a ball. An ol' feller pick' mih up to dance an' we did de castillan or somethin'."

"Since when yuh dancin' in public?" I ask incredulously.

"It was an exception." She pushes her sunglasses off the bridge of her nose onto the crown of her head. "Fuh one thing, everybody who wasn' playin' an instrument was dancin'. Ol' people, young people. An' de feelin' up dere . . . it was authentic. It was true-true Parang. De

Spanish lyrics an' de cuatros wid de African shak-shaks an' de drums. Yuh shoulda' see one a de ol' men on de stan'-up bass. He was ol' as de hills. No teeth, white hair, those blue-rim' irisis, yuh know what I mean? But he stan' up proud an' play de bass. Yuh could see he still feel de holiness in de music. None a dis modern Chris'mas wid presents at de centre fuh him. To him de Parang is still holy Chris'mas music. It move' me."

The road switchbacks, rising as it bends, then suddenly, through the foliage, a glimpse of blue. Ahead, through a break in the trees, we get a proper view of the vast, rocking Caribbean Sea. I sigh audibly and Nadia smiles. A woman and a boy are walking gingerly along the side of the road. The boy is carrying something large. Her hands are full too. "Le's give dem a ride," Nadia says, pulling up at the shoulder.

"Yuh wanna drop?" I shout, and they check for traffic before crossing to the jeep. They climb into the back seat.

"Thank yuh, young ladies," the woman says, breathing hard. "We come out too late dis' mornin' fuh de bus so Ah tell Roderick les' start to walk an' we might be lucky enough to get a drop. We goin' all de way to Maracas buh if yuh stoppin' before dat we glad fuh any little distance in de car."

"We goin' pas' Maracas so no problem," Nadia tells her as we drive off again. I turn to make conversation. She's nearing fifty. The bright cotton-print dress belies the tired lines around her eyes. She's clutching a Thermos and a folding table. The boy is eleven or twelve and hasn't spoken. In his lap he holds a shallow cardboard box that contains two large jars. In one of them are pickled pommecytheres and in the other are sugar cakes, pink and white.

"How much fuh de pommecythere?" I ask. The boy's arms stiffen and he looks at me furtively.

"I's nice a you young ladies to offer us a drop. Ah wouldn' charge yuh. Take out two dere, Roderick." He unscrews the lid and I take four single dollars from my wallet. He reaches in with a pair of tongs and places each fruit on a square of brown paper. I hand him the money. He looks at his mother. She's about to speak.

"Things too hard here for yuh to be givin' it away," I say. She smiles and nods. Nadia takes her pommecythere from me and I bite into mine. The sourness ties up my tongue for a few seconds. "Dis' really good," I say, turning to her, but her eyes are already closed. Roderick is looking out over the sea. Nadia glances in the rearview mirror at the woman, who clearly has fallen asleep. She looks at me, her eyebrows raised.

We drive on, bamboo arching overhead, shading us from the sun. In time, we pass the Maracas police station, then the Lookout. Shortly after we drive past a restaurant and bar with an open patio, the road rises sharply, and at the crest we see Maracas Bay below us. Nadia swings into the lot, already half-filled with vehicles, and parks. Roderick puts his hand on the woman's shoulder. "Ma?" Her eyes fly open. "We reach already?" she exclaims, a little flustered. The boy opens the door and climbs out. "Thanks," he says, leaning down to Nadia.

"Yeah, I hope yuh have a good day. Plenty sales."

"Thank you," the woman says when she is outside. "God bless, eh?" Nadia begins to drive away.

"Yuh mean we not limin' at Maracas with de beautiful people?" I ask, chuckling. This is the body-beautiful capital among beaches; chiselled torsos and tight behinds parade here every Saturday.

"Wid mih thin foot? Yuh doh know I'm a F.B.I.? A fine-bone' Indian?" We break into raucous laughter and drive over to one of a line of food stalls situated along the road. We order two shark an' bake and watch the young woman take the fish from a cooler packed with ice and deep-fry it in an iron pot. The dough for the bake she drops into another skillet with oil. I lace mine with lime and shado bêni, a pungent herb that tastes like coriander. You either love or hate it, no in-between.

"I had a cravin' for this about a year now," I say, biting into the crispy dough.

"But I thought yuh livin' in de Maritimes," Nadia says. "Wha' happen? No shark an' bake out dere?" She starts up the jeep.

"Go ahead an' laugh," I answer, feigning anger as I settle back in the seat for the rest of the drive.

From Maracas to Las Cuevas, a small fishing village, the curves in the road ease somewhat. It's a glorious day. The sky is brilliant blue and the sea breeze keeps us cool. As we head toward La Fillette, fields of heliconia appear, their spiky orange petals jutting out from among the tall grass. We'll stop on the way home to gather bunches for our mothers.

"By de way, I have a surprise fuh yuh," Nadia says without taking her eyes off the road. "Yuh always sayin' yuh want to talk to de really ol' people before all a dem gone. I' takin' yuh to meet a woman who use' to be our housekeeper. She's eighty-seven now an' she love to talk."

"Buh I doh have a tape recorder or anything," I say nervously.

"Yuh doh need one. Doh think a dis as research. I's jus' a place to start."

We drive past Damian Bay, waves crashing against the brown rocks that jut out of the water.

Mrs. Daniel doesn't look eighty-seven. To get to her house we've had to park the jeep on the shoulder of the road and climb an incline that seems to be at a ninety-degree angle. I wonder how she gets around. Her house is concrete painted a pale yellow and there's a kitchen garden in the front yard. She invites us to sit on the front porch and disappears inside.

"Nice up here, eh?" Nadia comments.

"Smells good. Green."

Mrs. Daniel comes out again carrying three glasses of ginger beer. She sits in the bentwood rocker and clasps her hands in her lap. "So, how is de family, Miss Nadia?" she asks.

"Everybody fine, Mrs. Daniel, Natalie's baby jus' turn' five."

"Time could fly, eh? Yuh mudder good?"

"Workin' too hard buh okay otherwise. She said to tell yuh she'll be up sometime this month."

"Nice, nice. Ah doh think Ah know dis frien'," she nods in my direction.

"I brought Michelene because she like to hear de ol'-time stories."

She frowns. "Wha' kin'a ol'-time stories?"

Nadia looks at me and waits.

"I' been writin' stories about Papa Bois an' Douenne an' dat kin'a thing, buh hardly anybody could tell mih anything about them."

She lets out a short, dry laugh. "Da's because a all de light it have now. All dose streetlight. When de place bright like it is nowadays, yuh tink people seein' spirit or anyting so?"

I smile and take a sip of my drink, crossing my legs.

"When Ah was a girl, Ah talkin' 'bout before de war, dey didn' have light like dis. In Port a Spain, was streetlamps here an' dere. Dey didn' have no big set a light, an' in places like dis? Oui fut! Only blackness. Spirit 'roun' every corner. La Diablesse make style wid plenty woman husban'. Mih brudder self had a brush wid dat shameless woman. He had never see her before an' he like how she dress an' de perfume she wearin', so he offer to walk her home. Lucky ting she trip on some branch on de groun' an' her dress liff up an Vernon see i's a goat foot she have. One foot good-good an' it have on a ladies' shoe. De other one is a hoof. Yuh could believe dat?" Mrs. Daniel cackles and Nadia grins.

"So, wha' Vernon did?" I ask.

"Run, nuh! Wha'else he go' do?" She laughs again and we laugh with her.

"Wha' I doh understan' is why all de women in dose stories so wicked. Soucouyant an' Maman de l'Eau . . ."

"Mama D Glo?" she asks, using the patois pronunciation. "She not really wicked. She's a protector a de rivers an de animals, like Papa Bois. She's a halfa-snake, halfa-woman an' Ah suppose everybody 'fraid snake buh she's only punish people who's trow dey rubbish in de rivers. Hunters who's trap an shoot roun' here have plenty respec' fuh Mama D Glo an' Papa Bois too. He doh wan' nobody damagin' de fores' eider. He'll punish yuh if yuh set fire or kill a animal fuh sport buh da's because he's de farder a de fores'."

She goes on to tell me who to beware of and why. She asks if I have children, "because if yuh take too long to chrissen yuh chil' it could become one a dem ghos'-babies, one a dem Douenne. Dey'll lure yuh chil' away." She says she knows a couple in La Fillette who waited one day too late. The child was two and walking when they decided to christen her. On the morning on which the church service was scheduled to take place, they found her small bed empty. Outside, in the dusty front yard, there were scores of bare footprints made by children leading into the bush behind the house. They never found her. "De Holy Spirit is protec' a chil' buh widout religion de poor little soul is wanderin' roun' in de dark where de evil spirits trivin'."

Beware of the Soucouyant, fire spirit. She'll hide in the flesh of an old woman, shed the skin at night, fly around in the shape of a ball of fire, looking for a victim whose blood she'll suck. Beware of Lagahoo, the shapeshifter. He protects friends and casts spells on enemies, and in the shape of the wolf, he is terrible. "Yuh say people duh remember de spirits again," Mrs. Daniel says. "Dat doh mean dey gawn, doh."

"No, it doesn't," I say, shaking my head.

The next day I take a route taxi into town and walk to the National Museum. I had forgotten or perhaps never noticed the colonial architecture. The museum is painted white, with the wooden shutters left their natural colour. The floors are a dark-stained hardwood. I make my way to the second floor with its large balcony, onto which a set of French windows open. They aren't shut today and gusts of wind blow through this room with its high ceiling.

I find the painting easily, and it's as haunting as it is in my memory. It's a forest scene in oils, and they're all present. Papa Bois is huge and forbidding. Mama D Glo, serpent from the waist down, stares out. A group of Douennes, straw hats covering their faces, are milling about under a silk-cotton tree. La Diablesse, in her turn-of-the-century frock, waits for a victim. In the background, Lagahoo is prowling, and hovering in the smoke-grey sky is a ball of fire. "Soucouyant," I say softly. I look for a few minutes more, then step out of the cool dark of the museum and into the sunlight.

I cross Keate Street and head down Frederick. It's one of the main arteries in the grid that is downtown Port of Spain, which was laid out by the English when we were a colony. Upper Frederick Street is calm. There are bookshops and art-supply shops here because a number of schools are located nearby. I'm always self-conscious walking these blocks because I attended an all-girls' school in this area for seven years. It's run by nuns, and though they had definitely loosened up with Vatican II, our intellectual and moral development was monitored very closely. I feel fifteen again until I cross Park Street to Lower Frederick, territory out of the jurisdiction of the Sisters of Cluny. Territory we were forbidden to wander at lunchtime.

It's teeming with life. Sidewalk vendors are selling handcrafted jewelry made from shells, copper, leather, and beads. A middle-aged woman wearing a polyester dress circa 1967 sits at the mouth of an alleyway behind a folding table. Her portable tape recorder broadcasts gospel music. I notice a cardboard sign propped against the legs of the table: HAVE YOU FOUND YOUR WAY TO JESUS? I keep walking. Woodford Square is ringed with the familiar red wrought iron. This is the People's Square. The homeless of this city congregate here, and individuals will regularly take the opportunity to air their views on politics and religion. A middle-aged man with matted dreadlocks crouches at a standpipe at the edge of the square. Wearing only a tattered pair of briefs, he is filling a Milo tin with water and pouring it over himself. Nobody appears to notice. I walk past fabric stores, jewelry stores, a fresh fruit-juice stand. A Black Muslim in the typical skullcap and loose-fitting white garments approaches me solicitously. "Yuh look like a sister who like to smell nice." He holds out a tray stacked with perfumed oils and incense.

"Does that mean I smellin' bad now?" I ask, walking on. He starts explaining himself but I keep walking.

I turn off Frederick at Independence Square and cross the street to the Drag Brothers' booths. The brothers are a group of leather craftsmen, many of them members of the Rastafarian religion. I'm looking out for Abu. He custom-made a pair of sandals for me last year and I'm hoping he has a strong satchel. He's in the same booth. I knock on the open door and enter. He's sitting at his work table rolling a joint.

"Hello, Abu, yuh remember me?"

He narrows his eyes for a moment.

"Sandals," I add. "Yuh made me a real nice pair 'bout a year ago. Yuh measured mih feet."

"Yeah," he nods. "Ah didn' really fuhget yuh, sister, jus' didn' recognize yuh dere. Wha' I could help yuh wid?" He's shirtless. His locks are tied back with a red, green, and yellow cord, the colours of Rastafari. "Yuh doh min' if Ah smoke?" he asks, but he's already lighting up.

"Nah. I was checkin' to see if yuh had any satchels." My eyes scan the shelves and the hooks on the walls. Sandals, handbags, wallets, caps, belts.

"Wha's dat?"

"A leather bag to carry books. Yuh know, wid a strap, strong."

"Nuttin so. Nobody go' buy dat here. Nobody carryin' 'roun' books." He exhales a slow jet of smoke and I clear my throat.

"Yuh think yuh could make one fuh me?"

"Yuh have books to carry 'roun' or i's jus' fuh style?"

"Books are jus' about all I do have, Abu," I say, laughing, and he smiles and searches among the scraps of leather and tools on the table.

"Draw it fuh mih," he says, handing me a piece of brown paper and a thick pencil with a stubby point that looks as though he has sharpened it with a knife.

I sketch a reasonable facsimile of what I'd like and figure out the dimensions. "Give mih an estimate," I say, handing him the paper.

"Yuh want sof' leather? De bes'?"

I walk over to a handbag and hold it up to him. He frowns, makes some calculations on the paper. "Somethin' like 220 dollars. No more than 250. An' it go' take 'bout three weeks."

"Alright, go ahead, then. Yuh want a deposit?"

"Ah want to say no buh dese days yuh ca' trus' a soul buh Jah." We decide on fifty dollars. He gives me a receipt and I head down Independence Square toward the maxi-taxi stand.

One of the few efficient systems in this country is transportation by route taxis. They service all of the central areas of Trinidad and charge a standard fare, which depends on the distance you're travelling. This stand is the starting and finishing point for service along the Port of Spain/Diego Martin route. All of the taxis are Japanese-made minivans painted an off-white. I approach the vehicle first in line.

"Family!" the conductor greets me. "We goin' Diego direck! Down de Four Shore, by-passin' St. James. Come! Come! Only four places leff!"

I hand him two dollars as I climb in and find a seat. The drivers who are lucky enough to own their own vehicles are proud of that fact. They exhibit this pride in a variety of ways. Some display photos of themselves leaning Hollywood-style against the front grille of the vehicle. Some name their vans and paste large letters on the back window. The younger, more macho men who were weaned on "kick-ups" (karate films), and who in recent years have been rushing to the cinemas to watch bulky Van Damme, Segal, and Schwarzenegger in action have dubbed their taxis First Blood, Punisher, Blue Steel. The older gentlemen who have already sown their wild oats and, perhaps, have found religion prefer more wholesome names such as Rock of My Soul and Blessed Assurance.

In this taxi the conductor does the communicating and handles the money. The driver waits wordlessly behind the wheel. He's dubbed his vehicle The Enforcer; the name is pasted in red letters on the back window. Dangling from the rearview mirror is an image on cardboard of a woman in a transparent teddy and garter belt. The driver wears leather gloves and dark sunglasses and occasionally glares eyelessly at the passengers in the mirror. Once I took a taxi called Flash. The driver sped all the way, dodging between the cars he found too slow, stopping in an instant when someone rang the buzzer. When one of his victims caught up with him at the light to shout abuse, Flash pulled a child's cap gun from his breast pocket and shot it at the irate man. But the young passengers love driving with these daredevils. They enjoy the element of speed and the fact that their vehicles are always equipped with good stereos. Woofers and tweeters lambaste you with rockers, hip-hop, and rap. Teenagers scorn the more low-key maxi-taxis that have only factory-installed radios for entertainment. They'll wait patiently in the rain for First Blood, Punisher, and Blue Steel while Blessed Assurance drives by half-empty, Johnny Mathis or Barbara Streisand barely audible from the tiny dashboard speakers.

We're moving, and as we drive out of the lot, the tunes are turned on. Heads instantly begin to bob. An older woman in the back scheupses in annoyance and presses the buzzer. The taxi jerks to a halt. She asks the conductor for her money back, and whether it's out of good business sense or respect for the Mother, he hands her the two dollars and she gets off. We drive away again and despite myself, my feet begin to tap, my fingers to drum on my knees. I give in and allow The Enforcer to entertain me all the way home.

Jeffrey and Nigel are Trini yuppies who, as far as I'm concerned, have way too much responsibility at work and too little time to relax. They're so tired by the end of the day that if they leave the house at all when they get home, it's only to take a leisurely drive through Port of Spain and then sit on a bench around the Savannah drinking coconut water. I must confess that that kind of thing is just my speed. So when I'm in Trinidad they'll often stop at my house to see if I'd like to join them.

Tonight we cruise down Western Main Road through St. James, the City That Never Sleeps.

"Look out fuh de roti lady," Jeff says to me in the back seat.

"Yuh jus' ate dinner, Jeffrey," Nigel says in disgust.

"I's Mich I was thinking of. She doh get roti up dere in de sardine province." Too true, and unlike Jeff I haven't eaten, so I keep my eyes peeled. This road is lined with bars and roadside vendors for whom business is best from around eleven p.m. till five a.m. the following morning. There's no "last call" in Trinidad, so most people don't roll home till around three a.m., and by that hour, especially after drinking, many are hungry; the food vendors do well. Nigel pulls off the main road onto a side street to park because he's spotted the roti lady. We all walk to where her low table stands covered with a white cloth on the sidewalk. She's accompanied by a daughter and by a burly son whose cutlass is placed subtly on the pavement behind him. He handles the money. On the table in one large bowl sits a huge circle of dough, and there's a plateen on which she fries the individual rotis. There are a number of smaller bowls containing the various curried meats and vegetables with which she fills the roti. The men have been drawn in by the aroma, and we order one shrimp and bohdi (green beans), one chicken, potato, and baigan (eggplant), and, for me, a beef and pumpkin.

"Pepper?" she asks innocently, and we all shake our heads.

"Le's eat roun' de Savannah," Nigel says as we walk back to the car.

We drive down St. Clair Avenue to get there. The Queen's Park Savannah, a park three miles in circumference, is one of the main hubs of activity in Port of Spain. It's a centre for sporting events, and at night, around its rim, corn on the cob, barbecued meats, fresh fruit, and oyster cocktails are sold by licensed vendors. We park between the rival coconut sellers across from Queen's Royal College, its clock tower looking out over the city through the night. Jeff can't resist a coconut water, so we watch as the man standing in the tray of his truck shakes a nut to check for liquid and chops it expertly with his cutlass so a neat hole is left, like the rim on a bottle. We sit on a bench under an ancient samaan tree to eat and watch the cyclists, strollers, joggers, and those driving past.

"Damn good roti," I say.

"I should'a bought two," Jeff responds.

"You have to be sick," Nigel scheupses.

"Was it las' year yuh were here for Hosay?" Jeff asks me, and then I remember that it was two years before that the three of us went to St. James together to observe the Hosay ceremonies.

A large percentage of the St. James population is East Indian, and some of those are Muslim, so Hosay is observed with enthusiasm in that city. It commemorates the death of Hussein, nephew of Mohammed, father of the Islamic faith. Young men practise on tassa drums for weeks in preparation for several hours of ceremonial drumming. Others build models of Eastern palaces known as tadjas, which are carried through the street as part of the procession on the night of Big Hosay. Sons of the families that have traditionally taken part must perform the dance of the moons. Two large crescent moons, one green representing poison, the other red signifying blood, are carried on harnesses mounted on the shoulders of two groups of men. The dancers spell each other as they grow tired or find themselves losing control of their burden as they spin. It's considered a sacrilege to drop the moon.

I stood amongst the crowd on the sidewalk with Jeff and Nigel, waiting. Some had been drinking in the St. James bars and had come out when they felt it was time for the ceremony to begin. It was near midnight when we heard the tassa drummers approaching. With their instruments strapped to their chests, they moved in procession and stood in staggered groups along the roadway. Intent on the rhythm, they did the ceremonial drummers' dance while their hands moved manically over the goatskins. The crack of the drums echoed, and I felt myself shiver. I moved away from Jeff and Nigel, pushed through the bodies to get closer to the sound. But I could feel the crowd responding to a movement that had started blocks away. A space was forming down the centre of the street and Poison was storming down it. Poison, half-naked, sweating, eyes wide, willing the green crescent to remain steady. And from the opposite direction came Blood, whirling like his counterpart, just as intent and driven. The crowd waited for the drama to unfold. Then the moons began to spin in wide circles around each other, in small circles alone, crazy as dervishes. As each man danced, his brothers moved with him, crouched, staring in dread up at the dancing moon, ready to take up the burden if the one chosen first should stumble.

I stayed watching till Jeff moved through the crowd and found me. They were ready to leave. As we walked to the car Nigel spoke. "Yuh notice how entirely male it was? It don' look like Muslim women participate in it. Yuh saw any a dem around?"

"No, yuh right," Jeff said, and I nodded.

Hosay in St. James

Every brudder wid a drum strap on, slappin
a angry riddim wid sticks or de heel
a dey han, an it crack
in yuh ear like gunfire, and de cymbals
trow in a ringin, leave
a feverish buzz.
Mohammed army jump twice on one heavy
foot, once on de nex,
sweat roll in dey eye an dey shake dey head
never miss a beat
face clench like fiss, 'dis
is serious business, dis is religion, brudder

Den Blood come, an Poison
an nobody could say who reach firs
because bote a dem big an bote a dem swirlin
bline an unbias as disease
disguise in de shape a moon, half circle spinnin
out. An who would tink
to link de sof white
curve a dat planet wid poison
wid blood
but a man?

"I suppose yuh want another coconut water," Nigel says to Jeff, "or maybe a boil' corn, or two roas' ones."

"Yuh such an ass," Jeff snaps. "Come on, le's go home so I could explode in comfort."

Nigel and I are doubled over with laughter as we follow Jeff to the car.

I'm leaving again. Again my father hovers in the doorway and my mother rushes about preparing pepper sauce and coconut sweet bread for me to take with me. Again my heart is fluttering and I'm anticipating the leaving. I wonder if there ever comes a point when the ache isn't quite so sharp.

My family drove to Piarco Airport to greet a relative who had been away for some time. I was five or six then and in those days there was a shallow pond in the shape of Trinidad in the open area in front of the entrance to the main building. There was moss around its concrete sides and I remember tadpoles darting among the stalks of the leaves that floated on its surface. I began to run around the rim of the pond.

Las Cuevas, Blanchisseuse, Macqueripe.

"Yuh goin' to fall in chil'!" my mother exclaimed.

La Brea, Brighton, Point Fortin.

I was too busy travelling around my country to hear. I set foot on Galeota Point twice, maybe three times. Hopped over Point Radix, passed Manzanilla, Matura Bay, Balandra. And then I slipped. I bellyflopped into Trinidad somewhere near the source of the Oropouche River. My brother and sister sidled away as my parents dashed over to haul me out. I was dripping wet, my dress bore traces of algae. I had been baptized in the font of Trinidad; I would be a child of hers from now on, no matter what.

So, I will always feel the urge to get there, once or twice a year. The longing-for-home dreams will come and I will spend my meagre savings or borrow the money for a ticket. The rhythm of tassa and the melody of steel pans will lure me and I will make a pilgrimage to Trinidad to pay my respects and to learn more of her texture and the many tastes of her. Despite how far I wander, a devotee initiated by water, I will be forever coming home.

KIRSTI SIMONSUURI

Kaamos, the Darkest Time of the Year

I have excerpted this story from my travel book Northern Notebook, *which was published in Finland in 1981. The story tells about my three-year journey to the north of Finland, more specifically to Oulu, a northern industrial town, and its surroundings.*

Finland is located between the latitudes of 60 and 70 degrees. Oulu is at 65 degrees, the Arctic Circle at 66.5. The North has always attracted me because of the extremes of its light. In winter the dark has a palpable presence which is related to some creative moments. I went to look for this, after many years abroad. When I was offered my first real job at the University of Oulu in 1978, I took it with an explorer's enthusiasm. My three years in Oulu revealed to me something essential about my own country, half of which belongs to this arctic region. The North shows sterner and somehow more real aspects of life than the southern part of Finland where I grew up. I would like to think of my journey to the North as one after which the traveller was not the same any more, "sadder and wiser" perhaps.

I

In the cold. The cold that nips, the dark that is pitch-dark, tarry. I jam myself into a steaming-hot train carriage. It is morning.

How can you tell. How can the people discern. Somebody must have informed them that it is seven o'clock in the morning, that it is time to undo the sandwich bags, to eat the bread quietly nibbling, and to peel an orange.

The metal tube dashes into the North. But how can you tell, there is no movement, for the black windows reflect only what there is inside the tube, dull strangers darkly dressed, on garish green seats. An amazingly singular-looking people with Indian features and thin blond hair.

They are as if transported somewhere, unwilling beings.

When the day breaks, vast expanses open. Nowhere is bleakness deeper than here. The grainfields are textiles, rough tow cloth, and above them hangs a grey gossamer, a rickety sky. What is visible is only a tiny fraction of what there is. The measure of frustration, as if the thin light visible above the horizon on a winter's day would try to suppress the real light.

All this must be learned again much more attentively than I could have foreseen. Behind language, there is something gigantic, monstrous, consolidated, the existence of which I could not imagine before.

Beyond Ylivieska there is only Oulu. When we arrive there, the day has brightened, and darkened again.

There is a long platform, immeasurable, its one end reaches north and its other end south. I stand there with my suitcase. My feet trample the whiteness, the snow squeals under my boots. I do not want to leave right away.

The city is bare. It is like a newly slaughtered skin that has been turned over, the wrong side up, so that all the veins and the dried bits of innards gleam on its surface. Lights flash as if in an amusement park, deserted by its patrons.

II

First there is the snowless season. But because the air is humid, the ground is covered with hoary frost, and a pale-grey veil lies over the lawns and the roadsides. The tall birches in the park are white, not bearing the burden of snow but frosted, showing every tiny branch and twig clearly. The air has a dark, bluish-grey hue. The sky of "kaamos" is a painting of fine, serene colours, a rug of violet, lilac, blue, red, salmon, rose, crimson, and turquoise stripes. Above the horizon the colours remain a tranquil whole until the red tones gradually fade, violets disappear, and the sky changes altogether into dark turquoise, and finally darkens, into blackish blue and black.

The sight never bores, never wears out, that play of the images of silence and negation, performed day after day.

Kaamos is the best season in the North, lasting from around the middle of November till the end of January. The best moment is when the snow does not yet stay on the ground.

The park has no life, no wintering blackbirds, no squirrels, no hibernating pheasants, no signs of life familiar from the December parks and woods of southern Finland. No people ever walk across the park, and yet, it lies in the vicinity of the town centre, and the marketplace and the harbour would be reachable through it by a short detour. The riverbeds and the tributaries which dried out already in late summer run across the park. They are meandering creeks which can be crossed by decorated wooden bridges.

It is silent and still. There is beauty because of the silence.

III

When I wake up in the morning, snow has piled up in mounds covering the bottom third of the windows. Even in the heart of the town one is on a journey to some unknown destination through snowdrifts, through a tunnel, in a large, dishevelled and forsaken depot of trams. The room is like a carriage, with half-veiled windows through which a white plateau opens, everywhere the same. The carriage rides smoothly, without sound, and it leaves no track.

Inside the room I have a vision of the summer, and it has a familiar, smiling face. *A mon seul plaisir:* in a sealed space without sensations, in a vacuum without stimulation, the senses need each other even more, they get closer to one another.

The day is short, it is a thought interrupted. Today I start my lecture by saying that humanism runs a permanent risk of getting buried under those snowdrifts, if that has not happened yet. I point to the row of windows on the upper partition of the lecture room. But I mean the human being, not humanism. I dislike the overcultivation of the word humanism. Its inflation has happened. It is used without a sense of history and with little critical judgement as a kind of panacea, to be prescribed when all other methods have failed to work. I mean perhaps that the perspective of historical change is incomprehensible and too abstract for those who have lived without history, constantly battling against inimical nature, devouring snowdrifts. It is difficult to separate the unity of human existence from concrete, mundane tasks and to perceive this unity also in mental aspirations. Humanism will stay in the snow.

I walk back. Hobbling along on a slippery Cavalry Road. Covering my face against the cold. I pass a shop for the blind, see its stark shield portraying a bat, and turn around the corner to Shoemaker's Lane, which is lined by colourful wooden houses. It could be the beginning of the century. The nocturnal town is startlingly empty here. Only a few blocks away a hellish merry-go-round of steely junk, the town youth, is swirling as every night.

The moon's dress is the same everywhere. Tear it open, and you will see how different everything is. The moon is a language.

IV

Darkness returns morning after morning. Darkness is a hand wearing a black silk glove, it penetrates everywhere and caresses you. Darkness wills no evil, it is alive and tender. I touch darkness.

But maybe for those who have always lived and worked here, darkness has lost its personal features, because they have become used to darkness.

I do not find darkness a vital principle. Living in the dark is like constant mild narcosis. Its benefits are that it simplifies things and shuts the unnecessary out.

Sylvia Plath's poem "Tulips" delineates a world seen from the hospital bed, which is for Plath, in the poem, a secure, happy world. It is painfully broken into splinters by a bunch of tulips, shining too brightly. Tulips ooze their red, sturdy vigour, too much information. What the tulips express by their sheer being is redundant and hurtful in the peace of the sickbed.

I listen to the music in the dark, and I wonder if darkness has ever been described in music, expressed in the language of music. I cannot remember any pieces. The seasons have not infrequently been written into concertos, but in their winter movements, darkness does not figure as a special element. Vivaldi's concerto describes commotion, cold, warmth, human activity, as does Mozart's. And in Haydn's oratorio *The Seasons*, winter is depicted as the time that kills all life.

Light is a central theme in music; but how could darkness be described there?

v

The white reindeer carries me farther over the fields of snow. The sun is glowing without mercy, and the crusts of snow become steel and glass. I ask the white deer where it is taking me. It replies: nowhere. I was afraid of this. But although it does not know it always gets there.

I leave for Sotkamo. During the journey my eyes notice new, fragmentary things. By the roadside a pack of spitzdogs like arctic white foxes attacks a huge animal corpse they have dragged into their enclosure. On the other side an auto-demolishing plant steams in an exquisitely serene snow valley.

Everywhere infinite snow-covered spruce forests, like cathedral spires clustered together.

Here the snow is a bed of feathers, a mausoleum. The pure crusts of snow, the slumbering hills. This far have I come: snow creates anxiety, not freedom. It is oppressive in its purity, in its colourlessness, and in its speechlessness. No, this is the anxiety of novelty, I have been away from it for so long. Snow does not live. It is the fantasy of many years, a dream landscape. In reality I have visited these places. In reality I have never been here. The scenery is familiar from some dreams. Some of them have been nightmares. I navigate in the landscape of symbolic powers. In reality. In the forest. On the crests of hills. On snowy mountaintops.

When the silent, snowy wood, devoid of people, extends around me, I realize how far I have travelled from my origins. Finding a habitat in the heart of the city, in the midst of people, settling down among coffee pots, cigarettes, good food, books, movies, and stony bridges. That has been the direction of my movement. In the midst of buildings erected by men, creations of brains and hands.

Here I am illiterate for a moment, I do not understand the language of the wild trees. I am puzzled. Then I realize that there is no need to read them, for they, too, are illiterate, and they do not bother to understand those who circle around their trunks. They do not even hear you up there. They do not ask anything except that you exist as you are, as no other, unchanging. And they do not wish anything except that no one would fell them.

A whistle, and the white deer jumps in through the window.

VI

A journey to the northern region. What can you understand of it? There is the snow. Snow tranquillizes. It is the state of repose. It is the rain of the land of death, regressing. I am going to leave.

All of a sudden the city has closed up, like a giant mussel, concealing everything, without revealing life, as during the first days. Something is always happening somewhere, the young people sit in the old American steel, the lights of the merchant hotel flash and glitter.

But I can see nothing of that, really. The city has slipped away from me, left me, fallen back to its distant peace where it had always been.

I walk toward the station. It is very cold and there is not much snow on the streets. Main Street has been decorated with Christmassy gloss, as glittering and tasteless as anywhere else.

At night I see a dream where I am wandering in a kind of classical garden, in Tiberius's Capri or Nero's Domus Aurea. Around a rectangular pond there are Roman imitations of Hellenistic marble statues, white human figures. All of a sudden the marble is transformed into flesh, first the toes and the fingers begin to move, and then all the statues are metamorphosed into people.

I wake up in the morning in a sweat of pain. The temperature goes down to -30°C. The city streets have become quiet in the grip of this unbearable cold. The exhaust fumes from the cars fill the sidewalks with vapours and then rise straight up to the cold, blue sky and disappear.

There is no going back. "Fasten your seat belts," the stewardess beckons.

JANICE KULYK KEEFER

Spain: Ghosts

The faces I saw in the mug shots produced by a seedy police station on a shabby side street have haunted me, wordlessly, for the past five years: what I wanted was not to exorcise those ghosts, but finally to raise them. If I couldn't give them back their faces, stolen from the bodies no one thought worth photographing, I could at least attest to the book composed of those faces, and the use to which it was being put. And acknowledge the two kinds of ghosts I'd encountered in Spain. Ghosts that had to do both with an experience of perfect freedom, and with something as miserably limiting as the law of gravity, but a man-made version and therefore immeasurably worse.

ON THE TRAIN FROM MADRID TO OVIEDO, THEY played *North American Grizzly;* on the bus from Oviedo to León, it was *Rio Grande:* thirty-one pairs of eyes caressing Katharine Hepburn's cheekbones, John Wayne's slow, stupid smile. You could tell I was the only tourist by the fact that my eyes were glued to different screens: the Escorial rising from plains flat and dry as face powder; mountains I'd always thought invented by painters of the lives of hermits and

ascetic saints: painters locked at sea level, fantasizing rocks into cy-
clones and tornado waves.

Thinking I was a traveller, not a tourist: this was the first mistake I
made in Spain. But then, travellers don't merely make mistakes: they
make their maps out of them. All travel is errant motion, a wandering
off from what is known and thus correct. No traveller wants to be correct, but there is such a thing as being careful. Especially for women,
travelling alone.

My first time in Spain, I am alert to everything, as though each pore of
my skin has become a new pair of ears and eyes. Spain has happened to
me by accident: an invitation issued long ago that suddenly I'm able to
take up. Having a hairsbreadth of the history; speaking nothing of the
language except what I pick up from an airport phrasebook on the flight
from Heathrow to Madrid. *Se puede pagar con la tarjeta de crédito?*

Exhilaration at the airport, when I collect my bag and hail a cab and
make my destination understood: a university residence downtown,
the same residence where Lorca had been a student. For all I can tell,
the very same commando of small, mustachioed women rules the dining room, doling out garlic soup and rolls so hard your teeth squeak
against the crust.

For three days I walk all over Madrid, my purse slung over my
shoulder, my hands in my pockets. So easy, so guiltless, this shedding
of the skins of husband, children, house, job that I can feel my bones
pushing closer to the air and light, as I stride down avenues and across
plazas. Too stubborn in my freedom, that first day, to take a bus, so
that I end up walking miles and miles along a road of ugly banks and
offices and billboard hoardings, breathing in huge squirts of diesel fuel
from cars packing six lanes of traffic. Arriving at the residence exhausted, yet on that high of absolute fatigue when it becomes impossible to sleep. In the narrow white bed in my narrow white room, I write
down the day in that extension of my eyes and hands: my notebook.

I write about the Velázquezes in the Prado; how seeing the actual
paint with the light and noise of the room mixed up in it was violently

real, violent as if all the reproductions I had ever studied were being ripped up in front of my eyes by the force of the canvases themselves. Dwarves and naked *majas;* infants with hair and skirts like giant dinner bells. Hapsburgs lapsing into a crowd of chinless, chubby degenerates whom even Goya cannot make any less sulkily stupid. Or Hugo van der Goes's *Deposition from the Cross:* all that anguish rammed into the small space of his canvas, twisting the bodies in upon themselves, making the Virgin's face not alabaster but grey, as if her grief were so extreme it had started to decay the living skin. After which *Guernica* seems as bloodless as that Virgin's face, and no more violent than a comic strip.

"Travellers' joy": the name of a wildflower I have found only in field guides. Joy has everything to do with luck: the luck I have arriving in the north of Spain in what should be the rainy season, February-miserable, but instead is dry and mild as early summer.

In Oviedo I am cared for; no longer a traveller but a guest, driven to an eighth-century hunting lodge once the haunt of kings, and a restaurant in the hills overlooking the town, where I learn how to drink the local cider. The waiter raises the bottle high overhead, then pours the drink so that it splashes and foams into the glass, which we share, passing it from hand to hand and mouth to mouth. I think of how similar the north of Spain is to Nova Scotia, where I live: the rough seacoast, the coal seams underground and the superbly militant miners who have worked them. But Asturias has no Baptists riding sentinel over its orchards, or the cider here would be nothing more than what it is at home: apple juice with benzoate of soda, incapable of raising a fizz even if poured off the top of a ten-storey building.

My friend Isabel lives with an Englishman who has a passion for mountains. They have been to the Andes together and are planning a trip to the Himalayas; she suggests that we spend Sunday strolling through the foothills of the Picos. My other friend Socorro, her husband, and their three children complete the party. And it is partylike, this setting off together into hills and valleys brown as hazelnuts. Bad for the farmers, Isabel says, and I am about to protest that, drought or no drought, no one could farm soil as thin as this, when suddenly my ears begin to pop. The valley falls away, like a stone tossed off a precipice. There is nothing ahead but air and rock and farmhouse, built from the same parched stones roughed so laboriously into fences.

To the ancient woman who owns the house we are all of us tourists, intruders: our boots will ruin the grass that belongs to her sheep. Even though Socorro assures her we will keep to the hiking trail and disturb nothing, the woman eyes us sourly as she raises the gate to let us pass, one by one. In the yard there's a lamb that can only be an hour old: its legs tremble as it butts against its mother. Her teats are absurdly pink, like chewed bubble gum; her eyes are the colour of mustard. The ewe and lamb are bathed in a shadow — not the shadow of a tree or bush, but that of a vulture sharpening its wings against the cool, dry air.

Metaphorically, literally, this is the high point of my travels in Spain. Here I am not a woman travelling alone, but a friend included in a family outing: a day's walk in the mountains. As though I just happened by, the way I might show up at any friend's house back home. With this difference: that here I am no longer deaf, blind, dumb to where I am, to whom and what I see. These two hunters, for example, dressed in soft leather, guns slung over their shoulders and chamois bags at their waists for the birds they'll shoot down. At their heels trot a pair of liver-spotted spaniels with bells round their necks. We hear them long after they've passed from sight, a blur of notes juggled by the wind.

The air in these parts goes straight to my head, I am drunk on wind and the view and the pain of climbing, though these hills have been chosen for the subtlety of their slopes — there are, after all, children on this walk: one of them is young enough to want to be carried. With each step I take I feel myself turning more and more insubstantial, exhaling not air but the very cells of my body. When we reach the collar of stones that forms the summit, sitting down to a lunch of bread and apples and hard, pale cheese, I seem to disappear entirely, into the line dividing this landscape into two. On one side the Europa mountains, looming white, improbable as angels; on the other, the

Atlantic, so sharply blue you can almost smell it. And from this line, another possibility — the leap into pure vertical, the native sphere of that most perfect kind of traveller: the ghost, who can pass invisibly through any obstacle or boundary, who speaks all languages in one: the silence of pure perception.

It takes a long time for my body to return to me, as we retrace our steps to the place from which we started. It takes a ceremony: we stop to pee against a ruined stone wall not far from the farmhouse, men on one side, women on the other. We are all laughing, except for the children. Isabel and Socorro joke about how the hunters will come back into view just as we unzip our jeans and hunker down; we agree that it is perfectly stupid, the design of women's trousers, making peeing out-of-doors so cumbersome and slow. And as we laugh, and as I leave this thin, insistent trace of myself over ground littered with parched sheep droppings, my body comes back to me. First my bones, and then my flesh tucking itself round them, the way I tuck my shirt back inside my jeans. A necessary, ordinary sort of miracle, to which I give less than a moment's thought as we head down the twisting road to Oviedo, in what has become the dark.

That night I jot down *vulture, lamb, liver-spotted spaniels* in my notebook, the same notebook I will take from my shoulder bag the morning I arrive in León. Writing the dizziness of my delight at the sugar spun cathedral, the storks perched on its pinnacles. White birds; white stones. And then a word insists itself onto the page, the way a sliver from a dream can work itself into your mind, though you've forgotten the dream, and the sliver has no meaning beyond its ability to provoke. The word is *ghost*.

If you are fair-haired they will spot you immediately as a tourist. It won't matter how suavely you negotiate the plazas and calles; or that your body, in generic jeans and sweater, shows no trace of camera, guidebook, even the slim betrayal of a map. They'll spot you before you've even left the hotel, they'll mark you out. It's business, O.K.? You're just one more appointment in their daybook.

It may be Isabel who says this, or Socorro. Maria del Socorro Perpetuel, warning me about street thieves in Barcelona. Or the voice of hindsight, warnings every mother shouts at her daughter as she waltzes out the door *to go heaven knows where staying out all hours you're just asking for trouble*. Warnings whispered now, hanging no heavier than feather earrings, but unshakeable as I make my decision, that first night in Barcelona, not to sit in my cramped, dirty hotel room just because I'm a woman, on my own, in a strange city. I have a map, don't I, and the common sense to stash my passport, tickets, credit card into the safety deposit box at the front desk. And I choose my route so carefully: the wide and well-lit streets that lead to the cathedral, where they're celebrating evening mass.

I blend in, I tell myself; with a scarf over my head, with my decent winter boots and coat I am as good as invisible. And perhaps I would have been, if I hadn't stopped on the cathedral steps to pull my notebook from my shoulder bag. I want to write something down before I forget, something about the geese kept in the cloisters, white geese huddled in a jungle of small palm trees and untended grass. And it is this that gives me away, not my scarf slipping down to show the colour of my hair, which is as far from the white-blond of my childhood as water is from snow. A notebook, conspicuous as any camera or map. They wait till I've set out along the wide, well-lighted street leading back to my hotel; they take an alleyway that links up with my bright, safe street filled with decent people walking home from mass. Who do nothing as the three men jump from the alley's mouth and get down to business. One of them grabs me hard by the shoulders, the other rips my bag from me, the third looks out in the unlikely event that anyone will try to interfere.

They sprint back down the alley, as I yell out, not "Socorro!" which is the only Spanish word I can remember, but, "You can't do that, you can't!" I go careening after them into the *barrio*, fury sharpening my heels. The alley twists like a snarl of black thread; at a curve blocked by garbage cans an old woman leans from a window, shaking her head at me, gesturing with both hands: *turn back and don't go running after worse trouble than you've got already.*

Everything that happens now is a cross between farce and night-mare. A policeman directs me down a street as dark and narrow as the alley from which I've just surfaced; once I find the police station, I have to fight my way past two men having a vicious quarrel over a huge dog. One of the men has a bandaged hand; the dog is rolling his eyes, and there are flakes of foam at the corners of his mouth. The officer at the desk tells me to try the station that stays open all night, the big one on the avenue Cristoforo Colombo. I thank him, leaving the men to their quarrel and the dog to its dis-ease. Once outside, I turn my back on the avenue Cristoforo Co-lombo and the police station in the harbour district, which is home of bigtime thieves and muggers, the ones who carry knives and use them more expertly than they do their fingers.

In my hotel room I sit up all night and rage. At how stupid I've been, how cowardly, how ladylike. I could have kicked the man who was wrenching my handbag from me: kneed him in the groin. I could have made a scene at the station instead of thanking the desk sergeant for his absurd advice. I would give anything to find myself just once again in that flash of knowing it was happening, and to me, what my mother had warned me of all those years ago. Not so I could run away, but so I could fight; it is physical lust, this rage to hit and kick and keep them from snatching what they have no right to, no possible need of. A handbag heavy with *The Phaidon Cultural Guide to Spain*, half a dozen pens, and my notebook.

A stranger is waiting for me in the lobby the next morning, an ac-quaintance of Isabel and Socorro, who have arranged that she should show me the sights of Barcelona. I ask her to take me back to the po-lice station instead. There I observe, for the notebook I no longer have, particulars I was blind to the night before: the shit-brown and banana-yellow in which the walls are painted, part of the systemically ugly decor of police stations here, the colour scheme a punishment in-flicted on criminals and victims alike. And then I see what no amount of travelling would have revealed to me, except in circumstances such as these: a photo album of suspects from which I'm asked to pick out my attackers. Every face in this album belongs to a North African, or to a South American of Indian blood.

Words in a foreign language flood the room, from the policemen's mouths, and the mouth of my companion, and from all the people waiting behind me in that morning's queue for justice. Words knocking against my head, so that I can't remember any more the proper terms in English for what I'm being shown — a rogue's gallery, no, mug shots. *An ugly mug like yours* — I remember that from an old B movie, an actor with a face like a dead bulldog. But mug also means to joke around, doesn't it — to put on a grotesque expression, just for the fun of it? The faces caught so neatly under the album's plastic sheets are anything but funny, or expressive. In fact, the only silence in this whole frantic room is coming from the faces of these men shot by a policeman's camera. Not travellers but migrants, isn't that the word? Undoubtedly thieves and possibly rapists, some of them, but under my eyes in that safe prison of the police station, nothing but blanks.

And though I keep saying, "No, no, the men who jumped me were Spanish, Europeans," the secretary who types out my official complaint and offers it for my signature with his hand obscuring everything but the line on which I am to sign, puts in "African" instead of "Spanish" under "racial origin of assailant." My companion shrugs when I ask her to make them tear it up and give me another, truer form to sign. Truth and forms have nothing to do with one another, her shrug says. Besides, they are finished with me; they are on to someone else: a young German couple who are making a formal complaint about the theft of an expensive camera. It's getting to be an epidemic, she explains: tourists who arrange to have their cameras stolen in Barcelona, so they can claim the insurance when they return to Germany. "It usually pays for their whole vacation." And then, as if to console me, the woman says, "They only get the money if they have an official form, like the one you've signed. The police will send a copy of that form to your consulate here, in case someone finds your purse in an alleyway and there's something left in it to identify you as Canadian. The consulate will get in touch with you."

She reads my eyes before I can speak.

"I wouldn't count on it," she says. "It's probably been dumped into the harbour, along with a million others."

At first I'd thought it was the violation of my freedom that had caused my rage in the hotel room that night. And sustained it for the rest of my time in Spain, inscribed in my new notebook — a cheap, small, spiral-backed affair that I kept hidden in the leg of my boots. How one night in Barcelona the inescapable fact of my gender had leaped out at me, no longer a seamless part of who I was but an outrageous double, a Siamese twin visible to everyone. *A woman travelling alone, stupid enough to go out at night in a strange city, a city equally famous for its flower stalls and thieves. She should have stayed home, as her mother told her. Why doesn't her husband take better care of her?* But now I know it wasn't that, or at least that those reasons didn't last, for I have travelled alone to many other places since, and walked out at night, though always with my purse tucked well inside my coat, and never again in Spain.

It was, instead, the theft of my notebook, its violent translation from the warmth of my shoulder to the cold, filthy waters of Barcelona harbour. The ink I used on its pages was indelible, and sometimes I imagine the words are still there, floating among all the gutted handbags and wallets and briefcases clogging the mud at the bottom of the harbour. I want to retrieve those words, or at least, I want to go back some day and shout into the water, add to the account of storks on cathedral spires white as icing sugar, or of newborn lambs huddling under a vulture's shadow, words for the blanked, black faces in a police album; the lies typed into official forms. I want to tell how there are forms of dispossession far more violent than theft; how I discovered who the real ghosts are, in Spain and elsewhere: the ghosts that no one wants to see, yet everyone believes in. Black faces on white paper; ink poured onto the bottom of the sea.

China

In 1965 I stood next to a fellow American traveller in northern Uganda as he took a picture of a destitute Karamojan tribesman who was, in fact, dying. The man was a refugee from ancestral lands to the south, now expropriated by another group, and forced to eke out what living he could in the barren north. He wore the briefest shredded loincloth, had at most a single tooth, and his eyes were covered with flies. He sat very still for the photograph (he had raised himself at our approach), and as we turned away held out his hand. The photographer gave him a quarter.

No doubt this memory is one reason I never travel with a camera. But another is my belief that human beings are already cameras, and that adding a second camera to the process of seeing (and remembering) shallows rather than deepens vision. I am saddened when the TV commercial declares Kodak "America's storyteller," because I realize our private culture is about to become as streamlined as our public one. But perhaps only poets and writers feel this.

In June of 1983, I went to China with a group of eleven American women writers that included Paule Marshall (our delegation leader), Nellie Wong, Blanche Boyd, Tillie Olsen, Lisa Alther, and my friend and travel companion, Susan Kirschner, who took many beautiful pictures of our trip with a "real"

35-mm camera. As she has shared her pictures with me, I wish to share these im-aginary or mental "snaps" with her, and with the other members of our group.

ONE

This is a picture of Susan and me at the San Francisco airport en route to China! We are leaning against the ticket counter furiously scribbling notes to our loved ones. I have chosen the same card for my daughter as for my companion at home. On a white background in large, black letters above a vibrant red heart are the words I AM SO-O-O HAPPY WITH YOU!

So why am I going to China?

How could anyone be foolish enough to leave the ground?

Whenever I fly I fear I will not return to earth except in shreds. As the plane lifts off I look at the earth with longing and send waves of love to cover it as I rise.

But you, I write to both of them, understand even this contradiction in me: that I must fly to see even more of the Earth I love.

TWO

In this mental photo, Susan and I are on the plane somewhere over the Pacific reading identical copies of *The True Story of Ah Q* by the immortal Lu Xun and drinking innumerable cups of Japanese green tea. In this 1921 story by the "father" of modern Chinese literature, a penniless peasant tries to impress the local villagers by pretending to be a revolutionary and they hang him for his trouble. Lu Xun depicts Ah Q as a foolish, childish person with no understanding of his emotions or his fate. We finish reading it about the same time and look at each other in quizzical disbelief. We feel Lu Xun has condescended to his character, in precisely the way white Southern writers have condescended to their characters who are women. He can't, in fact, believe a peasant capable of understanding his own oppression, his own life. Since the story is also exceedingly dull, we wonder what the Chinese value in it, beyond the fact that it is perhaps the first attempt to portray a Chinese peasant *in* fiction.

THREE

This one shows our arrival in Beijing. Not the actual landing and meeting with our interpreters and Chinese writer hosts but the long drive from the airport into town. It is our first awareness that, though China's people population is phenomenal, its tree population is more so: and they are a kind of planned magic. From the air, they're hardly visible because of the dust that sweeps down from the northern desert steppes, turning the landscape dun and yellow. And even when they first appear, they seem modest and young and one thinks of them in future tense. "How grand they will look at eighty!" and so on. But by the time one arrives on the streets of Beijing and notices veritable layers of trees five and six rows deep lining the broad boulevards, a wonderful relief comes over the mind.

For one feels irresistibly drawn to people who would plant and care for so many millions of trees — and a part of me relaxed. Because, for one thing, the planting of trees demonstrates a clear intention to have a future and a definite disinterest in war.

FOUR

In this one, five members of our group are standing around the limited but adequate bar (Orange Crush, mineral water, beer, Coca-Cola) on the end of our floor in a hotel in Beijing. It is the day of our first long outing through the dusty streets of the city. Everyone is hot and thirsty. They are trying to decide whether to have Orange Crush, mineral water, or beer, like Americans who are intent on being politically correct. The look of dismay on their faces is because I have just walked up to the counter and said to the barkeep: I'll have a Coke.

I take the Coke into the room I share with Susan, drink some, and pour some out the window in libation. I save the bottle cap with

"Coca-Cola" written in Chinese. Wherever I go in the world I buy one Coca-Cola in memory of the anonymous black woman who is said to have created it (probably on the theory that if you dope your masters — Coke used to have real coke in it — they're more pleasant).

I never heard of that, says Susan.

I tell her it is the one thing I remember from my high school graduation day. Our commencement speaker, Mr. Bullock, a horticulturist of stature from Atlanta, tried for thirty minutes to inspire pride of heritage in us by listing name upon illustrious name of heroic and creative black folk. People nodded. But when he said: Even Coca-Cola was invented by a black woman, everybody snapped awake. For didn't most of us drink this part of the heritage every day?

I tell Susan that in Callanwolde, the Coca-Cola mansion outside Atlanta, I remember seeing a statue of what appeared to me to be a black woman in the foyer, but nobody I asked about her seemed to know who she was or why she was there.

I laugh. It doesn't matter, really (though what a story there must be behind this story, I think). There's too much sugar in Coke. I'm sure the original was much better. It may even have been created as a medicine.

FIVE

In this one I am wearing a large mulberry-coloured coat several sizes too big, a long grape-coloured scarf, a Chinese peasant hat the size of an umbrella and am carrying a cane with a dragon carved on it. We have just stopped twenty miles upriver from the town of Guilin (a stunning boat ride through the mountains that look like stone trees), and the peasant merchants from the surrounding countryside have ambushed us on the shore. Their one American word is "hello," which they say with the same off-key intonation that I'm sure we say "Nee-How" (phonetic Chinese for "hello"). In their mouths it becomes a totally different word. It is like meeting a long line of people and each one solemnly greets you with "Elbow." I fantasize that my

"Nee-How" probably sounds like, say, the Chinese word for "foot" to them. So all during this trip I've been smiling and saying "hello" and they've been hearing "foot, foot, foot."

Looking closely at this picture, I see that I am also wearing very baggy pants. In fact, everything I'm wearing is several sizes too large. I realize we were asked by our tour leader not to wear tight, uncomfortable, or revealing clothes, but the overall looseness of my attire appears extreme.

But I suspect, looking at this picture, in which I look ridiculous, but regal, that this outsize dressing is typical of people — especially women — who grow up in families whose every other member is larger than they. Which is true in my family. We can't believe we're as small as we are. And so we dress ourselves as if we were them.

SIX

This is a picture of a university dormitory in Guilin. It is early evening as Susan and I walk across the campus on our way to visit families of Susan's Chinese acquaintances in Portland. As is true everywhere in China, there is no wasted electricity (lighting is mellow rather than bright: 40 watts rather than 100) and no unused space. In rooms smaller than those two American college students would share, five and six students bunk. Freshly washed clothes hang everywhere inside the rooms and outside the windows on long bamboo poles. The students we meet on the path are returning to the classrooms, which double as places of study at night. We watch rows and rows of them bent silently, intently, over their books.

Of course I think of Hampton Institute, Tuskegee, the early days of Morris Brown, Morehouse, and Spelman, black colleges started just after the Civil War in barracks and basements: poor, overcrowded, but determined to educate former peasants and slaves; schools which have also, like the Chinese schools, managed to do just that.

SEVEN

You would never believe, from this photograph, that I am sitting on the Great Wall of China. I look bored. I look unhappy. There is that tense line around my mouth that means I'll never come thousands of miles to see more of man's folly again. What I hate about the Great Wall is the thought of all the workers' bodies buried in it. I hate the vastness and barrenness of its location. I hate the suffering the women and children attached to the builders endured. I hate its — let's face it, I hate walls.

Susan dashes ahead of me looking for the best view. But the wall tires me, instantly. It is the concrete manifestation of so much that is wrong (a kind of primitive MX). What a stupid waste, I am thinking, in the photograph. A lot of flowers never sniffed. A lot of dancing never done.

The brochure about the Great Wall says that the invaders, finding it indeed impenetrable, got over it simply by bribing the guards.

The Great Wall is redeemed by only one thing: over each battlement portal (through which hand-propelled missiles must have whistled) there is a tiny decoration, serving no purpose whatsoever except to refresh the eye. And here is where the writer could benefit from having had a camera other than herself, because I feel deeply about this decoration, this modest attempt at art. I send mental salutations to the artist(s). But now I cannot remember what precisely the decoration is: Is it a curled line, horizontal and short, like those on the windows of brownstones? Is it the missing flower? Or is it two straight lines from a hexagram symbolizing war that I have mistaken for peace?

EIGHT

This one is of me and Susan walking across Tiananmen Square looking at the many fathers out for a stroll with their female children. They all look interested, relaxed, happy. Susan stops one little girl and her father and asks if she may take a picture. At first the father looks suspicious, or, more accurately, puzzled. We begin to *ooh* and *aah* over his child — a serene three-year-old with an enormous red ribbon in her hair. He understands. And beams with pride. Then we notice that street signs at crossings between the Forbidden City and the square depict just such a pair as we photographed: pearl-grey against a blue background without letters of any kind, the outline of a father and daughter holding hands, crossing the street.

We are made incomparably happy by this: I think of my daughter and her father. Susan, I know, thinks of her husband, John, at home with their girls. We look at each other with enormous grins. Thinking of fathers and daughters all over the world and wishing them luck.

NINE

This one shows us sitting down in the middle of the square looking dissatisfied. We look this way because we both really like Beijing. Miraculously feel at peace here. It is true that the dust gives us coughing fits and my eyes feel gritty from the smog, but overall we are pleased with the wide, clean boulevards, the rows of sycamore trees that sparkle like jewels in every breeze, the calm, meditative motion of thousands of bikers who pedal as if they're contemplating eternity rather than traffic. At night we, like the Chinese, are drawn to the streets. There is no sense of danger. No fear. People look at us mildly curious. We look back. Occasionally there is a spoken greeting. A smile.

What is it about Beijing that is so seductive? Susan muses. We consider the dimness of the lights at night. The way the few cars and trucks do not use their headlights, only their parking lights. The way homes seem to be lit by candles. How there is very little neon. Nothing that blinks, flashes, or winks. The softness this gives the evening. The night. How, strolling through this softness and hearing, through an open window, someone practising cello or flute is a satisfying experience. And how the mind begins to think religious thoughts but in a new way.

When we first arrived, we had thought Beijing a drab and ugly city because of the gray buildings and perpetual dust. Now, after six days, we find it beautiful enough not to want to leave, though neither of us speaks more than three words of Chinese.

In the West, Susan says, the cities are built to impress you with *themselves*. They are all-important. Here, the people are most important, and buildings are backdrop.

TEN

Something else occurs to me from this next picture. The one of me wearing both the Chinese ring and cloisonné bracelet I bought at the Friendship store. *People are more important than what they wear.* Everyone wears basically the same thing: trousers and shirt. And everyone is neat, clean, and adequately dressed. No one wears makeup or jewelry. At first faces look dull, as a natural tree would look if Christmas trees were the norm. But soon one becomes conscious of the wonderful honesty natural faces convey. An honesty more interesting than any ornament. And a vulnerability that makeup and jewelry would mask.

ELEVEN

In all of China there is nothing and no one more beautiful than the writer Ding Ling. She is short and brown and round. She is also "old." But these attributes alone, which connect her to great masses of women throughout the world, do not make her beautiful. It is a puzzle at first what does. In this photograph, she is listening to Madame Kang Ke Quing tell our group about the Long March and swinging her foot slightly as if to keep it awake. Madame has talked for three hours and told us most of the information about the Women's Federation (which she heads) we'd already read. (That the Women's Federation "re-educates" those who would practise female infanticide, for instance.)

I have drunk so much tea I am afraid to stand up. But Ding Ling — it is not tea she has drunk. She has drunk patience. Imprisoned by reactionaries and radicals, Kuomintang and Communists, presumed dead at least twice to national mourning, her young common-law husband executed by firing squad two months after the birth of their child, herself locked in solitary confinement for ten months by Mao Zedong's wife, Jiang Qing, imprisoned and separated from her present husband, Chen Ming, for six years under the Gang of Four, this small, brown, round, "old" woman — who claps her hands like a child when Susan asks if she will be photographed with me — has, through everything, including banishment to Manchuria to raise chickens among the peasants (whom she taught as they taught her), simply continued to write. Powerful story after story, novel after novel, over a period of fifty years. And though beaten bloody by the Red Guards during the Cultural Revolution (for having been, among other things, famous) and forced to parade through the streets wearing a blackened face and dunce's cap, she holds no bitterness, only saying, of all her travails — illnesses, children lost; books and notes destroyed — mainly, I lost time.

At nearly eighty she says things like: Oh, to be sixty-seven again!

TWELVE

In this picture, I have just been told by an editor of a Shanghai literary magazine that my novel *The Color Purple* is being translated into Chinese. I am delighted. Especially when she looks me warmly in the eye and says, in a beautiful Chinese accent, mocking my surprise: But Alice, it is a very *Chinese* story. She tells me further that two of my stories have already appeared in translation and that the woman who translated them (and who will translate the novel) wanted to meet me but was afraid I'd want to talk about copyrights.

I don't. What interests me is how many of the things I've written about women certainly do, in China, look Chinese. The impact of poverty, forced sex, and childbearing, domination as a race (before the Chinese revolution) and *still* as a caste. The struggle to affirm solidarity with women, as women, and the struggle to attain political, social, and economic equality with men.

But I am disturbed that a young Chinese writer of my generation,

Yu Luojing, who is writing stories and novels similar in theme to mine in China, is banned. Whenever we ask about her, there is a derisive response. She is only "writing out of her own bitter experiences" they say, as if this is a curse. "She is perpetuating bourgeois individualism." One of our hosts even goes so far as to accuse her of libel, because she allegedly published excerpts from letters she'd received from a well-known literary figure who was her mentor and lover.

Still, though we do not meet her, and her books (not yet in English translation) can be bought only on the black market, she is the writer in China, next to Ding Ling, who intrigues me. She has written, for instance, about being raped by her husband on their wedding night, and of her hatred of it; an experience shared by countless women around the world (by now we understand there does not *have* to be blood on the sheets). For this bravery alone, I feel the women of China will eventually love her — in fact, already do. For though she is scorned by the literary establishment — and by the Chinese Writers Association in particular — her books are underground bestsellers.

THIRTEEN

In this one, one of our hosts is singing "Old Black Joe" under the impression that this will prove she knows something about American blacks. There is deep sadness in this picture, as we realize the Chinese, because of China's years of isolation, have missed years of black people's struggle in the United States. No Martin, no Malcolm, no Fannie Lou. No us. I want to move closer to Paule Marshall and put my arms around her, and I want her to hug me back. Here we are, two black women (Thank the Universe we *are* two!), once again, facing a racial ignorance that depresses and appalls. Our singing host was once in America, in the fifties, she says, and was taught this song as part of her English lessons. This is one of the songs American-trained Chinese learned in America and brought back to teach others throughout China.

I explain the reactionary nature of the song. But the energy required to do this nearly puts me to sleep. Nor can I foretell that from

this point in the trip, everywhere I go I will be asked to sing. To teach
the Chinese "a new song." I sing (one of my secret ambitions, actually), the irony of being asked, as a black person, not lost on me for a
second. I start out with Reverend Dorsey ("We Shall Overcome") and
end up with Brother Lennon ("Hold On"). It is really James Weldon
Johnson's Negro National Anthem that is required ("Lift Every Voice
and Sing"); but I am embarrassed to say, I could not recall all the
words. This I consider the major personal failure of the trip.

Lift every voice and sing
Till earth and heaven ring
Ring with the harmonies of liberty
Let our rejoicing rise
High as the listening skies
Let it resound
Loud as the rolling sea.

Sing a song
Full of the faith that the dark past has taught us
Sing a song
Full of the hope that the present has brought us
Facing the rising sun of our new day begun
Let us march on till victory is won.

Stony the road we trod
Bitter the chastening rod
Felt in the days when hope unborn had died
Yet with a steady beat
Have not our weary feet
Come to the place, Oh, where our ancestors[1] sighed?

[1] I have replaced the original "fathers" with "ancestors," believing that Brother
Johnson, a sometimes progressive in his day (1871–1938) and an artist in any event,
would understand that our fathers were not by themselves when they sighed.

205

We have come
Over a way that with tears has been watered
We have come
Treading our path through the blood of the slaughtered
Out from the gloomy past till now we stand at last
Where the white gleam of our bright star is cast.

FOURTEEN

In this one, three young men from Africa are talking. They are from Chad, Uganda, and Somalia, and have been studying medicine in China for seven years. Soon, they will be going home.

"They teach us, but that is all," one says. "There's no such thing as going up to the professor outside the class."

"And if the Chinese should invite you to their home," says another, "they make sure it's dark and the neighbours don't see. And the girls are definitely not to go out with us."

"But why is this?" I ask, my heart sinking over the brothers' isolation. But marvelling that they all study medicine *in Chinese.*

"Because the Chinese do not like black people," one says. "Some are nice, but some call us black devils. They don't like anyone really but themselves. They pretend to like whites because that is now the correct line, and they're all over white Americans because they want American technology."

As we talk, I am reminded of Susan's face one evening after she'd been talking, for over an hour, with our interpreters. She was happy because they had appeared interested in and asked innumerable questions about American blacks. Only after I pointed out that they could have asked the same questions directly *to* American blacks (me and Paule) did her mood change.

"That's right," she said. "Damn it."

The next evening a continuation of the questions about blacks was attempted, but Susan was ready, and annoyed. "Any questions about blacks, ask Paule and Alice. Both are black and Alice is even a peasant!" she said. And that night her face was even happier than before.

FIFTEEN

This is a picture of our hotel room in Hong Kong. Susan is standing in the doorway preparing to leave. She is carrying a beautiful cello she bought for her husband in Shanghai (which she laughingly says is my colour *and* shape). But is it my tone? I reply.

I have been ill the last couple of days of the trip, and she has been mother, sister, and nurse (all of which has added up to: Let's get a doctor up here quick!). It is mostly exhaustion and I am spending my last morning in Hong Kong in bed. Later I will get up and catch a plane to Hawaii, where my companion is waiting to meet me.

Now that we are out of Mainland China, there is an eagerness to be gone entirely. I look down on the bay and hills of Hong Kong and all I can think about is San Francisco. China already seems a world away. And is. Only a few images remain: the peasant who makes 10,000 yuan (about $3,500) a year and has built a nice two storey house that fills his eyes with pride; the tired face of Shen Rong, the writer whose long short story "At Middle Age" (about the struggle of Chinese women professionals to "do it all") I watched dramatized on Beijing TV. The faces of people depicted in statues commemorating the Chinese Revolution: strong, determined, irresistible; Ding Ling; and the city of Beijing itself, which of all the marvels I saw is what I like best of the New China.

But the finest part of the trip has been sharing it with Susan (over the years we have incited each other to travel: Let's go to Mexico! Let's go to Grenada! Let's go to *China!* And now we have), now admiring, now cursing a rather large cello that grows larger by the second, that she's not sure she should have bought (Do you think they'll let it on the plane? Will it need its own seat? And are you *positive* you're okay?) striding out the door.

E. ANNIE PROULX

On the train to hell
and can't get off

The piece itself says all I want to say.

———————

*Rowe's Rule: The odds are five to six that the light at the end of the tunnel is
the headlight of an oncoming train.*

Paul Dickson
Washingtonian, November 1978

THIS IS THE PART OF THE WRITER'S LIFE THAT
has nothing to do with writing and everything to do with stress,
peril, ennui — the journey known as "the book tour" that occurs in
the peculiar weeks after a book's publication.

Drive, and there are the serial killer highways, chances of running out of gas at midnight in Montana, sticking in mud wallows,
dodging tornadoes and outrunning blizzards, eating cruel food in
Mud Butte or Biloxi. Fly, and it is paralysis in boa constrictor seats,
headache from oxygen deprivation, the salmonella sandwich, babble of

a lunatic seatmate, ice on the wings, lost luggage. Illness compounds these miseries.

I have the flu, a sinus infection, and a double ear infection. The book tour dates are cast in iron but my ears don't work, crackle, echo. Fluid behind the drums. No flying. Driving is too slow. It has to be the train, just Montreal to Chicago and back — cancel the west coast. I set out.

In the waiting room of Montreal's Gare Centrale I give a dollar to a young beggar in a red sweater because he says, piteously, "I'm an American." He rushes to the coffee shop joyfully calling "money, money, money!" to someone in the corner. I can hear him order a large cappuccino. I take an aspirin.

The train is clean in a sad, threadbare way. A baby-faced steward pushes soft drinks and mineral water. The landscape hurtles past, snowdrifts slumping in the spring thaw. We are in a region of broken, splintered trees, the wreckage of a blizzard ten days earlier.

For a brief moment I think I see a man's body half thrust out of the snow, the upper part of the torso in a red plaid shirt, the face blackened by exposure, one dark hand uplifted as though waving at the train. I press my burning forehead against the glass; have I seen this or imagined it?

There is nothing like travelling across North America by train in the early spring. The rivers brim with brown, quilted water. We pass an orchard in a lake. Ditches overflow, dirt roads along the track are gleaming mud. The mean architecture tilts away from leafless trees, the snow shrinks from clumps of grass like the dirt-clogged manes of dead horses. On the train clacks through old fields of corn, copses of sumac, angular branches bearing torches of black fruit. Another train rushes in the opposite direction, flashes of red-brown broken by yellow, green, blue, black.

The train horn plays again and again, not feathered, but strong and full, that haunting Canadian E-flat minor triad, as we rock past square hip-roofed farmhouses, leave them, and plunge into the industrio-socio crap of North America, visible by train as in no other form of travel: trash, shacks, tenements, discarded machinery, bus graveyards, rusted wire, long miles of transmission towers, gravel storage sheds - - odd, pointed buildings like enormous brassiere cups — the brute complexities of generating stations, torn chain-link fence, parallel highways fringed with paper wrappers, hubcaps, beer bottles. We pass an iridescent swamp dotted with scabby refrigerators and washing machines. On higher ground, car lots, scrap metal yards, and dismal houses.

The view is of plastic chairs on a flat roof, a "Square Boy Pizza" truck, a tenement house covered with fifty-year-old asphalt shingles, pipes, wires, cables, and fire escapes. The train drifts through an alley of transmission towers, enters a deserted village of storage units with metal doors, a raw housing development, roofs dotted with crouching pigeons. The transmission towers multiply, stride off in all directions through a coarsened landscape that seems charged with dangerous electricity. The sun strikes, a four o'clock disk in the cloud as the train sways sharply through a brilliant osier redness, then enters a channel of concrete. We are pulling into the station.

The next morning I walk past hundreds of tiny shops packed with mirrored vests, airbrush paintings of leopards, hooks, blood sausage. A black man sways toward me, each outstretched hand twirling a tassel, his entire body activated by private rhythms. Two middle aged men, stunted, dressed in slouch caps and layers of sweaters, talk in a clicking language. An elderly black man holds out his baseball cap. Both thumbs are wrapped in electrician's tape. His grey hair is braided into fifty or sixty small pigtails stoppered at the ends with varicoloured glass beads. He is singing short lines, swaying, holding the cap, nodding his head. The beads tremble. I put a two-dollar bill in his hat.

"What are you singing?"

"Nursy rhymes." He sings again and I catch the words. "Lil Bopee, los er shee, Rocksabye babee, Jack and Jill uppa hill, three bline mice, three bline micc."

I cross the street. Near the curb is a pool of wet blood about the size of a dinner napkin. I find the door I want. Wooden stairs, each with its own note, and at the top a dark warren packed floor to ceiling with books. A buzzer sounds intermittently and interminably. A woman cannot be interrupted, she is typing rapidly on an electric typewriter. In another part of the store a man bends over some papers. I ask for a book I have been seeking for years. I no longer expect to find it. But suddenly it is in my hands, a first edition, clean, the dust jacket crisp and unfaded, the pages pure. The price is modest.

On the next morning my illness has taken a new form, a sore throat and near deafness which I interpret as the psychological effect of staring out a train window. I go out, walk near the lake shore. There are geese in the water, they hiss and show their hard pink tongues. A woman wrapped in a pale-grey raincoat lies on a'bench. Her wild hair is almost the same colour as the coat. She is speaking loudly into the glare, her eyes shut, as she lies there.

". . . And then fooling around with three or four other kids, and that's it, isn't it, goddamn you!" Her face is maroon from crying. She is smoking a cigarette as she lies there and talks and weeps. Suddenly she opens her eyes and looks at me.

"Good morning," I say.

She sits up, a tiny smile appears. An hour later she is still there, lying on her side. A wave made up of curled, broken segments edged with foam crosses the calm water. Where it comes from I cannot understand. The sky is blue-violet. Against this sky is a glass building and it also is blue, but blue-green. Together the sky and the building give the impression that shades of blue are the only true colours.

It is astonishing how many women in this city wear red coats.

The woman on the bench sits up, opens a clear plastic sack and forages in it. She moves objects around without taking them out. She throws a paper napkin on the ground. She removes a smaller plastic bag, folds and returns it. Now she holds an orange. She peels it very slowly and places the peels on the end of the bench. When the fruit is naked she crosses her right leg over the left and begins to eat the sections, one by one. Her foot swings. She wipes her fingers on a paper napkin, then roaches back her hair. The sky behind the building is tremendously purple. A Chinese couple walk on the esplanade, their white shoes winking. The shadow of a bird glides over the ground.

At the station again I board another train, inferior to the first in appointments, services, and comforts. There is a ten-hour crawl through urban wilderness, vast lots of wrecked cars with holes in the windshields, two-storey crushers squeezing wrecks into cubes. The snow is reduced to occasional filthy wads My illness is receding as well, but I feel that it can, will, flare up again. The train stops beside another scrap metal yard, red mountains of odd geometries. Rain begins, less rain than acid drizzle.

The train arrives in darkness.

In the hotel room my illness returns, and I roll up in the comforter, watch the lights of the city glittering in raking sleet. A storm, in from the lake.

The next day there is the crackle of wildfire in my ears, my head and throat ache. I meet a woman for lunch in the hotel's dining room, keep saying what, what, drop the napkin, the silver. The waiters brush dandruff from one another's shoulders, hardly glance at our table where we wait hungrily and patiently.

That night I dress and go out. Wind roars off the lake and blows the doorman's fur hat into the street. The snow falls so heavily headlights resemble paper disks. Two blocks from the hotel the taxi spins and crashes forcefully into an immense boat of a car filled with drunken men. My nose bleeds, my glasses are broken, the left ear piece lost somewhere on the wet floor. The driver gets out. I grope for the ear piece. The men from the car push the taxi driver, his turban falls, rolls like some thick bird's nest blown out of a tree. I get out and go toward him. The drunken men stagger in the churned raw snow. They drive away. I notice the taxi driver's feet, encased in cracked white patent-leather evening pumps with dangling bows. He leans on the hood of his taxi. I walk back to the hotel.

The lobby is deserted, no one at the desk, the doorman absent, the empty elevator waiting. I ride in solitude to my floor, enter the room, and call the concierge. A voice comes on the wire. There is a man in the street, I explain. He's been in an accident.

"Is he a guest of the hotel?"

"No. A taxi driver."

"Ah," says the voice, "someone . . ." and trails off.

I call the friend I was to meet for dinner. The phone rings 137 times. I get my spare eyeglasses from a pocket in the suitcase. They are an old prescription and make objects seem smaller than they truly are.

In the morning the sky is brilliant, the lake tosses harshly. My nose is swollen. I have many appointments and each is saturated in an atmosphere of chaos; recording equipment malfunctions, telephone calls do not go through, an elevator in which I ride stops between floors, then jerks spasmodically up and down, up and down while I press the alarm button, pound on the wall and shout "stop this damn thing!" Suddenly it does stop and opens smoothly onto the crowded lobby. There is a pebble in the burrito I order for lunch. Later I walk up twenty-two flights of stairs. My heart pounds.

In a free hour before the train leaves I go to see an exhibition of works by a famous dead surrealist. But as I enter the first room a guard calls out that the museum is closing in ten minutes. I begin to rush through the rooms, harried by the booming voice, "the museum will close in five minutes, three minutes, the museum is closing now, please move to the outside room, please exit the exhibit, the museum is closed now." The rooms are empty. I stare at a painting of a rifle leaning against a wall. A guard pulls at my arm.

"Now, lady."

The station is a jam of travellers with weeping children. People swallow glass after glass of whisky and vodka purchased at a mobile bar in the centre of the concourse.

The train is an hour late. I board, find my sleeping compartment. The attendant says, "Oh boy, bad news. The dining car won't open until nine p.m." When nine o'clock comes I am ravenously hungry. I sit across from a fat young man who exudes a miasmic stink. I cannot eat, take a buttered roll and return to my compartment. The people in the swaying coaches already seem exhausted, sprawl in their seats with babies, blankets printed with words bunched over them, their bruised eyes closed, mouths gaping and choked. The car sways, the wheels roar.

At midnight, lying in the bed with the shade up, I see we are entering Toledo. And fall asleep before we arrive.

An hour after dawn I am awake. The train is motionless. I feel it has been motionless for some time. There is a breathy hissing. I dress in my stale clothes. The sky is cloudy, there is a view of graffiti on concrete. The sleeping car attendant comes with coffee and juice.

"Oh boy," he says, "oh boy, I have bad news. We are still in Toledo, we have been here all night. There is a problem."

"What?" The coffee is lukewarm, with a grassy taste as though from an infusion of hay.

"A boat is stuck under the railroad bridge at the Maumee River."

Up and down the train the passengers buzz. The sleeping car passengers laugh at first. The coach passengers, who have known for hours, are sullen, cramped in their seats with the hard armrests.

As the hours crawl by there is no information. Rumours seethe: the train will go back to Chicago; the train will be rerouted to the north; the passengers will all be sent on by bus or plane; the boat under the bridge cannot be freed; powerful tugs are coming down from Detroit to pull it out.

Free coffee and doughnuts for all. People are getting off the train and wandering into the station to telephone, to explain to bosses and spouses that although they should have been in Boston by now they are still — ha-ha — in Toledo, home of the Detroit Tigers' minor-league team, the Toledo Mud Hens. The train has no cellular phone. In the station only two telephones are working. There are long lines. No food in the station either, only vending machines displaying "empty" signs. The ticket agents know nothing. Yes, this has happened before, last November another boat was stuck under the same bridge.

I get back on the train. I pass through the club car. The attendant is piling bags of peanuts on the counter; on a napkin he writes the word

"FREE." The peanuts are intended as solace. I take some. In my cubby-hole I take up my book and read. The peanuts are stale.

All at once the train begins to move, cautiously but steadily. Inside the station the passengers waiting to use the telephones see the train leaving and they run out onto the platform. But it is no use. The train is on its way and they are left behind.

The train crosses the bridge. There is no boat in sight, no tugs, only splintered pilings and the rough brown current of the Maumee. We gather speed. The train is twelve hours late. I have missed my connection to Montreal. Everyone has missed everything. We pass a vast cemetery at the edge of a cornfield.

Things are seriously awry. The train has lost its slot in the great flow of rail traffic. The sleeping car attendant has dark circles under his eyes, answers the querulous complaints of passengers by saying, "I don't know, they don't tell us anything." The train chief, the conductor walk briskly through the cars, trying not to look at the bitter passengers. When their sleeves are seized, they grimace, say they are awaiting instructions, all will be made right. "That's as much as I know, ma'am." Then they are gone. Later, an insistent passenger demanding the train chief is told that he is sleeping, the poor fellow has been up all night.

In Cleveland we pass boats shrink-wrapped in royal-blue plastic near a cliff of scrap metal. The sleeping car attendant's eyes are bloodshot. He limps on swollen feet. At noon he brings his passengers each a bag of barbecue-flavoured potato chips and a cup of coffee. The train has run out of food. He brings each of us three mint chocolates of the sort hotels put on a guest's pillow.

We are the fly in the ointment, the drunk uncle at the wedding party. The train moves slowly past a desolate station. All the windows are broken — there is no pane intact in 504 lights. A fine, wind-streaked snow begins. This is a nerved-up, strained time of waiting for nothing but the cessation of waiting.

Sighing and groaning, the train halts in a wasteland, once a marsh and now a combination swamp-and-appliance-disposal depot. Toppled stoves and yellowed refrigerators lie in ice-rimmed water, in the sedges and cattails. A male mallard duck hovers and drops down through a maze of wires. A few minutes later he flies up with a female, into the wind.

A passenger is carrying on in the corridor, insisting he be let out to make a phone call. Perhaps there is a telephone booth in the marsh.

"Sir, the train will not wait. If we start you will be left."

I can tell when the train is going to start — there is a straining sensation, though without movement. I feel this strain now. The passenger jumps out. At once the train jerks forward and the marsh dissolves to an abandoned, ramshackle station. The passenger, halfway between the train and the station, looks back — his bag is on the train. It is snowing heavily and almost dark. Everyone is hungry. There is not even coffee now. The train glides through more wetlands. Snaking through the boggy ground beneath the high-tension wires are dirt bike trails crooked as dropped ropes. The handlebars of a motorcycle project from a scummed pool; is there a rider under the water? In the dusk we pass junkyard after junkyard, one of them filled with nothing but the cut-off tops of bulldozers and backhoes and graders. The word "CUT" is spray-painted on the doors. More ducks, like bowling pins with wings.

Outside Rochester the train stops again. The attendant, lurching and grey-faced, comes with more bad news; of the two eastbound tracks ahead, one is flooded. On the other a freight train has derailed and run over its own drawbar and behind it seven other freights have right of precedence over us. There will be a minimum wait of four-and-a-half hours to get the derailed freight off the tracks, and then the track repairs . . . The train is on a downhill run to nowhere. The crew lost their chance at the on-time bonus last night. There is no reason for getting this train to its destination aside from passenger anxiety and pleading — and that counts for nothing. It is money reward that runs the train and now the reward has shifted from the on-time bonus to the sweeter lure of massive overtime. In every car plastic sacks of trash block the corridors.

The car attendant is strung out and crazy. He is at the end of his rope. There is no food, no coffee, the chocolate mints are gone.

"Cheer up," says a second attendant, who has appeared from nowhere, "it can't last forever."

"It seems like it already has," the first says in a sullen, dropping voice. He coughs. "I'm going to change my clothes." I hear him go into the empty roomette across the corridor.

After a few minutes I take my aspirin bottle from my purse and open it. The lid cracks up noisily, the pills rattle. From the corridor the second attendant shouts in a rough voice, "John! What are you taking!"

"What?"

"What are you taking? I heard the pills rattle, goddamn you. You better not be taking anything!"

"What are you talking about?"

"You push me, I'll break that damn door down."

The voices have a delirious, feverish quality. There is a long silence.

"Don't go to sleep, John," says the voice of the second attendant close to the door, "you'll be up all night . . . John, what saved his ass was that flood. The general inspector coming on here like gangbusters. They couldn't get hold of him — he used the flood for an excuse. I tell you, John, this is unbelievable, unbelievable." There is a long silence.

"John, you want a beer? You got the white one, right? I'll tell you what I got now. John, you got a pen on you?"

"Yeah."

"It black?"

"We were out of Cleveland at 12:33."

"5:26. What time we pull up? 5:26."

Sleepily, four or five minutes later, "5:26?"

"Yeah." There is a long silence. "Hey. Open up!" The door opens and the second attendant goes inside. Their conspiratorial voices are clearly audible.

"O.K., Johnny. How many tennis racquets you got? I might borrow one from Tubby. You got balls? Want to play on Monday? I'll tell you something, John." The second attendant's voice drops. "Twelve hours overtime, that's like two days' pay! Two days' pay! Hey, Johnny. Did you call up Carmen when you were here?"

"No. I was thinking about her."

"Hey, the hormones getting to you."

"You see now, you tell me if he's thinking clearly? Where are you, Scotty?"

"Oh, I'm right across from Van Damme."

It is dark outside. Huge green letters appear. THE SPAGHETTI WAREHOUSE. I am starving. I have a headache and a ringing buzz in my ears like cicadas. The train slows, slows, and stops before a deserted station, a brick colossus in the dirty snow, the waiting room lit by a dim high bulb. Luggage trucks on the platform in random positions. The door across the corridor opens and the attendants come out, walk away. After a long time the first attendant, John, brings word to his few remaining passengers. He is startled to see me. "Oh. I thought you got off the train back there."

"No."

"Well, the conductor is holding up the train for some food."

"Better luck if he would hold up a restaurant. There isn't any food on the train." A feeble joke.

An hour passes. Two cars pull into the station parking lot. A few train crew people are on the platform, go into the dirty waiting room, come out again. A taxi cab arrives and they run to it. The driver opens the trunk. The train people pull out large cartons. The train chief, he who escaped the inspector's discovery of his illegal nap, strips small bills from a large wad of money and pays the taxi driver.

"Arunh!" A man grunts with the weight of the boxes. Money is in the hands of the vehicle drivers. More taxis, more boxes arrive, cartons of soft drinks, and someone brings up a baggage wagon. A voice issues from a loudspeaker.

"All train attendants. They're relaying the chicken to your cars. Please be ready."

John, enveloped in the perfume of salty, greasy Kentucky Fried Chicken, brings me a striped box. A dozen more taxi cabs pull up, disgorge other men. The vehicle drivers hang around on the platform staring at the train as though at a road accident. More taxis.

"They're changing the train crew," says John, yawning.

"You can finally get some sleep."

"No. The car attendants don't ever get relieved. We're on for the trip, even if it takes a million years."

Outside on the platform the train chief is staggering, perhaps with weariness, his stumbling figure backlit by the bulb in the open baggage-cart storage shed. In the corridor I hear the voice of the second attendant again.

"John, Johnny, we have to take care of each other. Right or wrong!"

I go to the club car. It is like a tableau from hell, crammed with flushed drunks, thick smoke, and the stink of dirty travellers. People are shouting, snoring, kissing, scratching, arguing, dealing cards, bending down, coughing, drinking rotating their glasses to make the ice swirl up the sides, tapping ash into striped boxes of bones and wadded napkins, throwing down torn magazines, picking up torn magazines, stumbling toward the toilet, standing in line at the toilet, vomiting inside the toilet. I buy a small bottle of warm white wine, think a moment, and buy another.

Back in the claustrophobic cubbyhole a terrible knowledge comes. Somehow, in Chicago, I have boarded the Train from Hell on its endless circling route, clanking and lurching through dirty days and nights until the universe runs down, and then on into the void. The passengers who debark along the route drop straight into the fiery pit. Here at least is greasy chicken and warm wine.

"Hey, hey Johnny, you see this? Saudis behead five?"

Mumble.

"Aw, give me a break!"

Mumble.

"We got time. They got this other crew waiting at Amsterdam. Imagine bringing this thing in?" His mocking voice drops to a whisper. "Amtrak is the besssssst. . . ."

In Syracuse the train holds up for more than an hour in a labour dispute. The question is, is it legally necessary to put on a new crew? There is an enormous wrangle on the platform while the passengers grow old. A woman in a white leather coat gets off the train, approaches the chief, and screams in his face that he and his fucking train are utterly, utterly fucked up. She gets back on. And so the second night grinds away, the train jerking forward, running for fifteen or twenty miles, then stopping in snowy junkyards, at way stations where crew members are replaced, where union representatives shake their fists, again and again.

"That's two complete changes of the train crew since yesterday morning," says John in dawn light. His face is ghastly, great black circles under his eyes, gaunt and stubbled, numb mouth.

On this second morning, as the sky lightens in the east, the train enters rural countryside in upstate New York. The landscape is grey and dense. The trees are plastered with clots and rinds of snow. There is a man coming down a steep path toward the railroad track, frowsy, half-asleep. He is carrying a white enamel pail, an old-fashioned object from the days before indoor plumbing — the thundermug, the slop bucket.

The chief tells me I can make my Montreal connection at the next stop. I carry my bag to the platform of the sleeping car. The train pulls in. I press money into John's hand. I cannot believe I am free of this train. In the station I present my ticket at the window.

"Montreal? There's no Montreal connection here. You should have got off at the last station. No, there's nothing going anywhere until tomorrow. You better get back on that train. At least it's going east. *Hurry!*"

I run for the hated train, the heavy bag pounding against my leg. John sees me coming, extends his hand for my bag. The train pulls out.

"What happened? What happened?" His distress is real.

"You can't get there from here."

The train lumbers on for hours, hopelessly compromised, filled with exhausted, reeking humans entering a curious state of mind — irrational, manic. Nothing that has once defined the journey counts any longer — tickets, arrival times, connections, accommodations, business meetings, family reunions, all are meaningless. The passengers' only hope is some compromise that will not leave them homeless in Yellowknife or hitchhiking north from Miami. A kind of euphoria sets in as the conductor shuffles along asking people where they want to go. Not that he cares. Passengers begin to choose strange new destinations that have nothing to do with their former lives.

"Let me off in New York, haven't been there for years."

"I was going to Schenectady, but I think I'll take Boston now."

My connection to Montreal is dead. Dead in an unmarked grave.

"White River Junction?" I murmur. It is only thirty miles from where I live.

"Yes," says the conductor, "get off at Springfield, there'll be a taxi to take you to White River Junction. There's other ones going."

Six of us disembark at Springfield. There is no taxi but we are off the train. The cold air smells wonderful. After long discussion with the ticket clerks — how clean and fresh they look, how energetic, filled with careless confidence in contrast to the demoralized, wretched passengers — a vehicle arrives, a small sedan driven by a 300-pound woman. We squeeze into the rump-sprung seats. Four of us sit in back. I am between a homeopathic physician who recites know-all accounts of Chinese herbal cures and a pair of teen sweethearts who kiss and fondle. In the front, next to the huge driver, is a businessman who says he has now conquered his fear of flying and a frail grandmother who seems unconscious.

This last hour-and-a-half is the worst of the entire trip: crushed against strangers, head swimming, in a car speeding over an icy road while the radio plays country and western and machine-gun advertisements to "get hooked on phonics," this final leg is nearly unbearable.

It is an eternity until I am in White River Junction eating burned eggs at the Polka Dot Diner and waiting for a friend to pick me up. I think it is over.

But the journey does not end, cannot end. A year later I am still on that train, you are with me, and there is no getting off. The train is a metaphor, bearing us through the junkyards and despoiled landscapes at the end of the century, past mean houses and the casually dead, through broken trees, deserted stations and transmission towers, a train staffed by the exhausted, the sly, the conniving, the uncaring.

CAROL SHIELDS

Encounter

The incident described in this piece — when it happened — seemed to signal something of the mystery and randomness of the world. Like many such transcendental experiences, it was hard to talk about, though I did once attempt to transform it into fiction, in a story called "Collision." It came out wrong: extraneous elements had crept in, and the central unexpected happiness of the moment had drained away and become something else. Why did I feel so forcefully a simple encounter with a stranger? I can only suppose that being in a strange place shakes loose our bearings and opens us to sensation. I find it curious, and also heartening, to think that "my stranger" and I were for a few minutes as intimately connected as human beings can be.

I WAS IN TOKYO TO ATTEND A CONFERENCE, ONE OF a thousand or so delegates — and that probably was my problem: the plasticized name card and the logo of my organization marked me as someone who desired only to be cheerfully accommodated.

The allotted two weeks had passed. A single day in Japan remained, and at last I admitted to myself that I was disappointed. The terrible banality of tourist desire invaded me like a kind of flu. Walking the

broad, busy boulevards, I caught myself looking too eagerly, too pre-
ciously, for minor cultural manifestations — the charming way the
bank teller bowed when presenting me with my bundle of cash, the
colourful plastic food in the windows of restaurants; these were items
I was able to record in my travel journal, touching them up in the way
of desperate travellers, shaping them into humorous or appreciative
annotation on the Japanese people and the exotic city they inhabited.

But Tokyo with its hotels and subways and department stores was a
modern industrial complex. Its citizens went to work in the morning,
earned money, and travelled home again at night. These homes, to be
sure, were impenetrable to me, but the busy working days bore the
same rhythms as those found in any large North American city. The
traffic noises, the scent of pollution, and the civility of people in the
street made me think of — home.

I had hoped for more; what traveller doesn't? Travelling is expensive, exhausting, and often lonely — the cultural confusion, the acres
of concrete, the bitter coffee, the unreadable maps, and the rates of
exchange that are almost always unfavourable. And then, like a punishment at the end of the traveller's day, there waits a solitary room, and
a bed that, however comfortable, is not your bed. What makes all this
worth the effort is the shock of otherness that arrives from time to
time, rattling loose your bearings and making you suddenly alert to an
altered world. But Tokyo was determinedly polite, fulsomely western,
a city with a bland, smiling face, ready to welcome me not on its terms
but on my own.

I already know that the banquet that was to conclude the conference would be a model of French cuisine. Seven courses, seven different wines. No rice, no noodles, no sushi, no hot radish. It was to be
held at the famous Imperial Hotel, which was fifteen or twenty
minutes' walk from the somewhat less expensive hotel where I was
staying.

I started out in good time. It was a soft spring evening, and the
thought of a leisurely stroll was appealing. I would be able to look

around one last time, breathe in a final impression that I could perhaps test against my accumulated disappointment, acquiring some fresh point of perception with which to colour and preserve my Japanese sojourn.

At that moment it began to rain. A few drops at first, then it came down in earnest, spotting the silk dinner suit I was wearing and threatening to flatten my carefully arranged hair. I looked about for a taxi or a roof to shelter under, but neither presented itself. The only thing to do, I decided, was to run as quickly as I could the rest of the way.

But a tall man was standing directly in front of me, a man with an umbrella. He was smiling tentatively, and gesturing, and his mouth was moving. But what was he saying? I wasn't sure, since the accent was unfamiliar, but it sounded like "Imperial Hotel?" With a question mark behind it. "Yes," I said, nodding and speaking with great deliberation, "Imperial Hotel," and at that he lifted his umbrella slightly, and invited me under.

The umbrella was large and black, resolutely standard, the sort of umbrella found in every city or backwater of the world. "Thank you," I said in Japanese — the only phrase I had mastered — but he only repeated what he had said earlier: "Imperial Hotel?" And tipped his head quizzically in an eastward direction. "Yes," I said again. And we began walking.

It seemed only polite to make an effort at conversation. Where was he from? Was he with the conference? Was he a stranger in Japan like myself? He shook his head, uncomprehending, and released a shower of words in an unidentifiable language. Now it was my turn to shake my head. After that, smiling, we continued our walk in a contained silence, as though we had each admitted to the other that language was absurd, that rhetoric was a laughable formality that could be set aside for this brief interval.

Suddenly careless of social taboos, and because it's difficult for a short woman to walk with a tall man under an umbrella, I took the stranger's arm. (Thinking about this later, I theorized that he must have gestured minutely with his elbow, inviting my intimacy.) Now, arms linked, we were able to walk together smoothly, stepping over and around the puddles without losing our stride, pausing at traffic lights, stepping down from curbs.

We had arrived quickly at our congenial gliding pace, left foot, right foot, left foot again, a forward rhythm with a very slight sideways roll like a kind of swimming. Our mutually constrained tongues, the sound of the pelting rain, and our random possession of a random moment in time, seemed to seal us in a temporary vacuum that had nothing to do with Japan, nor with gender or age or with Hollywood notions about men and women walking in the rain. This was good walking, though, I knew that much — walking that transcended mere movement. Hypnotic walking. Walking toward the unimaginable. And I found myself wanting it to go on and on.

But there we suddenly were, at the brilliantly lit entrance of the Imperial Hotel, caught in a throng of people arriving and departing, people who had come from every corner of the globe, and trailing after them their separate languages, their lives, their ribbons of chance connection. The stranger with the umbrella abruptly disappeared. I looked around for him but was unable to recall his face, how he had been dressed. One minute he was there and the next minute he'd vanished, leaving me alone with that primary shiver of mystery that travellers, if they're lucky, hope to hang on to: the shock of the known and the unknown colliding in space.

Notes
on the Contributors

MICHELENE ADAMS is a citizen of Trinidad and Tobago. She is currently completing a Ph.D. program in English at the University of New Brunswick in Fredericton.

HANAN AL-SHAYKH was brought up in Beirut and educated there and in Cairo; since 1982 she has lived in London with her husband and two children. Her novel *Women of Sand and Myrrh* was named one of the fifty best books of 1992 by *Publishers Weekly* and in 1993 was named one of the year's top ten novels by the International Feminist Book Festival.

   CATHERINE COBHAM, teaches modern Arabic literature at the University of St. Andrews. She has translated a number of contemporary Arab writers, including Naguib Mahfouz.

MARGARET ATWOOD is a novelist and poet. She was born in Ottawa in 1939 and almost immediately set out for points north in a packsack. She has since travelled by sleigh, car, plane, train, bus, and foot. Her most recent novel is *The Robber Bride*.

ANN BEATTIE has just finished her fifth novel, to be published by Knopf. In 1992 she was elected to the American Academy of Arts and

Letters. She and her husband, Lincoln Perry, divide their time between Charlottesville, Virginia, and Maine, with vacations to everywhere they can afford. She is five feet six inches tall; people usually exclaim that they thought she was taller.

CLARE BOYLAN was born in Dublin in 1948. Her early travels were restricted by the fact that her parents would not allow her to ride a bicycle. This resulted in a lifelong restlessness that keeps her almost constantly on the go, to London for business and friends, to France for pleasure, and everywhere else for discovery. She is the author of two volumes of short stories and four novels, the most recent of which is *Home Rule.* She also edited a volume of literary essays, *The Agony and the Ego.*

ROBYN DAVIDSON was born in Queensland, Australia. She worked variously in a bar and as a camel trainer before writing her first book, *Tracks,* which documents her six-month trek across the desert in western Australia. In 1989 Davidson published her first novel, *Ancestors.*

KATHERINE GOVIER was born in Alberta. In Washington, D.C., she had babies; in England she was perpetually damp in the laundry flat on a run-down estate. Now she lives in Toronto, where her most recent novel, *Hearts of Flame,* won the Toronto Book Award.

IRENE GUILFORD has published short fiction and poetry in journals and anthologies. She lives in Rockwood, Ontario, where she is at work on a novel.

JANICE KULYK KEEFER has published poetry, fiction, and literary criticism. She was born in Toronto in 1952 and has travelled to Stockholm, Kiev, and Jerusalem. Her most recent book is *Rest Harrow,* a novel. She teaches English and creative writing at the University of Guelph and makes her home in Eden Mills, Ontario.

SUSAN MUSGRAVE lives on Canada's west coast. Her most recent books, both published in 1994, are *Musgrave Landing* (essays on the writing life) and *Forcing the Narcissus* (poetry).

E. ANNIE PROULX writes fiction. Her novel *The Shipping News* won the Pulitzer Prize in 1993. She lives in Vermont, travels a great deal, and may be recognized by her yellow pencils, feedstore cap, and heavy suitcase full of books.

CAROL SHIELDS grew up in a Chicago suburb and moved to Canada as a young woman. She lives now in Winnipeg, where she teaches at the University of Manitoba and writes drama and fiction. Her most recent novel, *The Stone Diaries*, won the Governor General's Award for fiction and was shortlisted for the Booker Prize. She is more and more interested in writing about the lives of women, particularly those women whose history doesn't make the public record.

BAPSI SIDHWA was born in Karachi and raised in Lahore. She began writing in her twenties, self-publishing a novel called *The Crow Eaters* in 1968 in Pakistan. That book has since been published in India, England, the United States, and Russia. Most recently she has published *An American Brat*. In 1993 she received a $105,000 Lila Wallace–Readers' Digest Writer's Award. She lives in Houston, Texas.

KIRSTI SIMONSUURI was born in Helsinki, Finland. She teaches at universities in Helsinki and abroad. In Finland she has published several volumes of poetry, as well as novels and collections of essays. She has also translated foreign works into Finnish, including Virginia Woolf's *A Room of One's Own* and Aeschylus' *Oresteia*. She has lived and worked in England, France, the United States, and Germany, and has also explored the Mediterranean, particularly Greece.

YSENDA MAXTONE GRAHAM is a journalist living in London. She is a frequent contributor to the *Sunday Telegraph*, *The Tatler*, and the *London Evening Standard*. Her first book, *The Church Hesitant: A Portrait of the Church of England Today*, was published in 1993.

WENDY LAW-YONE was born in Mandalay and grew up in Rangoon in what is now Myanmar. Her short stories have appeared in *Grand Street* and in such anthologies as *The Gates of Paradise* and *Slow Hand*. She is the author of two novels, *The Coffin Tree* and *Irrawaddy Tango*.

ALICE WALKER won an American Book Award and the Pulitzer Prize for *The Color Purple*. Her other novels include *The Third Life of Grange Copeland*, *Meridian*, and *The Temple of My Familiar*. She is also the author of two short-story collections, four volumes of poetry, and two volumes of essays.

Sources

Adams, Michelene, "Where Mih Navel String Bury," copyright © 1994 by Michelene Adams. Reprinted by permission of the author.

Al-Shaykh, Hanan, "Cairo Is a Grey Jungle," copyright © 1994 by Hanan al-Shaykh. Reprinted by permission of the author.

Atwood, Margaret, "Islands of the Mind," copyright © 1988 by O.W. Toad Ltd. Originally published in *Quest*. Reprinted by permission of Margaret Atwood.

Beattie, Ann, "The Occidental Tourist," copyright © 1988 by Iron and Pity, Inc. Originally published in *Esquire*. Reprinted by permission of Ann Beattie.

Boylan, Clare, "A Journey with My Mother," copyright © 1994 by Clare Boylan. Reprinted by permission of the author.

Davidson, Robyn, " Alone Across the Outback," copyright © by Robyn Davidson. Reprinted by permission of Rogers, Coleridge & White Ltd.

Govier, Katherine, "In Fez Without a Guide," copyright © 1994 by Katherine Govier. Reprinted by permission of the author.

Guilford, Irene, "The Cold Sea," copyright © 1994 by Irene Guilford. Reprinted by permission of the author.

Zami
A new spelling of my name
Audre Lorde

In this classic autobiography Audre Lorde combines elements of history, biography and myth to tell her own story. A young black girl grows up in thirties Harlem, a teenager lives through Pearl Harbour, a young woman experiences McCarthyism in fifties Greenwich Village. In and out of this lyrical chronicle move the women – mothers, lovers, friends – who are Zami: 'Every woman I have ever loved has left her print upon me, where I loved some invaluable piece of myself apart from me – so different that I had to stretch and grow in order to recognize her.'

'Lorde is a convincing, powerful writer. Her prose speaks directly to the heart of racism, self-acceptance, mother- and womanhood.'

A Phoenix Rising
Impressions of Vietnam
Zoë Schramm-Evans

In this thoughtful, informative and very personal account of a journey from Ho Chi Minh City and the Mekong Delta to Hanoi and Halong Bay, Zoë Schramm-Evans delves behind the cliché-ridden images of Vietnam, to discover a country poised on the brink of the most remarkable social and economic change. On her journey she meets former Viet Cong fighters, students, journalists, civil servants, street children, prostitutes, entrepreneurs and, of course, fellow travellers.

Throughout her travels she observes with humour, and occasional despair, the energy, the excitement, the struggles and the sometimes surreal juxtapositions of old and new, East and West, which are Vietnam.

The Yeats Sisters

A biography of Susan and Elizabeth Yeats

Joan Hardwick

In his autobiography and letters the Irish Poet W.B. Yeats gives the impression that he had one rather shadowy sister somewhere on the fringes of his life. In actuality the poet was for many years largely dependent on his two sisters, Susan (Lily) and Elizabeth (Lolly). The family home in which he lived was for very many years sustained only by the earnings of Lily, who worked as an embroiderer for May Morris, and Lolly, who taught in a kindergarten and gave lessons in painting.

Joan Hardwick's insightful and carefully researched biography reveals not only the artistic talents of these women – one a remarkable embroiderer, the other a skilled painter, teacher and printer – but also their great resourcefulness. With determination and acumen they achieved an unusual financial independence by means of their business Cuala Industries, at a time in Irish history when attempts at female self-determination were at best tolerated, and more often derided.

ZAMI	0 04 440948 6	£9.99	☐
A PHOENIX RISING	0 04 440965 6	£12.99	☐
THE YEATS SISTERS	0 04 440924 9	£8.99	☐

All these books are available from your local bookseller or can be ordered direct from the publishers.

To order direct just tick the titles you want and fill in the form below:

Name: _____

Address: _____

_____

_____ Postcode: _____

Send to: Thorsons Mail Order, Dept 3, HarperCollins*Publishers*, Westerhill Road, Bishopbriggs, Glasgow G64 2QT.
Please enclose a cheque or postal order or your authority to debit your Visa/Access account –

Credit card no: _____

Expiry date: _____

Signature: _____

– to the value of the cover price plus:
UK & BFPO: Add £1.00 for the first book and 25p for each additional book ordered.
Overseas orders including Eire: Please add £2.95 service charge. Books will be sent by surface mail but quotes for airmail despatches will be given on request.

24-HOUR TELEPHONE ORDERING SERVICE FOR ACCESS/VISA CARDHOLDERS – TEL: 0141 772 2281.